S0-AFB-392

Sights on the Sixties

A volume in the series *Perspectives on the Sixties*
Edited by *Barbara L. Tischler*

SERIES EDITORIAL BOARD

Clayborne Carson, Stanford University
William Chafe, Duke University
Morris Dickstein, Queens College, CUNY
José Limón, University of Texas, Austin
Elaine Tyler May, University of Minnesota, Minneapolis

Sights on the Sixties

edited by

Barbara L. Tischler

FLORIDA STATE
UNIVERSITY LIBRARIES

JUN 15 1993

TALLAHASSEE, FLORIDA

Rutgers University Press
New Brunswick, New Jersey

Contents

Acknowledgments

I n April of 1990, the New England American Studies Association held its annual meeting at the University of New Hampshire. The theme was "Out of the Sixties," and the workshops for teachers, panels, dramatic presentations, films, and even the sixties dance party (at which there seemed to be as much talking as dancing!) all explored interesting and challenging aspects of the period. Some of the articles in this collection were featured as papers at the NEASA meeting. Sarah Way Sherman of the University of New Hampshire's English department and then president of NEASA made the preliminary program and lists of conference participants available. She and NEASA were early supporters of this project, and their tangible assistance helped to turn a good idea for a 1960s anthology into a real book.

A week after the NEASA meeting, the Charles DeBenedetti Memorial Conference took place at the University of Toledo. The weekend proceedings included tributes to the work of this young scholar, along with the presentation of much new and original work on the antiwar movement. Conference organizers, Mel Small of Wayne State University and Bill Hoover of the University of Toledo, deserve special thanks for making the list of presenters available to me, even as they were engaged in putting together a collection of papers from the conference. Their forthcoming volume, along with *Sights on the Sixties*, highlights how much good work is currently being done, and how much there is yet to do, in the area of sixties scholarship.

Individual contributors to *Sights on the Sixties* have requested the opportunity to thank a number of colleagues and institutions, including, in alphabetical order, Donald Altschiller, Michelle Azimov, Charles Beard and the staff of the West Georgia College Library, Fay Bellamy, Martha Berryman, Joseph Boskin, Brandeis University's Crown Fellowship in the History of American Civilization, the City University of New

York Graduate Center, the Contemporary Culture Collection at Temple University's Samuel I. Paley Library, Robert Fernea, Ray Franklin and the Center for Labor and Society at Queens College of the City University of New York, V. P. Franklin, Fred Giffin, Evelyn Hammonds, Marty Hanlon, Albert S. Hanswer, Gordon R. Hough, Gloria House, Marty Jezer, Jose Limón, Dorie Ladner, Joyce Ladner, Chana Kei Lee, Kibibi Mack-Williams, Diane Nash, Martha Norman, Susan Ostrander, Gwen Patton, Judy Richardson, the Rockefeller Archive, Chris Smith, the Social Sciences and Humanities Research Council of Canada, the Southern Regional Education Board, Rosalyn Terborg-Penn, Steven Tischler, the University of Alberta, the University of Central Florida, Philip R. VanderMeer, Joan S. Whitfield, and Eugene Wu and the staff of the Harvard-Yenching Institute Library.

The following four chapters have been previously published and appear here with permission: Morris Dickstein's piece is a revised version of the introduction to the 1989 Penguin edition of *Gates of Eden*; Jonathan Goldstein's chapter is a revised version of his article in *Peace and Change* [11, no. 2 (1986)]. Stephen J. Whitfield's appeared originally in the *Virginia Quarterly Review* [66, no. 4 (Autumn 1990)]; and Stephen A. Kent's appeared in an earlier version in *Sociological Analysis: A Journal in the Sociology of Religion* [49, no. 2 (1988)]. Amy Swerdlow's chapter is a revised version of a talk she gave at the Charles DeBenedetti Conference in 1990.

I would like to thank Marlie Wasserman, Associate Director and Editor-in-chief, and Ken Arnold, Director, of Rutgers University Press for taking on the challenge of an anthology. Naturally, they were right about the pitfalls inherent in producing a multi-authored volume, but they were also quick to see how lucky we were in this instance to have contributors who produced great work on time! Marlie offered helpful advice, lots of encouragement, and great conversations about issues as well as the details of production. Judith Martin Waterman attended to the numerous details of copy editing and helped all of us create sharper prose, a usually thankless task that deserves special mention. Cartoonist Ted Rall took time from his developing career to create the cover illustration for this volume. Ted's presence here is especially significant, as he is a May 1991 graduate of Columbia University's School of General Studies who took my seminar on "America in the 1960s" The students in this course shared their enthusiasm for the period with me, along with their comments on earlier versions of some of the articles that appear here.

The success of any multi-authored volume depends on the cooperative spirit of the individual contributors. Each author in this collection endured numerous reminders regarding deadlines, editorial changes, and the details of style. To all of those who willingly ordered their word processors to double space *everything,* I offer sincere thanks.

Barbara L. Tischler
May 1991

Sights on the Sixties

Barbara L. Tischler

Introduction
"It Was Twenty Years Ago Today" or Why We Need More 1960s Scholarship

More than twenty years after the end of the 1960s, scholars are beginning to examine the events and ideas that characterized the period and to make some judgements regarding the historical and cultural legacies of this tumultuous time.[1] *Sights on the Sixties* contributes to the assessment of the politics and culture of the United States in the 1960s with essays from a variety of disciplines. Some cover topics that have been considered before, while others analyze aspects of the period that have received little or no attention.

As the twentieth century draws to a close, the need to understand 1960s political and cultural idealism can be found in many areas of life in the United States. Although it is popular in some conservative quarters to argue that a continuing struggle for racial equality is no longer necessary, the quest for social and economic justice remains an imperative in our own time. As racial tensions intensify, we see little of the confidence of the early sixties that racism could be overcome through nonviolence. Idealism has been replaced by cynicism, and even liberal efforts to address racism have degenerated into battles over discourse, as buzz words like "cultural diversity" often replace serious efforts to eradicate racism in the broader culture. Students and young people throughout the country often express little optimism about the real prospects for transcending prejudice to achieve equality. Further, these young people find themselves facing an economy in which they feel they will not find a place. For many, despair over the realization that mobility can be downward as well as upward predominates. Unlike their parents, who belonged to a generation that reached maturity in the mid- to late-1960s, today's youth no longer can assume a degree of material comfort which might allow them to focus their efforts, even if only for a short time, on the issues of their time, as their parents focused their efforts on realizing equality, attaining voting rights for the disfranchised—specifically African Americans and young people—and ending the Vietnam War.

✳   ✳   ✳

In 1991, with the United States still high from a popular victory in a distant desert war, comparisons with a faraway jungle war that ended nearly two decades ago reveal many contrasts that remind us that this is a different time. Unlike United States involvement in Southeast Asia, which was incremental over a period of years, the fighting in the Persian Gulf involved a massive mobilization of forces in a short time, a quick battle effort, and a relatively expeditious withdrawal of more than half of the troops within a few months of the end of the fighting. Even opposition to the Persian Gulf War was subsumed in a cry for support for American fighting forces, and "love the troops, hate the war" was an idea that could be embraced by those who flew the American flag and those who wore peace signs. Without a draft to bring the immediacy of the war home to young people and with the enemy embodied in a person (the "Butcher of Baghdad") rather than an ideology (communism in Southeast Asia), unequivocal opposition to the war wasn't always easy to find. Clearly, the Persian Gulf War was not like Vietnam, and those who opposed the fighting in the Persian Gulf had to struggle to find their own voice. This was a challenging task indeed, given the popularity and brevity of the war and the fact that the United States and the Allies "won."

It is clearly unfair to expect our own time to replicate the patterns of a period that has left its mark on politics and popular culture. Each generation needs to find its own voice and its own vocabulary for political, social, and cultural change. The 1990s are not necessarily going to be like the 1960s, but with so many of the issues and questions of the earlier period still unresolved, the debates over what seem to be old issues form the basis for political positions and strategies in our own time. I recently asked students in my seminar, "America in the 1960s," at Columbia University to articulate what they thought were the most important unresolved questions about the period. Overwhelmingly, the responses fell into two categories, What went wrong? and When (or perhaps, why) did the 1960s end? As we discussed variations on these two themes, it became clear how much we *know* about the 1960s, but how little we understand the political, social, and cultural questions that were raised, but not necessarily resolved, in such a short time span. The seminar discussion reminded me of the need to analyze the 1960s from numerous disciplinary perspectives so that we can interpret the period in the way scholars have mined sources from the 1840s, the Progressive Era, or the late 1930s. As more sources become available, it will be possible to frame the debates about the importance of the 1960s as an important historical moment.[2]

For those of us for whom "it was twenty years ago today" refers not only to the first line of a Beatles song, but to the approximate time of our college graduations, it is important to engage in serious debate about the most appropriate and useful ways to study recent history. We must do this in order to revise what is rapidly becoming a 1960s canon established by major news magazines, television, and what many of us have called the big books by big men about big movements that have set the tone of both popular thought and serious scholarship. The first wave of sixties books, some by activists in various movements, contributed significantly to the process of consciousness raising and to the growing acceptance of the 1960s as a legitimate period for analysis. It is now time for more local studies that will encourage a discussion of the 1960s in places other than the two coasts, big cities, and major universities. Scholars and students need to transcend the good sixties–bad sixties typology which valorizes the optimism and energy of the early part of the period while excoriating the excesses of the later years, placing the beginning of the United States's "downhill slide" at the precise moment of the Tet offensive, the deaths of Martin Luther King, Jr. or Robert Kennedy, the 1968 Chicago Democratic National Convention, or the emergence of the Weathermen.[3]

It is also critical that scholars contribute to the creation of a more sophisticated analysis of the 1960s in the popular memory. Particular reflections on recent history can be as numerous as the historical actors and analysts themselves, but two equally simplistic clusters of images of

America in the 1960s predominate in the popular mind. The first is a view of the 1960s that stresses the conviction that the social mission of the New Deal could finally be accomplished. For those who look back at the period with nostalgia, a number of phrases and slogans evoke *Big Chill* memories of a good-sixties ethos that is no longer in fashion in the 1990s. These include Camelot, "Freedom Now!," student power, the summer of love, and the War on Poverty that *could* be won. In contrast, other Americans remember the 1960s as a decade when the United States strayed from its proper path. The goal for proponents of this view has been to "correct" the aberrations of the period in order to "put the United States back on track" in terms of both its foreign policy positions and government involvement in the domestic economy. Those who see the 1960s as a period out of phase with the orderly progress of American history focus on phrases, labels, and slogans that emphasize the bad sixties, including Black Power and "Burn, Baby, Burn," SDS (Students for a Democratic Society) and the Weathermen, yippies, hippies, gay activists, feminists, and other nonconformists. These commentators see ignominy, if not actual defeat, in Vietnam, a war lost because of political constraints placed on an otherwise valiant military.

In considering these perspectives, and in trying to avoid both the nostalgia and hostility that romanticize and vilify the 1960s, scholars are beginning to consider the period as part of the broader spectrum of American history, not simply as an isolated episode of political radicalism, social experimentation, or cultural craziness. Without being bound to restrictive historical periodization or concepts such as Arthur M. Schlesinger's "cycles of American history," it is nevertheless true that the period we have conceptualized as "the sixties" was characterized by the continuation and extension of many cherished political and social traditions. What could be more American, for example, than revolutionary political protest and confidence in the ability of the nation to solve its most pressing social problems? But the 1960s was also characterized by important departures from "the way things had always been," since groups without a voice in the culture at large—African Americans, Asians, Latinos, homosexuals, women, and young people—found a place at the center of the political and cultural action.

The dynamism of the 1960s, and the conviction that the nation was ready for rapid and unconventional reform renders the decade almost unique in twentieth-century history. Not since the Depression had the nation experienced such dramatic tension and conflict over the legitimacy of institutions and individuals in positions of power to make policy. It was this tension that inspired many calls for meaningful social reform. As the major reform causes, racial justice and the Vietnam War, seemed increasingly resistant to resolution through the courts or the traditional political system, that tension contributed to generational, ethnic, and class conflicts.

The overlapping political, cultural, social, and intellectual histories of the 1960s raise questions of how to frame the period chronologically. The passing of the 1950s and the emergence of the Me decade of the 1970s hardly provide adequate starting and ending points within which we can define the 1960s. Many of the essays in this volume analyze events, issues, and personalities that predate the election of John F. Kennedy, while still others discuss issues that could be described as part of the legacy of the sixties that has affected contemporary culture at the end of the twentieth century. Indeed, it would be possible to frame the sixties in a variety of ways, each with a different time frame, focus, pivotal events, and historical actors. Consider just a few of the many ways to define the 1960s:

1954–1973   VIETNAM: from Dienbienphu to the withdrawal of United States military forces

1954–1966   THE CIVIL RIGHTS MOVEMENT: from the *Brown* decision to the expulsion of whites from the Student Nonviolent Coordination Committee (SNCC)

1966–1969   BLACK POWER, THE FORMATIVE YEARS: from the emergence of a Black Power movement to the murders of Fred Hampton and Mark Clark in Chicago

1960–1968   CAMELOT AND THE GREAT SOCIETY: a period of intense political and cultural optimism that America's problems were amenable to judicial and political solutions

1957–1969   TECHNOLOGY ASCENDANT: from the launching of *Sputnik* to the Apollo moon landing

1964–1984   THE NEW FEMINISM AND WOMEN'S LIBERATION: from Title VII of the 1964 Civil Rights Act to the most recent defeat of the Equal Rights Amendment

1963–1972   THE BEATLES TO THE BEAT: from the early days of the

"British invasion" in popular music to the emergence of
disco

Of course, there are many other possible ways to place analytical boundaries on 1960s reality.

This multi-theme approach contributes to disagreement over the all-
too-simple question, What were the 1960s about? Typical answers, as I
have indicated, are obvious: some responses focus on the good sixties of
freedom rides and a high moral purpose in the struggle for civil rights, an
economy of abundance that could, if only for a time, support a war on
poverty, childlike "flower power," and a cold war foreign policy that mandated tough talk and covert action rather than all-out war. Other answers
to the question emphasize the bad sixties of black hostility to white
America and a backlash against the idea of helping the dispossessed, the
counterculture's angry challenge to the authority of its parents, and a
shooting non-war that was lost because of a "lack of national will."

The effort to analyze the United States in the 1960s from a variety of
disciplinary perspectives brings us to the reason for adding another book
to the growing number of explanations, justifications, and scathing critiques of individuals, movements, and institutions. Existing 1960s books
have documented and analyzed major political and movement leaders,
cultural and countercultural representatives, and major events that we
have read about before. What is needed is an exploration of the meaning
of local events, lesser-known movements, and historical actors who
played smaller parts.

Sights on the Sixties begins this process, as many of the essays provide students, interested readers, and scholars in the field a broader sense
of the sixties by looking at less familiar events or uncommon sources. The
emphasis on local events, lesser-known historical actors, and aspects of
everyday life emanates from the no longer "new" social history and from
approaches to disciplinary and interdisciplinary scholarship "from the
bottom up" that were themselves the result of upheavals in the academy
in the late 1960s and early 1970s. As the work of fifteen authors who
draw on familiar and new methodologies in American studies, anthropology, film studies, history, literature, sociology, and theater, *Sights on the
Sixties* is not a text. Rather, it is a collection of case studies, which makes
no claim to be an analysis of all, or even most, of the subjects available to

1960s scholars. Many areas remain for other collections. In this volume, for example, the focus on race is on African Americans, with the recognition that the Chicano, Asian-American, and Native-American movements were and remain important agents for the emergence of multiculturalism in the West and Southwest. The rise of the student movement and the emergence of revolutionary political parties on the Left also deserve more serious discussion. While the latest developments in contemporary cultural studies are not represented in this volume, practitioners of the new scholarship have not yet turned their critical attention to this period in order to develop a large body of theoretical monographs. The essays that appear here were selected for their broad interest to students and scholars rather than avant-garde insights. Some of the essays in this volume have appeared before, while others represent new scholarly efforts. All have been written for readers who want to learn more than the "big books" or textbooks, which can devote only limited space to the 1960s decade, can provide.

*   *   *

What made the 1960s seem so special? In "After Utopia: The 1960s Today," Morris Dickstein reflects on the remarkable political and cultural climate of the period and on the legacies of its activism, experimentation, and openness to diversity. With a particular focus on "the change in the texture of our lives, the shifting sensibility and moral climate of the era," Dickstein explores issues he raised originally in his 1977 book, *Gates of Eden*. In response to critics who take delight in the "failure" of the utopian dreams of many writers and activists of the 1960s, Dickstein reminds us that "Utopians not only express a vision, a set of hopes, but they sketch out distant goals for more practical people to achieve." Many 1960s activists left a valid, if not always an immediately viable, agenda for later generations to realize.

One of the political legacies of the 1960s has been a skepticism about old and traditional ways that began with a challenge to familiar party politics in August of 1964. Mark Stern's "Lyndon Johnson and the Democratization of the Party Process" analyzes an important crisis at the Democratic party's nominating convention. The case of the Mississippi Freedom Democratic party (MFDP) and its efforts to transform the political process through the high moral purpose of the civil rights crusade is told here as a political narrative and as the story of a struggle against racism in Mississippi. The impact of the MFDP crisis on the delegate selection process reminds us, in Stern's words, that mortals, "not angels, conduct the affairs of government and politics."

By the end of the 1960s, campus protests against government-funded war research were common, and students often made campus recruitment difficult, if not impossible, for corporations whose technological research and development contributed directly to the Vietnam War effort. In "Agent Orange on Campus: The Summit–Spicerack Controversy at the University of Pennsylvania, 1965–1967," Jonathan Goldstein documents the serendipitous discovery of chemical and biological warfare research and the early resistance to such research at a major institution of higher learning. Using internal documents and press sources, Goldstein traces the discovery of what had been secret war research. He then looks at the emerging public debate over the role of the university and its board of trustees in facilitating the creation of chemical and biological weapons through its computer-based analysis of their production and effectiveness.

Campus opinion on the Vietnam War was often revealed through teach-ins, rallies, and other public expressions of divergent views. On many campuses, student newspapers became forums for debate on the war. Clifford Wilcox analyzes the relationship of campus debate on Vietnam to the structure and degree of student control of campus newspapers at two midwestern state universities in "Antiwar Dissent in the College Press: The Universities of Illinois and Michigan." Students also expressed their feelings about the Vietnam War by creating their own cultural events whose ethos emphasized countercultural rather than mainstream cultural values. Glenn W. Jones explores the origins and realization of one such festival at the University of Texas in "Gentle Thursday: An SDS Circus in Austin, Texas, 1966–1969." With music, clowns, balloons, food, and costumes, Gentle Thursday stood for four years in nonviolent, noncompetitive contrast to the war and the society from which it had emerged.

Ellen Herman asks us to consider some of the sources of 1960s countercultural and political movements that lie outside of the realm of politics. In "Being and Doing: Humanistic Psychology and the Spirit of the 1960s," she discusses some of the intellectual origins of movement and countercultural thought. Steven J. Whitfield provides a portrait of one of the exemplars of counterculture and action in "The Stunt Man: Abbie Hoffman (1936–1989)." As a champion of "an ethos of liberation from the benign, civics-text assumptions that were once pervasive in America," Hoffman bequeathed a legacy of ideas, including the rather "subversive" notion that freedom is "not only something to be protected; it is something to be used." Sociologist Stephen A. Kent finds some of the activist energy of the 1960s subsumed under the rubric of new religious impulses in the 1970s, and he analyzes this phenomenon as a social movement in "Slogan Chanters to Mantra Chanters: A Deviance Analysis of Youth Religious Conversion in the Early 1970s."

Artists in various fields have often been among our more radical, if not always political, visionaries, and David Sanjek and Alexis Greene illustrate how the arts were called into the service of social and political criticism in the 1960s. In "Apocalypse Then: Apocalyptic Imagery and Documentary Reality in Films of the 1960s," Sanjek analyzes various 1960s film genres and their contribution to a broadly based critique of modern society. From depictions of "bikers on the road" to documentary and dramatic portrayals of the 1968 Chicago Democratic National Convention, commercial films challenged audiences to reflect on broader crises in American society through film imagery. In "The Arts and the Vietnam Antiwar Movement," Greene demonstrates that many painters, poets, and playrights in the late 1960s and early 1970s used the war as a subject and inspiration for individual expression. When many attempted to "bring the war home" in their own ways, they came to realize the extent to which the antiwar movement itself was divided. They responded with "images of utter fragmentation in their art."

The new feminism and the rise of women's liberation have received increasingly serious scholarly treatment in recent years, but some women and their activist organizations have received more attention than others. In "Not My Son, Not Your Son, Not Their Sons: Mothers Against the Draft for Vietnam," Amy Swerdlow describes the organization and activism of Women's Strike for Peace (WSP). These middle-class women were committed to opposing the war in Vietnam, and they did so as *mothers.* Swerdlow argues that a study of the activities of WSP "provides fresh evidence that female culture can provide a source of strength, creativity, militancy, and commitment in radical movements, despite its failure to address the over-arching issue of gender equality." Gerald Gill's essay, "From Maternal Pacifism to Revolutionary Solidarity: African-American Women's Opposition to the Vietnam War" traces growing resistance to the war by women and the black community in general in the latter half of the 1960s. Gill discusses the role of African-American women as spokespersons in their own right for an antiwar point of view. In my own essay, "Voices of Protest: Women and the GI Antiwar Press," I discuss women's growing articulation of a feminist agenda through their opposition to the war and, more specifically, to what they regarded as the overwhelming sexism of the military. As women began to identify their gripes as legitimate feminist grievances, they spoke with the same force, although not with the same eloquence or erudition, as their academic and professional colleagues who comprised the new middle-class feminist movement.

Opposition to the Vietnam War grew in this country in the late 1960s, but opposition within the military carried risks. Despite these risks, GIs and officers began to express their reluctance to fight a war they could neither win nor support. In Gerald R. Gioglio's essay, "In the Belly of the Beast: Conscientious Objectors in the Military during the Vietnam War," he discusses the difficulty of gaining conscientious objector status once a soldier had enlisted or had been inducted into the service.

In the concluding essay, "The Legacies of the 1960s: New Rights and New Lefts," Barbara Ehrenreich discusses aspects of 1960s politics that have been transformed into neoconservative ideology. Examining the emergence and current popularity of the New Right, she concludes that "it is our job . . . to resurrect the alternative vision of human liberation that had just begun to be developed by the New Left and the civil rights movement in the 1960s. This is a vision of *radical* democracy [that represents] the best (and perhaps the last best) hope for humankind."

✳ ✳ ✳

Scholarship on the 1960s is still in its early stages, as new sources are made available and a new generation of students begins to challenge the assertions of the earliest books on the period. With its combination of familiar and new topics, traditional disciplinary methodologies and new sources, *Sights on the Sixties* represents a bridge between older traditions and new scholarship. The purpose of this volume is to raise questions and to encourage those who use this work to mine the sources for themselves and to revise and refine our stated "wisdom." As scholars begin to formulate interpretive frameworks for the sixties, debate over the vital issues of the decade can continue.

Morris Dickstein

After Utopia
The 1960s Today

O ne remarkable thing about the decade of the 1960s is how much it is still with us more than twenty years later. The activists of the era keep reliving their youth by writing books about it, while their conservative opponents, sour amid all their successes, never tire of invoking it as the root of all evil. Just as every bank failure or mortgage foreclosure makes people think of the Depression, any sign of social activism, antiwar protest, or sexual hijinks quickly brings the sixties to mind. Though many of the events of the decade belong to another world—to a raucous party that lasted long but ended badly—the sixties remain a tangible myth, a set of burnished memories, a point of departure for every kind of social argument, as well as the source of values widely diffused throughout our culture. Some revolutions fail by succeeding; this one seemed to succeed by failing. How did this happen? *Why* did it happen? How do the 1960s continue to influence us today?

The books published on the subject in recent years dealt mainly with the political side of the sixties—with the Vietnam war, with student radicalism and the growth of SDS (Students for a Democratic Society), with the civil rights movement and the antiwar movement, with bloody riots, assassinations, street demonstrations, and university uprisings. My own approach in *Gates of Eden* (1977) was somewhat different. Without ignoring the politics—who could do that?—I emphasized the changes in the texture of our lives, the shifting sensibility and moral climate of the era. The periodic resurgence of antiwar demonstrations during the

Reagan and Bush years showed one facet of the sixties legacy, a set of political reflexes and an arsenal of protest strategies. But the revolution in feelings and mores is where the values of the 1960s have proved most enduring. The sixties were not simply a time when young people grew long hair and took to the streets; it was also when many others dramatically reexamined their lives, with consequences that can still be felt to the present day.

This change in the landscape of feeling extended to politics as well. The political *forms* of the sixties have proved perishable; the *attitudes* that developed have cast a long shadow. As a national movement, the sixties Left came to an end when SDS destroyed itself in the streets of Chicago, when the McGovern campaign was swamped by a Nixon landslide, when the end of the war and the draft undercut the basis for large-scale protest. These tactics have been revived only when issues like nuclear arms, Apartheid, Central America, or (much more ambiguously) the Persian Gulf War evoked intense passion or moral outrage. The sixties left behind not a mass movement but a deep sense of skepticism and suspicion directed at our military and political leaders, especially on questions of war and peace, on environmental issues, on official lying and corruption, and on threats to individual rights.

Still, the pendulum shifted dramatically: as economic issues became more pressing in the early seventies, a conservative reaction set in, including a middle-class tax rebellion, and Ronald Reagan sprang forth as its spokesman and beneficiary. More traditional values—religion, family, patriotism—came to the fore, and many Americans recoiled from the carnivalesque instability of those times.

Culturally the sixties seemed to expire as well, for many leading figures found it difficult to survive the era. Writers as different as Allen Ginsberg and Kurt Vonnegut, Bob Dylan and Thomas Pynchon, Ken Kesey and John Barth, did not thrive in the quieter, more "normal" atmosphere that set in by the mid-seventies. Beat poetry and black humor, which crystallized the sensibility of one era, were quite marginal to the period that followed. Some political art began to look dated, overheated, but the cooler culture of celebrity typified by Andy Warhol went on and on. That part of the sixties would always continue to sell.

For artists and performers in the sixties, drugs and booze were a major occupational hazard. Self-destructive figures like Jack Kerouac, Lenny

Bruce, Jim Morrison, and Janis Joplin burned themselves out. For others, nature took its course: the pied pipers from an earlier generation—Paul Goodman and Herbert Marcuse, for example—exhausted their message and passed from the scene. Others like Timothy Leary and Jerry Rubin became professional clowns, turning their *shtick* into show biz (not far from what it always was). Radical comedians like Abbie Hoffman and firebrands like Mark Rudd were forced underground as others like Rubin and Tom Hayden navigated their celebrity and ambition toward the mainstream.

Among writers, perhaps the strongest survivors were the realistic novelists formed in a slightly earlier time, such as Philip Roth and John Updike, who simply took the changing scene and the ebb and flow of their own lives as their fundamental subject. Higher journalists like Tom Wolfe and Normal Mailer, ever-watchful observers of cultural change, were also able to adapt to a climate in which radical was no longer chic, in which style and consumption were the motive forces, not political commitment. It was easier for those who had come of age in the fifties to adapt to the seventies and eighties.

Few writers and filmmakers were able to make much of the topical concerns that agitated people in the 1960s. Much later, a flood of long-delayed novels and films about Vietnam, including powerful if simplistic works like *Apocalypse Now*, *Platoon*, and *Born on the Fourth of July*, showed that the popular imagination could at last come to terms with our national trauma. But only a handful of gifted writers like Tim O'Brien, Michael Herr (in *Dispatches*), and Hunter Thompson, as well as Mailer and Wolfe, were able to find a style that responded directly to the turmoil of the era.

But if Mailer and Wolfe kept going creatively as the sixties disintegrated, it was only by turning to quite different subjects, Mailer to the frighteningly bleak and bland American heartland of *The Executioner's Song*, written in a documentary style far removed from his usual first-person baroque, and Wolfe in his gee-whiz treatment of the space program (*The Right Stuff*) and his satirical reportage from the urban frontier (*The Bonfire of the Vanities*), which showed how the criminal justice system and the media were unfair to Park Avenue WASPs. Although his work was immensely readable, Wolfe was a journalist masquerading as a novelist. His strength was a mastery of the nuts and bolts: the operational and human details of the space program, the social intricacies of the urban jungle from top to bottom. With his conservative politics, his dandyish detachment from his subjects, and his glib fascination with money, class, and cultural style, Wolfe was the only sixties writer who was able to make a seamless transition through the Reagan era—an achievement, like Andy Warhol's, that underlined his limitations.

The sixties were a period of wild and sometimes ephemeral experimentation in the arts, reflecting the instability of daily life: from Fluxus and Happenings to postmodern fiction and psychedelic rock lyrics. At first the aftereffect of this carnival of sounds and images was to engender its opposite—the eerily effective low-key blue-collar realism of Raymond Carver, reminiscent of Hemingway, and the chic minimalism of Carver's young admirers; the smooth pop sound of the disco era and other machine-tooled rock of the 1970s; the revival of figural painting beginning with photorealism, with its flattened picture-postcard abstractions of everyday life. This pendulum effect, marked by a seeming return to more conservative styles, managed to mask the real impact of the sixties in the arts, which was to open the floodgates to a wild eclecticism and cultural pluralism in which no single style could predominate. This was liberating to some artists, disquieting to many critics, but to the entrepreneurs of culture, especially art dealers, it became a good way to turn a dollar.

Thanks to an endless appetite for cultural novelty, the avant garde became good business, at once commercial and prestigious, chic and austere. As culture and money grew more and more intertwined, as corporations became the powerful and sometimes intrusive supporters of museums, arts festivals, and public television, as the booming art market became a virtual offshoot of the booming stock market and the real estate market, the avant garde as an iconoclastic and oppositional force began to lose its meaning. In this as in many other ways, the seventies and eighties were a caricature of the sixties, whose experimental energy had made them possible.

But there's a positive side to this anarchic proliferation of styles, a new openness that took hold amid these wild swings of novelty and fashion. For more than twenty years now, in an atmosphere charged with the heady pursuit of the outrageous and the unconventional, abstract painting has coexisted with representational painting, experimental fiction with realistic fiction, free verse with formal verse, hard rock with soft rock, atonal with tonal music, modernism with postmodernism and anti-modernism. Detached and difficult artists like Robert Wilson have become fashionable, but so have impassioned traditional storytellers like Cynthia Ozick and Robert Stone.

Performance artists like Karen Finley, artists like Hans Haacke, rockers like Bruce Springsteen, and writers like Stone (in *A Flag For Sunrise*) and Robert Coover (in *The Public Burning*) maintained the political thrust of sixties art. The anger and machismo of black male writers, a keynote of the sixties, became shrill and repetitive just as the anger and tenderness of black woman writers, such as Toni Morrison and Alice Walker, began to move people deeply. Feminism, the most legitimate heir to the sixties idea that the personal is political, came into its own just as the New Left, grown increasingly rigid and ideological, was expiring as an organizational force.

But the success of feminism as a *movement* was atypical of the post-1970 era, when movements had trouble finding adherents and gaining attention. Like so much that had preceded it in the 1960s, especially the civil rights movement, feminism was an unstable mixture of politics and culture—legislative goals and economic goals along with deeply personal changes in self-image, the sense of identity, in sexual as well as social relationships. Contemporary feminism began with concrete issues of inequality and discrimination but also with polemical works of social history (Friedan's *The Feminine Mystique*) and literary history (Millett's *Sexual Politics*) that had real impact on how individuals thought about their lives.

Feminism reached more women through media coverage and personal contact, such as small consciousness-raising groups, than through large organizations like NOW (National Organization for Women). Women sought and achieved better control over their own bodies and more freedom from demeaning roles and stereotypes. Abortion rights became a battleground between feminists and religious conservatives, and the accelerated entry of married women into the work force made day care an urgent economic issue. Even when feminism stumbled politically, as in the campaign to ratify the Equal Rights Amendment, its cultural influence spread. Thanks to the mass media, feminism touched a nerve in many women who joined no organization and who probably did not consider themselves feminists. This is the way many sixties values seeped into the mainstream.

By remaining loyal to the sixties ideal of self-development through political as well as personal effort, women were laying claim to a terrain that young men had virtually abandoned. In *Making History*, Richard Flacks, an SDS founder, describes the balance of values on the sixties Left between an "ethic of self-expression" and an "ethic of social responsibility." The seventies and eighties proved far more congenial to the ideal of personal growth than to any form of altruism. The free-market faith of the Reagan administration made self-seeking legitimate, even socially desirable. Losing its political bearings in an era of economic strain, the counterculture of the sixties turned into the narcissistic Me Generation of the 1970s and the ambitious, self-involved young professionals of the 1980s. Despite their starting salaries and carefully planned lives, these young people remained children of the sixties, when they were born. Snorting coke instead of smoking joints, jogging and joining health clubs instead joining communes, seeking utopia on Wall Street rather than in rural Vermont, they stayed curiously bound up with the sixties values they seemed to caricature—above all, the search for self-fulfilment in the here and now.

The most faithful carrier of the values and attitudes of the 1960s has been the sixties generation itself. Near the end of *Gates of Eden* I predicted that "we'll hear from it yet, for noisy and visible as it was, it hasn't fully had its say. The members of a generation which made its mark collectively and individually at an abnormally young age have yet to make their mark separately and personally. . . . Most have disappeared into families, guilds, and professions in every area of society." At the twenty-year reunion of student strikers who had taken over the Columbia campus in April 1968, it was remarkable how many of them had somehow remained true to their old ideals. Their hair was shorter, but none wore ties and jackets. They had had their children late—and brought them all along. Some who had seen themselves marching bravely toward a new society had probably never expected to join nuclear families at all.

Beneath the easy informality, they seemed touched by a feeling that they were *special*, for they had been cast, however briefly, in a historic role. There were no signs of the dramatic deconversions that had marked the middle-aging of the Old Left. Few of these radicals were still politically active but many had become socially concerned writers, editors, teachers, filmmakers, or labor organizers, bringing old commitments into new professional lives. Others had gone in for local activism, serving on school boards or community boards, organizing campaigns to stop a highway from being built or open land from being developed. Few, it seemed, had just gone for the money, despite the Gilded Age ethics of the Reagan years. It was clear that some sense of communal responsibility would continue to shape the remainder of their active lives.

As members of this generation have moved into positions of authority, their ideals have transformed institutions as well as individual lives. To neoconservative polemicists, these sixties people are a Hydra-headed monster popping up everywhere, distorting American values, warping our educational system with their political agendas, fraying the fabric of American capitalism, and sapping our will to police the world. In their view, the death of the New Left and counterculture merely camouflaged a subterranean triumph, an insidious integration not only into the universities and other cultural institutions but into the American heartland. Like many exaggerations, this updated version of the Red Menace contains more than a grain of truth.

Anyone who remembers the quiet conformities of the 1950s will be quick to see how much the attitudes of the sixties and the arrival of a new generation have affected the press, the universities, advertising, the film industry, and even the Church and Congress. On issues like nuclear war, new weapons-systems, and armed intervention in Central America— issues which raised the ghost of Vietnam and the cold war—the press kept asking disrespectful questions it would never have broached before. Meanwhile, the Church continued to speak out and organize on matters of conscience, helping Congress find the will to resist the executive branch. All through the eighties, despite strong pressure from a more conservative Pope, the Church remained in the forefront of agitation for human rights, land reform, and democracy in Latin America.

At the same time, the universities, where many radicals of the sixties found a niche, became centers of political dissent as well as unconventional scholarship, which at times hardened into a new orthodoxy. Social history and interdisciplinary study prospered, along with new fields like black studies, women's studies, gay scholarship, and literary theory. Unlike the radicals of the sixties, who had warmly appealed to neglected

Western values like tolerance, diversity, equality, and nonviolence, the academic radicals did scant justice to the books on which they had been raised, the deep traditions that had nurtured their kind of dissent. They showed how easily the libertarian ideas of the sixties could be betrayed by becoming institutionalized. As Tzvetan Todorov said in his epitaph for this kind of theoretical radicalism, "it is not possible, without inconsistency, to defend human rights with one hand and deconstruct the idea of humanity with the other."

Major scandals like Watergate and the Iran-Contra affair, involving large-scale official deception and abuse of power, helped keep alive the spirit of skepticism that developed during the Vietnam War. Eight years of patriotic rhetoric over Central America, far from laying to rest the "Vietnam syndrome," showed that most Americans remained in doubt about such adventures unless our vital interests were at stake. Even Reagan could not always play the anti-Communist card, or restore an unquestioning faith in American virtue. The depth of Congressional resistance to arming the Nicaraguan rebels showed how much American liberalism had shifted since the days of the cold war. Nor would Congress allow the Administration to ignore official atrocities in El Salvador, Chile, or Guatemala. The impressive congressional debate on authorizing the Gulf War, haunted by still-vivid memories of Vietnam, showed how even conservatives in Congress had grown wary of unchecked executive authority and open-ended military intervention, a caution that would be forgotten in the euphoria of quick and painless victory. After the war began, both the generals and the protesters had Vietnam on their minds. So did the president in speech after speech when the conflict ended. His message was simple, if somewhat wishful: "The spectre of Vietnam has been laid to rest in the sands of the Arabian desert." Thanks to the breakup of the Soviet Union, the United States, despite its worsening domestic problems, became an unchallengeable force, the arbiter of local conflicts throughout the world. Only time will tell whether victory in the gulf will lead to new interventions and perhaps new protests.

On domestic issues liberalism was on the defensive throughout the 1980s and beyond. Here the Reagan presidency transformed the political arena beyond recognition as ill-conceived tax cuts, huge budget deficits, and runaway military spending made new social programs unthinkable. Instead, as Kevin Phillips demonstrated in *The Politics of Rich and*

Poor, the right achieved a significant redistribution of income in favor of the rich. The tax "reform" of 1986, while closing some loopholes, gutted the key liberal principle of progressive taxation. The big battles of liberals, on court appointments for example, were fought to halt retreat, not to make fresh advances.

While radicals turned academic and liberals were in disarray, conservative intellectuals, fostered by corporate largesse and a receptive political climate, developed a sweeping vision of "democratic capitalism" as a dynamic social and economic force. "Thus, ironically," writes Richard Flacks in *Making History*, "the left, previously the most explicitly ideological current in American political culture, now operates in pragmatic, piecemeal fashion according to the rules of pluralist interest group politics, while the right presents itself as the moral, visionary force." Marx was out, Adam Smith was in vogue, and much of the world suddenly dreamed of capitalism as the magic key to both freedom and affluence. The flight from Communism in Eastern Europe at once heightened the ideological confidence of this evangelical conservatism yet dissolved the glue that held it together, which was anti-Communism and the Soviet military threat.

Of course, "pluralist interest group politics" is really no novelty for the American left. It was the staple of the New Deal, which first created the modern liberal coalition. But during the Depression this was combined with an acute sense of national crisis and an active pursuit of the public interest. The New Deal used public works to create jobs but also to improve our physical environment and, in its arts programs, to foster a unifying sense of the American heritage. Nor was the New Left really an "ideological current" so much as an inchoate moral force, stronger in protest and resistance than in its own social initiatives. This helps account for why it went under, for protest movements inevitably wane when their immediate goals are achieved. As Barrington Moore has written, "moral passions without material interests rarely if ever suffice to move large bodies of men and women in a way that leaves a deep mark upon the historical record."

The New Left could work to stop the war and end discrimination, but it was the old-line liberals who pushed through the social programs of the Kennedy-Johnson years while the Warren Court was dramatically expanding the scope of individual rights. The New Left began as a movement with practical as well as visionary goals, as the freedom rides and community organizing projects show. But the war and the Black Power movement transformed moral witness and local activism into protest and finally rage; this gradually severed the New Left from the political arena and insured its ultimate demise.

Despite this political failure, many of the fundamental rights we now accord to women, gay people, and blacks belong to the legacy of the sixties, which conservative administrations could impede but not reverse. The same could be said of the impact of the peace movement in the early 1980s and, even more markedly, the environmental movement, which is now a permanent part of our political landscape. In spite of the fundamentalist backlash against the new freedoms of the 1960s, the Reagan administration made little headway in pushing its social agenda—as in its attacks on pornography, abortion, and the separation of church and state. Even in the age of a rampant AIDS epidemic, Americans seem unwilling to turn back the clock on the sexual freedoms they won in the 1960s, especially the freedom of expression. Instead, the threat of AIDS brought a dramatic new frankness to public discussions of sex, even with children. Though sex itself became suddenly more dangerous, the old hypocrisy and repression seemed a thing of the past.

The passage of time has made it easier for us to take a long view of the events of the sixties. The gradual acceptance of women's equality, the relaxation of sexual mores, the rise of the divorce rate, the changing relationships between parents and children, the growth of a separate youth culture with a great deal of disposable income, the vast expansion of higher education and its influence, the growing importance of technology and the mass media—all these trends can be documented in earlier periods such as the 1920s or 1940s. In the sixties such developments took a sharp political and cultural form, but they were part of larger social changes that lay hidden beneath the conservatism of the postwar years.

There was certainly a dark side to much that happened in the 1960s. No one will be nostalgic for the bloodshed and social conflict that resulted from the war—or the violence in the ghetto, whether it was born of new hope or sheer hopelessness. No one should shed a tear for the inflammatory rhetoric of the era, or the self-righteousness of some student radicals, which few as yet have seriously reexamined. At the Columbia reunion, Mark Rudd, describing the final descent into rage and violence, which had left friends dead or in jail, commented: "We were completely out of touch with reality. I now believe the Vietnam War drove us crazy." Yet aside from attributing some of his radicalism to his Jewish roots and to the Holocaust, he gave no sign of having reflected much on anything he had done. Understandably, he had too much invested in the drama of his own past. The simplistic public television series *Making Sense of the Sixties* (1990), despite some rare footage and good interviews, also enshrined the participants' view of themselves as a noble, idealistic, and happy-go-lucky generation, proving once again that oral history is not history.

The naiveté of some of the millennial dreams of the period is breathtaking today, yet somehow this vision remains one of the most attractive features of the sixties. Though it led at times to drugs and violence, to sexual anomie and moral smugness, it also fostered an ideal of community and equality that will always be ahead of its time. As a college freshman in 1988, my daughter wore a pin that read, Desperately Clinging to Utopian Illusions. That somehow seemed to strike the right balance, at least for her generation. *Credo quia absurdum est.* Today, in an ironic reversal, the "free market" has become just such a utopian illusion, a desperate talisman for many people around the world. Yet not long ago the president of Czechoslovakia, Václav Havel, told students at Columbia that he had been inspired by the spirit of their 1968 uprising. According to interviews they gave, the leaders of the brutally suppressed democracy movement in China in 1989 also took their tactics and ideas from the Western student movements of the sixties.

Utopians not only express a vision, a set of hopes, but they sketch out distant goals for more practical people to achieve. Unlike the Old Left, with its tenacious illusions about a mass-murderer like Stalin, the New Left and the counterculture did few people any harm—except, at times, themselves. Yet even the drugs of the sixties, principally grass and LSD, seem relatively harmless compared to the coke, crack, heroin, and (again) alcohol that became epidemic in later decades. Here the yellow brick road led not to paradise but to hell, a road not even paved with good intentions.

Mark Stern

Lyndon Johnson and the Democratization of the Party Process

L yndon Johnson was a president in search of election to the presidency in his own right. The 1964 Democratic National Convention legitimized his right to lead the Democratic party, and the 1964 general election legitimized his right to lead the country. His actions during the presidential election season of 1964 were set in the context of his ambition for office and for the legitimation of power. At least one major consequence of these actions, the solution which he mandated for the Mississippi Freedom Democratic Party (MFDP) challenge at the 1964 Democratic National Convention, profoundly influenced the future course of the Democratic party.

Lyndon Johnson (LBJ) was anything but lacking in ambition from the time he entered politics until the time he became president. Brought to the White House by an assassination, LBJ was keenly aware of his need for the 1964 election to provide a mandate for his accession to power.[1] Barry Goldwater offered him the perfect foil against which to win a great electoral victory and a popular mandate. At the same time, Goldwater's right-wing views allowed LBJ to redefine the political center, and bring a liberal, Democratic majority into Congress on his coattails. A liberal Congress would realize the president's plan to update Franklin Delano Roosevelt's (FDR) New Deal into the Great Society, with its myriad of social programs for the cities, the poor, the uneducated, and the elderly.[2]

But the challenge from the predominantly black Mississippi Freedom party to the seating of the segregationist Mississippi state Democratic party's delegation at the 1964 Democratic National Convention might have led the South to walk out of the convention and to bolt from the party in the general election. If he had denied the MFDP challenge, Johnson might have alienated the liberal wing of the Democratic party which had but recently gained faith in him after his support of the Civil Rights Act.[3] Johnson's mandate and his plans for the Great Society could all have disappeared if the MFDP challenge had torn the Democratic party apart.

*   *   *

On August 4, the Mississippi Freedom Democratic party held a state party convention in Jackson, Mississippi, and elected forty-four delegates and twenty-two alternates, including four white Mississippians, to attend the Democratic National Convention.[4] Freedom Summer had already caught the nation's attention and had produced results for the black movement. More than fifty thousand black Mississippians participated in the MFDP party system. The deaths of Goodman, Schwerner, and Chaney, as well as the founding of the Freedom schools, brought before the nation the terrible tragedy of black life in the Magnolia state. But the attention wrought by the MFDP did not bode well for Lyndon Johnson.

The president, like much of the nation, focused his attention in July of 1964 on the GOP's presidential nominee. The moderates of both political parties were dismayed at what had transpired. Barry Goldwater, the leading GOP contender of 1963, ran the gamut of state primaries in 1964 that, according to journalist Theodore White, "exceed[ed] in savagery and significance any other in modern politics."[5] Despite a series of defeats by GOP moderates, Goldwater narrowly won the June 2 California primary. This sealed his nomination, as the moderates were out-organized by the Republican right-wing in almost every convention state, and the Goldwater forces sewed up their delegations.[6]

Goldwater laid out his brand of conservatism in his book, *The Conscience of a Conservative*. He denounced federal intrusion into the states, federal intervention in the economy, and the establishment of the liberal welfare state. His position on the federal effort to integrate education was forthright, and appalling to the civil rights community. "The Federal

Constitution," he maintained, "does not require the states to maintain racially mixed schools. Despite the recent holding of the Supreme Court, I am firmly convinced—not only that integrated school are not required—but that the Constitution does not permit any interference whatsoever by the federal government in the field of education."[7] He was Mr. Conservative.

Throughout the year, the Goldwater campaign strategy was to "go hunting where the ducks are." He publicly argued, "The Republicans do not have the Negro vote. It is our own fault. We lost it in the thirties. I think we will lose the vote in the big cities, and I don't think we can change it this year."[8] The East Coast, as far as Goldwater was concerned, "could be sliced off and set adrift."[9] Its social-welfare beliefs and softness on defense represented all that was destroying the fiber of the country. The Eastern Establishment was a special target of his ire as its leaders—Henry Cabot Lodge of Massachusetts, William Scranton of Pennsylvania, and Nelson Rockefeller of New York—fell before his juggernaut. The South and the West were the targets of his strong posture on defense, his economic conservatism, and his appeal to rugged individualism. His advocacy of states' rights and his explicit decision not to go after black votes, won him special favor in the South. Despite Everett Dirksen's personal plea that "You just can't do it. You can't do it to yourself and you can't do it to the party," Goldwater voted against the 1964 Civil Rights Act.[10] Time and again he argued that states' rights demanded that civil rights could not be tampered with by the federal government.

On July 16 Barry Goldwater mounted the GOP convention podium to a tumultuous roar. He was Galahad and his acceptance speech that day reflected the purity of his vision. *"Extremism in the defense of liberty is no vice. . . . Moderation in the pursuit of justice is no virtue,"* he declaimed.[11] As the nominee gave his address, a reporter turned to Theodore White and marveled, "My God he's going to run as Barry Goldwater."[12] "I'd rather be right than president," Goldwater commented time and again. And he was going to be right, if only by his own light, but he was not going to be president. He realized no one could defeat Johnson, and his was a campaign for the future direction of the Republican party, not really a campaign for the presidency. His candidacy drew thousands of young, ideologically committed activists into the ranks of the GOP, especially in the South.[13] Nothing at the GOP convention detracted from Goldwater's conservatism; nothing at the convention detracted from Johnson's vision of a perfect fall campaign.

The Goldwater campaign was based on the argument that the major parties did not differ much over issues: they both had accepted the liberal welfare state. "A choice, not an echo," became another Goldwater theme. George Wallace, the southern racist who repeatedly stated, "There is not a dime's worth of difference between the two parties," now found a difference. Within days of Goldwater's nomination, the Alabama governor publicly withdrew from his effort to make a third-party run for the presidency and announced his support for the states' rights Republican.[14]

The Goldwater nomination was met with a chorus of excoriation from the mainstream white and black leadership. Moderate leaders feared the GOP abandonment of the center. "With the nomination of Barry Goldwater for the Presidency of the United States," the *New York Times* editorialized, "the right wing of the Republican Party has won a great victory. . . . It has succeeded in naming as leader of the party and standard-bearer in the national election a man who is the very symbol of radical reaction."[15] The civil rights forces feared the end of the Second Reconstruction could be at hand, and much, if not all, of their recent gain would be lost. The black leadership, for the first time in the history of its major organizations, openly opposed a major party nominee. "It is both unfortunate and disastrous," Martin Luther King, Jr. told the press, "that the Republican party has nominated Senator Barry Goldwater as its candidate for the presidency of the United States. I have no alternative," he continued, "but to urge every Negro and white person of good will to vote against Mr. Goldwater and to withdraw support from any Republican candidate that does not disassociate himself from Senator Goldwater and his philosophy."[16] In this matter the black community was virtually unanimous.

Within days of the Goldwater nomination black riots broke out, first in New York City's Harlem and then Bedford Stuyvesant, after a black teenager was shot and killed by a white police officer. Black rioting then shook areas of Rochester, New York; Philadelphia; the Chicago suburb of Dixmoor; and several cities in New Jersey.[17] As the rioting spread, and the demonstrations across the South continued, the White House grew concerned about the specter of white backlash. The president met with Goldwater to discuss the black riots and the fall campaign. The GOP nominee told LBJ it was wrong to play to people's racial fears, and he did what politicians rarely do: he gave up the use of a politically advantaged position because he believed it was wrong to use it. This issue would be kept out of the contest.[18] But, both the White House and the black leadership recognized that continued demonstrations or riots would provide aid and comfort to Goldwater's campaign.

The administration and most of the black leadership converged on a common strategy: demonstrations and riots had to be halted. Hobart Taylor Jr., a black White House aide, urged LBJ, to contact black leaders and "make a major and organized effort to direct their thinking along a proper course, . . . demonstrations and picketing can be avoided through personal contact and explanations of the seriousness of the problem."[19] The black leaders were already getting organized to deal with this concern. "It is of [the] highest importance," Roy Wilkins telegraphed the leaders of the major black organizations on July 22, "[that] we take counsel at [the] earliest moment . . . to ensure we do nothing to produce votes for Goldwater."[20] In fact, after the Civil Rights Act signing ceremony, LBJ privately told the civil rights leaders this law made "demonstrations unnecessary and possibly even self-defeating."[21] The president repeatedly called the black leaders to let them know of his concern over the disorders and his belief that they would hurt the implementation of the Civil Rights Act and weaken his campaign against Goldwater.[22] In addition, Johnson had a lengthy telephone conversation with Wilkins on July 27 and called him again on July 28, the day before the black leaders convened in response to Wilkins's telegram.[23]

The better part of the discussion at the black leaders' meeting centered on bringing organized demonstrations to a close until the presidential campaign ended.[24] While James Farmer of the Congress of Racial Equality (CORE) refused to stop his organization's demonstrations, Wilkins, Randolph, King, and Whitney Young agreed to "call upon our members to voluntarily observe a broad curtailment, if not total moratorium, of all mass marches, mass picketing and mass demonstrations until after election day, November 3." The demonstrations had to be halted because "[they saw] the whole climate of liberal democracy in the United States threatened."[25] Three days after the call for a moratorium, the *New York Times* headlined an article, "Campaign—Major Issues Are Coming Into Focus, Civil Rights Held Major Factor."[26]

Yet, the Gallup polls never showed the president's election to be seriously threatened by Goldwater. To the contrary, they indicated strong public approval—57 percent to 21 percent outside of the South—for Johnson's civil rights policy, and a consistent 70 percent to 30 percent majority who would vote for him over Goldwater. In the South, Goldwater was slightly favored over Johnson in the early summer, but by August even that support withered.[27] Johnson was going into the Democratic National Convention with a free hand to control the party platform and to name his running mate. Only the Mississippi Freedom party challenge loomed as a spoiler on his horizon.

✳　　✳　　✳

After the August 6 MFDP state convention, LBJ's thinking about the Freedom party challenge changed. John Stewart, who became intimately involved in this conflict as one of Hubert Humphrey's closest aides, recalled that "Johnson of course had figured: 'For God's sake, how could all of these people come making all this trouble when I've been the president who got this historic bill through?' He saw it as ingratitude." When he realized they were coming to challenge the regular Democrats, LBJ understood that chaos could ensue; southern white delegates could leave the convention, as their predecessors had done in 1948. Furthermore, Joseph L. Rauh, Jr., one of the players who instigated the liberal civil rights plank that caused the 1948 walk-out, was the MFDP's attorney for this challenge. Stewart continues, "LBJ's old nemesis, Joe Rauh, was going to be leading the charge, and it was going to be on TV, and it was going to be just awful. It was going to ruin LBJ's convention."[28]

In May, the MFDP had established an office in Washington, D.C., and sent out representatives to line up support for the convention challenge.[29] Convention delegations in California; Colorado; Massachusetts; Michigan; Minnesota; New York; Oregon; Wisconsin, and Washington, D.C., passed resolutions of support for the MFDP challenge.[30] By early June the MFDP had lined up enough members of the credentials committee to bring a minority report to the convention floor. White House pressure to stop the challenge was applied, especially to Rauh.[31] But the party forces were fighting a believer who felt he had little to lose and much to gain simply by taking on the mighty. "Everyone says that [to continue this battle] took a lot of courage and principle, but I don't think anybody realized how much fun this was to really get into a real battle like this, to have troops and to have a real fight with all the power," recalls Rauh. "You had the whole Democratic political machine, the President . . . and the whole labor movement trying to stop a few little Mississippi Negroes and me from making a little stink at the Democratic Convention.[32]

For Johnson, this was no "little stink." The president had the FBI place electronic surveillance devices on the MFDP's Atlantic City convention office. He was continually informed of the Freedom party's activities as the bureau kept abreast of them.[33] Johnson was not going to let his convention be disrupted, or possibly destroyed, by open battling between the civil rights forces and a southern state Democratic party.

At the end of the first week in August, LBJ ordered the Democratic convention credentials committee chair, Governor David Lawrence of Pennsylvania, to get to work on a solution to the MFDP problem. Lawrence conferred with the national party chair, John Bailey, who in turn contacted Harold Leventhal, the attorney for the national Democratic party; Jack Conway, the deputy director of the Office of Economic Opportunity; and Joe Rauh to set up a meeting at Lawrence's office. Lawrence reiterated that the president wanted a solution to the MFDP problem that did not cause an undue disturbance within the party. Rauh, in turn, made it clear that the MFDP challenge was not going to just disappear. The major discussion of the meeting centered on how the procedural aspects of the credentials committee hearing would be handled and how much time would be allocated to the MFDP counsel. The meeting ended with the understanding that the challenge would have a hearing before the committee.[34]

On August 11, Lee White, the president's counsel, told Rauh that LBJ wanted to know his position on the challenge. Rauh responded that the MFDP would consider accepting the compromise seating of both Mississippi delegations. The beauty of this proposal, as Rauh noted, was that it was consistent with most precedents for convention seating challenges, including the 1944 seating of both the Texas Regulars and the pro-FDR Texas Loyalists, who included LBJ as one of their delegates. This appeared to be agreeable to the president's counsel.[35] John Bailey and David Lawrence also agreed that this was a reasonable solution to the problem. But they did not speak for LBJ. The Mississippi delegation was determined to leave the convention if blacks were seated under their state banner, and LBJ feared that many of the other southern delegates would follow them. On

August 12, the president told Mississippi's Governor Johnson that his delegation was going to represent Mississippi at the convention.[36]

The president's men were scrambling. "There were so many hatchet men," recalled Rauh, "that you had to stand with your back to the wall." On August 14, another presidential envoy spoke with Rauh, and another element was added to the quarrel. Walter Reuther, the president of the United Auto Workers and a liberal ally who employed Rauh as the UAW's general counsel, told Rauh of LBJ's repeated threats to keep Humphrey off of the ticket if the challenge continued. Reuther argued, "the Hubert vice-presidency rode on the settling of the Mississippi thing to the satisfaction of the president." Rauh remembers Reuther telling him, "I would have Hubert's blood on my hands, if I did not stop this thing." At one point Reuther threatened Rauh with the possibility of losing his UAW job if he did not back down.[37] In fact, on the same day as Reuther spoke to the MFDP counsel, Hubert Humphrey met with Rauh, and they agreed that the seating of both delegations made sense. Humphrey had not yet gotten the word from the president that this was unacceptable. The New York Times called for the seating of both delegations, with the state's vote to be split equally between them.[38] As the convening date of the convention approached, Humphrey was drawn deeply into this fight.

Humphrey was called to the White House. He already knew that he was Johnson's likely running mate and that background checks had been done on him. Almost all of the president's advisers favored Hubert Humphrey for the vice-presidential slot.[39] After LBJ removed Robert Kennedy from consideration as his running mate on July 29, Humphrey was the liberal choice for this position. He was the Happy Warrior of the liberal-labor alliance and a major leader of the agricultural Democrats. The Johnson-Humphrey relationship went back to the early 1950s, and although the two men were sometimes at odds on the issues, they were also often allies both in the Senate and in the party. "Lyndon Johnson had tremendous love and affection for Hubert Humphrey," recalls Harry McPherson. "He had immense admiration for his heart and for his brains. He had a rather low estimate of his judgement and felt . . . that he was not tough enough."[40] On August 19, the day before Humphrey's appointment, Johnson met with a group of black leaders, including Wilkins of the National Association for the Advancement of Colored People (NAACP), and they told him the White House had to make concessions to the MFDP's challenge. Johnson lectured the black leaders on the need to stop the MFDP demonstrations and the need to abort the credentials fight. The black leaders maintained their support for the MFDP challenge.[41] When Humphrey arrived at the White House the next day, LBJ told him that he had to get the civil rights leaders to change their position.[42] Now Johnson was going to see if Humphrey was "tough enough."

Humphrey understood he had to swing his liberal friends over to the president or his vice-presidential chances might well disappear. John Stewart remembered his boss's words as he returned from the White House, "Now we've got this one to work out, too. They finally accept the fact that there's a problem, and the president has said I'm to work it out— so get going."[43] Humphrey later wrote, "Johnson was testing me one more time."[44] It was one of the toughest jobs he ever faced. His cause was civil rights. In order to fulfill his ambitions he had to find a safe passage between the needs of his long-time comrades-in-arms and the demands of Lyndon Johnson.

On August 22, the Freedom party presented its case before a nationally broadcast session of the credentials committee. Rauh's remarks emphasized the publicly announced intention of the Mississippi regulars to support Goldwater in the fall election. He also spoke of the refusal of the Mississippi regulars to allow black Mississippians to participate in their party processes. Finally, he introduced the testimony of brutality and vote fraud that was to be presented that afternoon.[45] The nation sat transfixed as witnesses provided details of police cruelty and state repression.

The hearing reached a crescendo as Fannie Lou Hamer, the MFDP vice-chair, told of the ordeal she faced following her arrest for aiding voter registration efforts. She was taken from her jail cell and, on the orders of a Mississippi state highway patrol officer, male prisoners hit her. "The first Negro began to beat and I was beat. . . . After the first Negro was exhausted the State Highway Patrolman ordered the second Negro to take the blackjack. The second Negro began to beat . . . I began to scream and one white man got up and began to hit me on the head and tell me to 'hush.'" Hamer's testimony continued, "All of this on account we want to register, to become first-class citizens, and if the Freedom Party is not seated now, I question America." Theodore White recalled, "as her fine mellow voice rose, it began to chant, with the grief and sobbing that are the source of all the blues in the world. The hot, muggy room was electrified. . . ."[46] The president called a televised news conference in the middle of Hamer's testimony, but that evening the networks rebroadcast her tragic account of Mississippi justice. Telegrams and telephone calls of support for the Freedom forces inundated Atlantic City and Washington. The morality play had the spotlight and the president's forces pressed harder to find a solution that met their needs.

As the convention began on Monday morning, Humphrey met with the MFDP leadership and leaders of the other major black organizations. While there was a discussion of possible compromises, no movement occurred. The liberal firebrand of the 1940s and 1950s could not get the radicals of the 1960s to alter their demand for seating as Mississippi delegates. "The meeting was a total flop," recalls Rauh, "everyone was disappointed. No one budged on their positions."[47] Humphrey could not press hard enough and, as Jack Conway saw it, he never really had a chance. He did not have the power to make a bargain. "That Hubert Humphrey meeting was a disaster," recalls Conway. "Everyone was mad. Hubert was sitting there talking, but he could not say anything. It was a vacuum. The whole objective was to get this challenge thing dealt with," recalls the administration's liaison, "but there was no one to talk to. The thing that struck me was that there was no one representing Lyndon Johnson that you could talk to and say 'Will you take this?' We needed someone who could communicate with the president." The president did not trust Humphrey to do the job even though he gave him the job. LBJ needed someone there whom he could trust.[48]

Word about Humphrey's meeting filtered back to the White House. LBJ called Walter Reuther, who was in the midst of contract negotiations with the president of General Motors. President Johnson demanded that Reuther go to the convention and bring the civil rights forces into line. Reuther halted negotiations with General Motors and, that evening, flew to Atlantic City to help bring LBJ's convention back into order.[49] The Reuther-Johnson relationship went back to the days when LBJ was a young congressman. Although Johnson seldom went along with Reuther on labor issues, they did maintain a friendship, and they respected each other. "Roy Reuther and I used to tear our hair out because we could never get anything out of Johnson," recalls Conway. "Yet Walter stayed the course with him."[50] Now Johnson turned to this tough negotiator. He would bargain for the president: because the president demanded it and because, LBJ assured him, Humphrey would get the nomination if the MFDP imbroglio was settled in accordance with Johnson's needs.[51]

Rauh stopped at Humphrey's headquarters that evening, much as he would each evening of the convention, and asked Humphrey how his vice-presidential campaign was coming. "At this stage," Humphrey responded, "honestly, I'm so tired of it, I honestly don't care too much anymore. I'm so tired of it all. I'm never at ease." Rauh told him, "Hubert, you got to give us more time. You got to give it some more if you don't want to get beat."[52] But the Happy Warrior was dispirited, and he had little to give to the battle.

That night and on into the next day the president's forces, now joined by Reuther at the convention, continued to search for a solution. Early Tuesday morning Reuther, Humphrey, Conway, and Walter Mondale, a young political ally of Humphrey's, met to discuss strategy. The general idea, "to balance the unbalanceable," as Walter Mondale recalls, "grew out of discussions and debates and sort of evolved over the few days before the convention and into the beginning day or two of the convention." There were repeated telephone calls between the White House and its agents at the convention as their compromise proposal was worked out.[53]

There was no doubt about "the clear moral credibility and strength of the Freedom Democrats' charges. But," Mondale noted, "the Freedom Democrats were not a political party. They were a collection of people who came up to the convention to make this case. For symbolic purposes we chose to seat the two MFDP representatives." (The MFDP wanted to seat forty-four delegates and twenty-two alternates.) Seating the MFDP delegates was one important element in the final administration proposal. Another important element was that the Mississippi state Democrats would pledge their support to the national Democratic ticket. A final, critical part of the proposal, was that future state party delegations to national conventions could not be chosen in a racially biased manner. The national Democratic party would establish a committee to ensure that this provision was carried out. This was central to Mondale's thinking. "I really wanted to make certain that, when these rules went into effect, there would be energetic enforcement of them. I wanted to make sure the door would be held open for black delegates." The Minnesota liberal recalls, "These rules contemplated affirmative participation by minorities." As for the broader implications of the creation of a national party committee which would set the standards for the selection of state delegates, Mondale recalls, "I don't think we spent much time on that."[54]

Jack Conway recalls, "We bowed to Lyndon Johnson's will. There had to be a compromise: that he have the Southerners in the party and yet the liberals had to be there, too." This was the key to the solution, as Conway remembers. "There was a lot of discussion about the importance of a loyalty oath, but there was no discussion about the ramifications of the agreement for the party. We had a job to do. There was a convention to get in order and a campaign to get underway. We just did what we had to do to get a solution for what was confronting us." Mondale worked out the details of the proposal, referred to afterwards as the Mondale compromise, and Reuther secured the president's agreement.[55] Now it was time to bring the civil rights groups into the fold.

On Tuesday afternoon, Rauh was waiting for the credentials committee meeting to begin the MFDP hearing when a committee member, Representative Charles Diggs of Michigan, approached him: "Joe, you are to call this [telephone] number. Walter Reuther." Chairperson Lawrence agreed to hold off on beginning the meeting until Rauh and the president's man had spoken. Reuther told the MFDP counsel, "This is the decision: they are going to exclude the [white] Mississippi people unless they take an oath which they said they won't take. So they're going to be excluded. They're going to give you two delegates, so you've won that. They're going to give you a pledge they'll never seat lily-white delegations again. The party will set up a committee to ensure that this promise is carried out." The UAW leader concluded, "This is a tremendous victory. And I want you to take this. The convention has made its decision."[56] Of course, "the convention" had not made any decision as yet, but Johnson had made his decision, and this was his convention.

Although Rauh thought this was a victory for the Freedom party, he could not accept the proposal on the spot. He had agreed with Aaron Henry, the NAACP state chair and the MFDP chair, that neither of them would make a decision without the consent of the other. In addition, Rauh believed that the administration had made a grievous mistake by not permitting the MFDP to select its own floor representatives. The White House chose two of them as delegates-at-large: Aaron Henry and Reverend

Edwin King. The Mississippians wanted to choose their own people for their own positions. The MFDP represented the poor and the sharecroppers, like Fannie Lou Hamer, and they would not accept a middle-class pharmacist, Aaron Henry, and a white professor, Edwin King, as their sole representatives. He asked Reuther to have the committee hold up its meeting, "Then I can come back and make the proposal to make it unanimous after Aaron Henry tells me he agrees with it." Rauh needed time to talk with Henry.

The White House would not give Rauh the time he needed. They were not interested in giving him or the MFDP anything more. They had been reasonable and they wanted to get away from the battling and on with the celebration. Rauh knew, "they had given enough now so that from now on we looked like the greedy [ones]. . . ."[57] The White House allies prowled the halls to ensure acceptance of their proposal. Sixty-four of the sixty-eight Mississippi regulars left the convention that day, rather than pledge support for the national ticket. The Alabama delegation also left. But all of the other southerners remained with LBJ's forces.[58]

When the credentials committee convened, its members voted to recommend the Mondale amendment to the convention. Rauh, a voting committee member as a Washington, D.C., delegate, and six others opposed the recommendation. On Tuesday afternoon, as the committee met, Reuther and Humphrey spoke with the MFDP leaders and the mainstream black organization leaders. Aaron Henry was at this meeting while Rauh was at the credentials committee meeting.[59] Humphrey was talking with Bob Moses when they heard that the Mondale amendment was accepted by the credentials committee. The MFDP leader was infuriated. He believed he was bargaining in good faith with the Johnson forces and now he learned that the outcome of the bargaining had been decided elsewhere. Aaron Henry and Fannie Lou Hamer were also adamant as Humphrey tried to persuade them to go with the administration offer.[60]

Walter Reuther persuasively argued with Martin Luther King, Roy Wilkins, and Bayard Rustin that they had to accept the administration proposal. After all, Reuther told them, we helped you in the past, and if you want our help in the future you have got to help us out now. The financial largess for the movement, he noted, was not as likely to be forthcoming from his liberal friends as it had in the past. They agreed to help him try to bring the MFDP leaders to accept the White House offer.

They believed it was a reasonable compromise solution.[61] Reuther returned to Detroit soon after this meeting ended. His job was done. He knew the Mondale compromise would be broadly accepted and that Humphrey had the vice-presidential nomination.

The next day, August 26, Rauh, Martin Luther King, Jr., Bayard Rustin, and James Farmer met with the MFDP delegation, and all of them spoke in favor of the compromise. Both Rustin and Wilkins were asked by Humphrey to attend the meeting and help get the compromise accepted.[62] King said he believed it was a fair deal, but he would not tell the delegates how to vote. Rustin urged the delegates to "think of our friends in organized labor, Walter Reuther and others, who have gone to bat for us. If we reject this compromise we would be saying to them that we didn't want their help."[63] The Freedom delegates were angry. They were believers, not compromisers. James Forman told the Freedom delegates, "There may be a difference between protest and politics, but . . . we must try to bring morality into politics." As one MFDP members saw it, the outside supporters of the deal, including the counsel, Joseph Rauh, were dealt with by the MFDP leaders "as if they were the archenemies of the Freedom Democrats."[64] The MFDP leaders never seriously considered taking the deal.[65] Aaron Henry and Edwin King officially turned the deal down on behalf of the MFDP.[66] The challenge was over, and the seats in the Mississippi delegation area were removed from the convention floor after a brief MFDP sit-in.

*   *   *

On August 29, Aaron Henry wrote, "We went to this Convention armed with the greatest might one could have on his side—the might of truth! We presented the truth. . . . It took the personal hand of President Lyndon Johnson to keep this . . . from our grasp." The MFDP chair continued his argument, "It was not that the President was against us, however, he took the position that he would lose the states of [the South] . . . if the Convention voted to seat us, we of the Mississippi Democratic Freedom Party. Thus," he concluded, "the issue within the administration was purely political. Our victory on moral and legal grounds was overwhelming."[67] He later remarked, "Lyndon made the typical white man's mistake. Not only did he say you've got two votes, which was too little, but he told us to whom the two votes would go."[68] For many of the Freedom

Democrats this was the end of their faith in liberalism. The spiral of black nationalism and alienation moved ever upwards.[69] Liberalism meant compromise, even of basic values and integrity. Liberals would not fight for principle when they could get a deal. Johnson chose to make sure he was president, rather than be right on the issue. Joseph Rauh, who had been invited aboard *Air Force One* and to the White House as a guest of the president during the early months of the administration, now found that his relationship with LBJ was over. "I really trace the end of it pretty much to the '64 Mississippi thing. After that it was never the same," he recalled. "It was really back to pushing for things from the outside."[70]

For most mainstream liberals the avoidance of a floor fight with a reasonable compromise, which put their champion over the top for the vice-presidency, was a victory.[71] On July 26, Johnson flew to the convention with Humphrey to display his running mate. The Johnson-Humphrey ticket was acclaimed by the convention delegates. A great eulogy for John F. Kennedy on August 26 was followed by an audacious birthday party for Lyndon Baines Johnson on August 27.

*   *   *

The 1964 general election campaign did run according to LBJ's script. "From the beginning," White House aide Richard Goodwin recalls, "the only issue was not victory or defeat but the size of the inevitable triumph."[72] Johnson seized the middle ground, and the Democrats won an overwhelming victory for both the presidency and the Congress. As LBJ commented on election eve, "it seems to me tonight . . . that I have spent my whole life getting ready for this moment."[73] While Goldwater carried the five deep South states of Mississippi, Alabama, South Carolina, Louisiana, and Georgia, as well as his home state of Arizona, Johnson carried 375 of the nation's 435 congressional districts. More important, the Democrats gained two seats in the Senate, for a 68 to 32 margin, and 37 seats in the House, for a 295 to 140 margin. As Richard Rovere concluded in his review of the election results, LBJ did not have to depend on the South the way FDR, Truman, or Kennedy had, and, in fact, "Johnson's power base is far more secure than Roosevelt's ever was."[74] The Great Society was put in place, and the Johnson campaign strategy of 1964 was vindicated, for the moment.

One of the most significant events of the 1964 Democratic National

Convention was almost overlooked amid the passions and celebrations of the moment. The Special Equal Rights Committee, the first of a series of reform committees which were to be spawned as an outgrowth of the 1964 MFDP compromise, was mandated into existence.[75] This became the critical, long-term result of the Mondale amendment. The 1956 Democratic National Convention had mandated that delegates would be "pledged formally and in good conscience to the election of those Presidential and Vice-Presidential nominees under the Democratic party label . . ." This established the principle that the national party could "impose national rules on what kinds of persons will be selected."[76]

The 1964 convention expanded on that precedent in a manner that had profound consequences. The Mondale amendment mandated that the national party would impose standards that state parties had to meet in the selection of their delegates to the national party convention. The call for the 1968 convention and all future national Democratic conventions would contain the following language: "It is the understanding that a State Democratic Party, in selecting and certifying delegates to the Democratic National Convention, thereby undertakes to insure that voters in the state, regardless of race, color, creed or national origin, will have the opportunity to participate fully in Party affairs. . . ."[77]

At the 1968 Democratic National Convention the credentials committee, supported by vote of the convention, removed the regular Mississippi state Democratic party delegation and replaced it with the nonsegregated, Loyal Democrats of Mississippi. The McGovern-Fraser commission was appointed by the party after the 1968 convention, and it expanded the Democratic national party rules to include eighteen guidelines that had to be met by state parties in the selection of their delegates to the national conventions.[78] Women, the young (under 30), and minorities all substantially gained access as delegates to subsequent Democratic national conventions.[79] Direct primary elections and proportional representation replaced winner-take-all state-wide delegate selection processes, as democratization was carried even further along.

Lyndon Johnson was busily grappling with the problem of his nomination and election to the presidency and the maintenance of a unified Democratic party when the Mississippi Freedom Democratic party challenge confronted him. He wanted, and believed he needed, a convention that did not stir up Northern versus Southern hostilities. As a consequence, Johnson demanded a solution to the MFDP challenge that would satisfy the liberals but not alienate much of the South. In pursuit of this demand, the Mondale amendment was worked out and accepted by the 1964 convention, and Johnson went into the 1964 general election with the Democratic party intact. The Mondale compromise and its consequences also remains intact. The democratization of the Democratic party is still going on as the Democratic party revises and re-revises its delegate selection rules between each successive presidential election and as it defines and redefines its responsiveness to open, participatory democracy. That is the fundamental, unanticipated consequence of the Johnson response to the MFDP challenge.

In the 1990s, with democracy and democratization as the international passwords of new-found respectability, it may once again be useful to remind ourselves that democracy is predicated on politicians as self-interested individuals. Political reform is often the by-product of veiled self-interest and is habitually unpredictable in its consequences. The origins of the reformed Democratic party delegate selection process and the course it has taken over the past quarter century can only serve to remind us that men, not angels, conduct the affairs of government and politics.

Jonathan Goldstein

Agent Orange on Campus
The Summit–Spicerack Controversy at the University of Pennsylvania, 1965–1967

The current debate over compensation to American Vietnam War veterans whose health was apparently impaired while they sprayed Agent Orange has diverted the concern of many Americans from the impact of that spraying on a large civilian population. This ethical concern received more attention during the 1960s than it does today. In 1966, twenty-two U.S. scientists, including seven Nobel laureates, petitioned President Johnson to end "the employment of anti-personnel and anti-crop chemical weapons in Vietnam." This and other representations were without effect, as use of Agent Orange continued until nearly the end of American military presence in Vietnam.[1]

Public disclosure, in 1965, of chemical- and biological-warfare (CBW) research at the University of Pennsylvania produced a twenty-month campus controversy over the propriety of such weapons and whether such research ought to be undertaken on campus. While not actually producing weapons on campus, Penn was involved in the sophisticated, computer-assisted analysis of production, delivery, and effects, including political and psychological consequences, of the entire spectrum of CBW weaponry: chemicals incapacitating to humans, herbicides, and toxic bacteria. Until 1967, when Penn's board of trustees cancelled the University's Pentagon CBW contracts, the viewpoints of the contending factions were symptomatic of the clashes of moral and academic values among

43

American academics at large. To comprehend the Penn experience as a microcosm of debate among U.S. academics, one should view the Penn episode as the product of several factors: the development of U.S. CBW research, the processes whereby such studies became "married" to American universities, the Indochinese–American War, and the introduction, by the mid-1960s, of CBW as a weapon for counterinsurgency, rather than for traditional battlefield combat. This last element ignited a particular concern with CBW research which might not have otherwise arisen. Apart from a brief and undocumented article in the October 1967 *Nation* magazine, no history of Penn's experience has analyzed each of the factions involved in the controversy.[2]

*   *   *

By the 1950s, according to *Science* magazine investigator Elinor Langer, the nuclear age military establishment regarded the U.S. Army Chemical Corps as custodian of a probably useless and potentially embarrassing arsenal. Battlefield use of poison gas had been commonplace in World War I. But as industrialized nations developed protective defenses against such weaponry, the use of poison gas became increasingly obsolete. In the years after World War II, the Chemical Corps, with its CBW arsenal, received increasingly bad publicity. According to Langer, CBW was easily misunderstood by the general public who considered it, correctly or incorrectly, a dirtier kill than shooting or bombing.

Because of this negative public image and perceived obsolescence, the Chemical Corps subsisted on budgetary dregs of about $35 million a year. Its most active support came from the Chemical Warfare Association, a group, supported by chemical companies, of military and industrial executives. The corps continually feared disbandment.[3]

In the 1950s, with the onset of limited counterinsurgency warfare, rather than direct battlefield combat between industrialized states, the corps saw an opportunity. In 1959, it launched Operation Blue Skies, a public relations and media effort stressing the advantages of aerosol-spraying of herbicides and incapacitating agents as an effective means of waging limited war in an era when the nuclear powers were reluctant to use atomic devices. The corps' pleas for expansion were endorsed by the American Chemical Society (ACS), an industrial lobby with a financial interest in CBW. An ACS newsletter editorial summarized the "humane" argument for CBW: "In the cave and tunnel warfare of the jungles there seem to be significant possibilities for riot-control agents used on mobs in the U.S. and elsewhere. To flush all parties out of hiding, temporarily unfit for combat, seems a desirable alternative to indiscriminate slaughter."[4] Knut Krieger, a professor of chemistry who directed CBW research at Penn for fourteen years, argued that chemical-biological warfare was a little less inhumane than conventional, and especially atomic, weapons.[5]

By the mid-1960s, as guerrilla warfare escalated in Indochina, the "humane" counterinsurgency argument advocated by the Chemical Corps and its allies in government, industry, and academia resulted in a comprehensive upgrading of U.S. CBW capabilities. In 1961, the research and development budget for CBW in all three military services was about $57 million. By 1964, it had risen threefold to about $158 million, a level maintained through 1967. A clear commitment had been made to simultaneously developing this old method of warfare and atomic and traditional battlefield weapons.[6]

*   *   *

According to the official Air Force history of its use of chemical weaponry in Indochina, Operation Ranch Hand was authorized by President Kennedy in November 1961. By the time it ended nine years later, some eighteen million gallons of defoliants, such as Agent Orange, had been sprayed on an estimated 20 percent of South Vietnamese jungle.[7]

The American public knew little about the herbicide program in the early 1960s. There were allegations by the Hanoi government about the use of CBW, but these reports had limited circulation in the United States.[8] As late as July 1965, Defense Secretary Robert MacNamara publicly denied any U.S. use of CBW in Vietnam.[9] It was only on November 1, 1965, that Deputy Secretary of Defense Cyrus Vance publicly admitted that "we are making limited use (of cyanide and arsenic compounds) in the Southern part of Vietnam, but not yet in the North.[10] According to investigator Langer, by 1967, five hundred thousand acres of cropland had been, in Department of Defense (DOD) parlance, "treated with herbicides."[11]

From the fall of 1965 on, then, it was publicly known that the United States was using chemicals in waging its war in Vietnam. That use became a major question of conscience for many Americans. Under these conditions, CBW research on American campuses could no longer be considered as theoretical and uninvolved with the war.

*   *   *

Extensive government contracting of classified war research to universities began during World War II. During that conflict, Penn's faculty constructed ENIAC—a pioneer digital computer, and a minisubmarine capable of penetrating antisubmarine nets. War research at universities proved important enough that the practice continued after the war, and by 1964, Defense Department grants to American universities totalled $401 million. [12]

From the vantage point of a large private university like Pennsylvania, the acceptance of government research contracts was sound fiscal policy. In 1964, Penn ranked eleventh in the dollar value of DOD contracts to U.S. universities. As of August 1966, government grants provided $25 million of a total university budget of $90 million, and represented the single largest source of Penn's income. [13]

From the inception of government research programs, Penn trustees, and some of its administrators and faculty, recognized a university obligation to national defense, an attitude that remained essentially unchanged until 1967. Professor Krieger argued that "if the University depends for its freedom on a free society, it has some responsibility to defend the free society [through government research contracts]. I like to believe that we are making some small contribution to the national defense." [14] Thomas Sovereign Gates, Jr., Penn trustee-for-life and ex-U.S. defense secretary, summed it up. "War is immoral to begin with. What's immoral about [CBW] compared to a flame thrower or atomic bomb? The whole goddamn thing is immoral." [15]

Acting under such major premises, Penn accepted its first CBW research contract in 1951. The overtures to Penn were made by William Day, special assistant to the United States secretary of defense, an engineer, and a Penn alumnus. Day's initiative was prompted by suspicion that the Chinese were developing "vectors," or delivery systems, for CBW in the Korean conflict. [16]

There were contacts in the summer and fall of 1951 between Penn administrators, engineering faculty, and Air Force personnel to discuss the project in more specific detail. Consequently, a secret CBW contract was negotiated and given the code name Project Benjamin in honor of Benjamin Franklin, the university's founder. When the contract was officially signed in December 1951, the code name was shorted to Big Ben in deference to DOD preference for two-syllable code names.[17]

According to trustees' minutes, Big Ben was "a study of biological and chemical warfare from all standpoints—social, political, technological, scientific."[18] A 1956 Big Ben annual report described the project as "an independent evaluation" for the Air Force recommending future research and development programs in chemical as well as biological (bacteriological) weapons.[19] Big Ben operated from January 1952 until January 1958, when it was terminated by a cutback in Air Force funds. Professor Krieger served as principal investigator, heading a team of thirty-seven employees, consultants, and members of a planning council. $2,900,000 was expended on Big Ben, including Air Force funds and an Army Chemical Corps stipend for field studies.[20]

Big Ben made Penn a center for CBW research and development. The university established the Institute for Cooperative Research (ICR) to house the parent CBW project and to attract other research projects. This institute offered the pooled resources of various university departments plus promised protection against security leaks. Project Summit, undertaken in 1955, involved "analysis of air-delivered CBW agent–munition combinations in counterinsurgency situations" and "development of mathematical models for computation of weapons effects." A 1963 version of the Summit contract mentioned evaluation of offensive and defensive CBW systems in "acceptable target situations."[21]

In 1961, two additional Chemical Corps contracts called for research to "develop through pharmacological research, data for new CW lethal and incapacitating agents." At this time ICR contracted with Penn's Foreign Policy Research Institute to produce a study of the psychological and political implications of CBW.[22] Finally in 1963, the Air Force contracted with ICR to investigate air-delivered chemical and biological munitions for counterinsurgent operations. This project, which paralleled the earlier Summit contract for the Army, was given the code name Spicerack. This contract was specifically concerned with counterinsurgent CBW in

Vietnam. Eventually, enough became publicly known about Spicerack and Summit to tie them both to the Indochina war.[23]

✳   ✳   ✳

Until September 1965, there appears to be no public record of dissent concerning the propriety of CBW research at Penn. Trustees, administrators, faculty, and staff privy to the knowledge that CBW research was going on all appear to have shared Trustee Gates's opinion that, not only were such projects proper, but that the university was an acceptable place for such study. Even those academics privately opposed to CBW research refrained from public opposition. Provost David Goddard, professor of botany and the university's highest ranking academic officer, asserted that "from the early days in which the university accepted the Department of Defense contracts, I had been personally opposed to CBW research." He went on to explain why he remained quiet about his opposition by saying that administrative leadership was necessary. "Were the president and provost perceived in public opposition to each other, this unity would have been destroyed."[24]

Such presumptions were challenged, however, through a chain of events beginning in the summer of 1965. Robin Maisel, a Penn undergraduate affiliated with the Trotskyist Young Socialist Alliance (YSA), was employed as a college bookstore clerk. He discovered ICR's offices, out of public view on the second floor of a Mercedes-Benz dealership. He then reviewed the list of ninety books ordered by the ICR over a six-month period, noticing a concentration on rice crop diseases and Vietnamese politics. Maisel concluded that he had stumbled upon a university-sponsored CBW research project. Gabriel Kolko, Maisel's history professor, independently verified the substance of Maisel's suspicions and organized a faculty protest group, the University Committee on Problems of War and Peace. Maisel also took his information before the Penn-based Committee to End the War in Vietnam (CEWV), a group to which YSA members, as well as non-Trotskyists, belonged. Jules Benjamin, a graduate student working in Penn's Foreign Policy Research Institute (FPRI) and a member of CEWV, reconfirmed Maisel's suspicions. Benjamin sent background material on the ICR, Spicerack, and Summit to *Ramparts* and *Viet-Report*, both antiwar publications that gave Penn's involvement with the contracts widespread national publicity.

Based on confirmation from Kolko and Benjamin, CEWV sent a letter to Penn's president, Gaylord Harnwell, requesting that he terminate the contracts as "immoral, inhuman, and unbefitting to an academic institution," and calling for the closing of ICR. Immediately afterward, Maisel was fired from his bookstore job, and Benjamin was relieved of some duties at FPRI. President Harnwell and Professor Krieger also publicly justified the CBW research and unwittingly became de facto publicists of the anti-CBW viewpoint. Harnwell was quoted to the effect that Summit and Spicerack were "used in Vietnam to develop dispersal systems for defoliants." Krieger told reporters that Spicerack scientists were "carrying out field research on the effectiveness of chemical warfare in Vietnam" and "developing delivery systems" for toxic chemicals in Vietnam, specifically arsenic and cyanide compounds and chemical defoliants. Such disclosures through the media established the direct link between Penn research and the Indochina war.

The anti-CBW movement was enhanced in the fall of 1965 when Penn acquired a chapter of Students for a Democratic Society (SDS). By 1965, SDS had become a nationwide student antiwar organization. Its Penn chapter cosponsored anti-CBW activities with CEWV, and agreed with the Trotskyist argument to oppose CBW, not because it was classified, but because it was CBW research, commissioned for counterinsurgency use in an unjust war. The Penn student movement maintained a united position emphasizing the ethical and moral consideration of the CBW issue throughout a twenty-month struggle.[25]

The Penn campus also had an official chapter of Young Americans for Freedom (YAF), a student group whose goal, according to its Penn chair, was "for anti-Communist college students—left, right, or center—to confirm their support for the President's policy in Vietnam." In October 1965, National YAF organized a demonstration in Washington, in support of American war aims, that brought together five hundred students from forty colleges in twenty states, including representatives from the Young Republicans and Young Democrats. Though numerically small at Penn, there are some indications that YAF's viewpoint, at least in the fall of 1965, may have been widely shared. A *Daily Pennsylvanian* (*DP*) poll of ninety-six randomly contacted students indicated that 84 percent supported the U.S. policy in Vietnam. Of course, the official policy at that time was ambiguous, as war aims included prominent statements calling for an honorable peace. Until May 1967, Penn YAF never undertook campus protest as the left-wing students did. After all, they had no reason to protest for they stood on the side of the president of the United States, and Penn's president, trustees, and some of its faculty.[26]

By December 1965, at least four factions with differing views on the propriety of CBW research had emerged at Penn. The ensuing struggle, between 1965 and 1967, paralleled a debate among other American academics over the propriety of the Indochina conflict and the means to be used in fighting that war, including the use of CBW for counter-insurgency.

One faction was Gabriel Kolko's faculty group, the University Committee on Problems of War and Peace. It utilized the campus; local, national, and international media; teach-ins; and faculty forums to spread its contention that CBW was both immoral and illegal and that CBW research at Penn should be terminated immediately. The committee favored Penn's immediate and permanent divestiture of all CBW research, whether classified or not, whether publishable or not. The politics of the Kolko committee was radical, measured against the goals held by most other Penn faculty. Significantly, the members did not necessarily see themselves as radicals in the ideological sense. Edward Herman stated that "some of us thought we were defending law and primary values, à la Thomas Jefferson, who would perhaps have been on our side. Some of us were plain liberals."[27]

Defenders of the status quo comprised a second faction: President Harnwell and the trustees, administrators and faculty who had brought CBW research to Penn in 1951 and had nurtured it for fourteen years, and some student and off-campus supporters, such as the campus chapter of YAF. "We should engage in the business, secret or not," argued Trustee Gates in defense of such research. "We were meeting a national requirement of vast importance." Defenders of secret CBW research maintained, furthermore, that to deprive faculty members of the right to choose their research meant violating their academic freedom, which could be defined as the right to study anything.[28] This was the group that found itself under attack and, eventually, was forced to concede defeat.

A third faction, led by faculty senate chair Julius Wishner (psychology), may be described as mainstream faculty concerned with publishing CBW research in the open scholarly literature and not only as classified documents. According to this group, secret CBW research was inappropriate at Penn, apart from any moral or legal consideration.[29] Clearly Wishner defined academic freedom differently than did the defenders of the status quo.

Radical students constituted a fourth interest group. Their general objectives paralleled those of the Kolko committee and were summarized, at the time, by two Trotskyists in an interview for the *DP*: "We oppose CBW research not because it is classified but because it is CBW research, commissioned for use in an unjust war. We would be no less opposed if its results were wholly public."[30] Radical students were not wholeheartedly supported by the student body at large. On the one occasion when student radicals attempted to launch a political party of their own in the student government, their effort was overwhelmingly defeated at the polls—despite the endorsements of the campus newspaper.[31] However, student radicals were more successful in procuring off-campus support—local, national, and international.

*   *   *

Once the issue of CBW research had been raised by Penn's students, faculty members became embroiled in a debate, among themselves and with others, over the propriety of the research.

Kolko's committee sent out detailed circulars about its position on CBW research to all faculty members prior to the first faculty senate meeting in the fall of 1965. Even before that meeting on November 3, the physics department voted unanimously in favor of banning classified research on campus. The physics department formally disassociated itself from President Harnwell, a member of the department, and from his scientist allies in the chemistry department, ICR, and engineering schools. One physicist, Sidney Bludman, became a particularly strong supporter of the Kolko committee's effort and its spokesperson at faculty meetings and before professional organizations such as the Federation of American Scientists.[32]

Julius Wishner opened the first faculty senate meeting of 1965–1966 by crediting Kolko with having first brought to his attention the possible existence of secret research on campus. Despite the efforts of the Kolko committee, faculty attention quickly turned to the issue of the secrecy, rather than the morality or the legality, of that research. For some this was the essence of the debate, but for others preoccupation with secrecy may have been a safe way to express a real opposition to CBW and its counterinsurgency use in Indochina.

President Harnwell responded to the faculty concern about secrecy and authored a resolution designed to win faculty concurrence without harming ongoing CBW research. The resolution stated:

> The University imposes no limitation on the freedom of the faculty in the choice of fields of inquiry or the media of public dissemination of the results obtained. It is the obligation of the faculty member to make freely available to his colleagues and to the public the significant results he has achieved in the course of his inquiries. [The faculty] will assume full responsibility in the public dissemination of their results through appropriate media to insure their maximum utility and to minimize the propagation of error.[33]

Harnwell defended the freedom to study anything. His reference to appropriate media was immediately lauded by Krieger and the CBW supporters. "Anything" could include CBW, and thereby, facilitate, in Krieger's word's, "the responsibility of the University to contribute to national defense." "Appropriate media" could include classified reports. Kolko and his supporters damned the Harnwell resolution as too elusive. They proposed an unsuccessful counterresolution for specific condemnation of classified research and the development of chemical-bacteriological weapons.

In the year following the passage of the Harnwell resolution, Wishner, with the guidance of a constitutional law professor, developed and gained senate approval of specific criteria for acceptable research, as outlined in broad form in the Harnwell resolution. A faculty senate resolution of November 10, 1966, established a special committee to advise the administration on the acceptability of research. Its guiding principle was that scholars could study anything, but results had to be publishable in the open scholarly literature, not only as classified documents. In accordance with this principle, it was argued that Penn should not accept contracts with clearance requirements that entailed approval from any agency outside the university before results of a study could be submitted for open publication or before certain personnel could be hired to work on a research project.

According to Wishner, the November 1966 resolution, which tightened the November 1965 Harnwell resolution, should have eliminated Summit and Spicerack. But faculty senate resolutions were only advisory, never binding. Wishner stated later that he underestimated the tenacity with which President Harnwell would ignore senate advice in order to protect "old friends" to whom he was "personally committed" since Big Ben days.[34]

The Kolko faction had no faith in the nonbinding and vague Harnwell resolution, which changed nothing at Penn. They also doubted whether Harnwell would implement the Wishner resolution. Having been unsuccessful in faculty debate, they continued their efforts to challenge the administration in the local and national press. They distributed materials to such publication as *Scientific American*, *Science*, *Scientific Research*, and the *New York Times*.

As already noted, it was Penn's radical students who initiated the protest against CBW; attracted the support of sympathetic faculty; and focused media attention on the issue, first in the campus press (*DP*) and subsequently in the nationwide left-wing press (*The Militant*, *Ramparts*, and *Viet-Report*).[35] The student radicals used a variety of tactics in their protest.

After their letter to Harnwell, CEWV was responsible, in October 1965, for the first international negative publicity that Penn's contracts received. The forum was the International Vietnam War Teach-in in Toronto, sponsored by a coalition of Canadian and U.S. antiwar groups, including CEWV. At that teach-in, University of Michigan professor Richard Mann, cued by CEWV, suggested a connection between ICR's studies and the Vietnam War: "When I see the ICR at the University of Pennsylvania trying to find out how to poison a nation's rice supply, then I must protest."[36] Later that month, CEWV marshalled a protest march to ICR's inconspicuous building, as part of the International Days of Protest against the Indochina conflict. On November 8, CEWV descended on the ICR a second time. Featured speakers included a YSA spokesperson who emphasized opposition to "genocidal CBW, whether secret or not."[37] On December 10, SDS and CEWV, took their demonstrating to the very heart of the Penn campus, the circle directly outside Harnwell's office. Signs at that demonstration advocated: No Genocide Research for Vietnam and Stop Johnson's Dirty War, Krieger's Dirty Research. The demonstrators clashed with other students and nine student pickets were injured. Both SDS and CEWV capitalized on this confrontation. Claiming violation of their right to protest, these groups held a much larger rally on the same spot the following day. They emphasized their anti-CBW position as well as freedom of speech.[38]

In addition to the spectacular SDS–CEWV protests which drew national and international media coverage, the groups organized, as a regular feature on campus, weekly bitch-ins on the CBW–Indochina war issues. Bitch-ins were held in Houston Hall's open plaza Tuesday mornings at 11 A.M., the only time during the normal college week when no classes were scheduled. Prowar and antiwar harangues were the normal bill-of-fare. A guitarist who composed, performed, and produced a record album of songs about counterinsurgency, CBW, and Indochina was introduced by YSA–CEWV. One composition, titled "ICR Song" reflected the philosophical orientation of YSA–CEWV by mocking an ICR professor, possibly Krieger.[39]

Other student protests reflected similar intensity. On Penn's Founder's Day, January 1966, Harnwell was greeted by a contingent of CEWV pickets, prompting the *DP* headline "Harnwell Gives Honorary Degrees as Pickets March Outside." The following month, a city-wide demonstration outside the Federal Courthouse reemphasized the link between the issues of ICR and the Indochina war. In March, the linkage was republicized as a second International Days of Protest demonstration outside Independence Hall, at which CEWV, SDS, YSA, and the newly formed Veterans for Peace in Vietnam cooperated. The Philadelphia Committee for November 5, 1966, Mobilization was formed by CEWV and held a City Hall march and rally on that date. The following month there was a public debate on the propriety of CBW between a YSAer and two Penn YAFers. In March 1967, prompted by the CEWV–SDS actions, pacifist groups, including the American Friends Service Committee and the Fellowship of Reconciliation, held an Easter Peace March from the ICR building to the Capitol building in Washington, D.C., via the Army Chemical Corps installation at Fort Detrick, Maryland. They were addressed by faculty activist Albert Mildvan at the ICR building.

The student newspaper was another force moving to eliminate CBW research. The *DP* was run by a self-perpetuating board of editors, although it subsisted on a stipend from the administration. Throughout the CBW controversy, it took an anti-administration view, most notably in its anti-Harnwell editorials such as "The Many Faces of GPH" and "An Old Man." The latter column advised Harnwell, because of his insistence on keeping CBW at Penn, to "step aside" in favor of a man "closer in outlook to the students for which the University exists." The newspaper, moreover, through its daily news coverage, reported horrors of the Indochina war, which had inescapable associations with the campus controversy. In the two-year period from August 1965 to August 1967, only fifty-four issues of this daily paper did not mention the Indochina conflict. Most issues were replete with news of antiwar and antidraft protest and perceived abuses of demonstrators' civil rights.[40]

The *DP*, then, working independently of the student antiwar movement, functioned as an additional force pressuring the administration and trustees toward the elimination of CBW research. A survey of its editorial positions from October 1965 to August 1967, reveals, at first, a desire that the administration disclose all relevant information so that a rational dialogue could take place. Instead of forthrightness, the newspaper staff felt that it was hearing double talk, and thereafter was suspicious and careful of its contacts with the administration. On October 18, 1965, a *DP* editorial spoke to this point: "First we were told that the projects were not secret; then we were assured that a statement would be issued following an administrative meeting; then the meeting was cancelled; finally, we are told that no disclosure can be made because the information is classified. Equivocations only add fuel to the arguments of the project's foes."[41] In November 1965, when the DOD acknowledged large scale aerosol-spraying of Viet rice fields, the *DP* prodded the administration further: "Can it be said any longer that the studies of the ICR into the uses of chemical and biological agents in warfare are being done to get a better understanding of 'defensive' measures? A continued silence on [ICR] can only validate all that the protestors have said."[42] When several weeks later the administration proposed "resolving" the issue by transferring Summit and Spicerack from the ICR to the University City Science Center (UCSC), a private corporation of which Penn was principal stockholder, the

DP criticized the administration for "skirting the moral issue."[43] By the end of 1966, the *DP* was editorially calling upon the administration to halt all classified research.[44]

*   *   *

Mainstream faculty, led by faculty senate chair Julius Wishner, had maintained confidence in President Harnwell after his November 1965 resolution on secret research and the November 1966 implementing resolution of the faculty senate. They believed Harnwell would divest Penn of secret research when he abolished the ICR in late 1966. As *Time* and *Newsweek* pointed out, the transfer of research to another part of the university only eliminated the apparent target for shrill and divisive faculty-student protest. Harnwell's maneuver in no way terminated Summit and Spicerack, which remained contractual obligations between Penn and the DOD.[45]

In late 1966, according to Wishner, Harnwell gave oral assurances that there had been no request for the renewal of Summit from the Chemical Corps, hence it would terminate in March 1968. The university would, furthermore, divest itself of the Air Force's Spicerack contract. Since Spicerack contained both types of clearance requirements forbidden under the November 1966 faculty senate resolutions, Wishner was gratified by Harnwell's assurances and conveyed his gratification both to the senate's research oversight committee and the senate itself. Despite these oral assurances, Spicerack was renewed in March 1967. According to Penn's federal relations coordinator at that time, Donald Murray, it was renewed to assure the continuation of USAF funding of Spicerack at its probable new home, the USCS. A letter to Wishner and others explaining this reasoning was en route to them when the Philadelphia *Bulletin* learned of the renewal through an inadvertent remark by Harnwell, made during a general interview, and published it in its Sunday, March 19, 1967 edition.[46]

News of the renewal reached Wishner via that Sunday morning's news story, and he received a number of calls from upset faculty. Wishner was outraged at what he considered Harnwell's breach of trust, and convened the steering committee of the faculty senate, with Harnwell present, to deal with the matter. According to Wishner, Harnwell was asked to explain what had happened. Wishner stated that Harnwell's explanation was

> very verbose. He seemed to be saying "I sort of signed it in a careless moment or something." [We were] outraged at this and asked the president to put in a call to the Air Force, while he was sitting there, that rescinded his signature. He proceeded to do it. We had him send a telegram on top of the telephone call, since by that time I suppose we couldn't be sure to whom he was talking and whether he was reporting accurately to us.[47]

After the meeting, however, the administration continued its efforts to have Spicerack relocated to the UCSC. Apparently Harnwell still differentiated between research undertaken at the university proper and at the University City Science Center. Most faculty, by this time, did not make such a distinction.

From mid-March 1967, moderate and radical faculty, plus radical students and the *DP*, were united, for the first time, on the single objective of forcing a cancellation of the Spicerack contract; transferral to some other quasi-university body was not an acceptable option to them. Even the continuation of Summit through 1968 became secondary to the issue of Spicerack's fate. Aroused faculty became more militant than ever. One professor threatened to wear a gas mask at the May commencement. Kolko, in a letter to the *DP* of April 5, argued that CBW research

> has given Penn a national reputation which is positive only in that it serves as a tocsin to other universities not to walk the same path. In the end, the University will lose its chemical warfare research, even if it is moved to the Science Center, and that Penn-controlled organization will become the new focus of controversy. That fight may take years, but the administration should now assume in its planning a struggle it will eventually lose.[48]

Student protest reached a critical stage after the revelation of the secret renewal of Spicerack in the March 19 Philadelphia *Bulletin*. On April 4, 1967, a solitary pacifist student commenced a short-lived one-man stand-in in front of Harnwell's office. He held the placard: End

University Support of War Research. Between April 8 and 15, Benjamin of CEWV co-chaired Penn participation in National Vietnam Week. A teach-in on CBW at Penn featured Carol Brightman, the author of extensive *Viet-Report* articles on CBW, and Kolko committee member Herman. The week culminated in a massive antiwar demonstration outside the United Nations Building. On April 26, the university's traditional Hey Day rites were interrupted when, in addition to customary canes and straw hats, some marchers donned gas masks, and stood in silent protest during Harnwell's address in Irvine Auditorium. According to a student organizer of that protest, "the only way to make the University cease its action in C–B warfare [was] to embarrass it in public."[49] By mid-April 1967, students formed an ad hoc organization called STOP—Students Opposed to Germ Warfare Research. STOP included veteran CEWV participants such as Benjamin and the Hey Day marchers, but was led by college junior Joshua Markel, a relative newcomer to the student antiwar movement. As STOP protestors occupied Harnwell's office on April 26 and 27, Markel compared the Penn president to Adolf Eichmann who, "having been told that gassing people is immoral, agrees, but says he has to honor his gas contract anyway."[50]

From March 19, 1967, on, radical student protest received the endorsement of the *DP*, which had not previously advocated nonviolent direct action. In March 1967, the *DP* reemphasized that students and faculty were "entitled to know where their university [stood] on the topical issue of chemical and biological warfare research." Not receiving an adequate response from the administration, the *DP* endorsed some of the most extreme demands of the radical students. One editorial stated that, after twenty months of equivocation, Penn could only cleanse itself by "saying farewell to all forms of inhumane research, whether on campus or at an off-campus front institution." Since the administration still seemed unwilling to budge, the campus newspaper took the editorial position of wholeheartedly supporting, on moral grounds, direct-action protest against the scheduled transfer of Spicerack to the UCSC. One of their editorials was entitled: "Let's Help STOP Now."[51]

During the period of radical students' and *DP* protests, Wishner convened a faculty senate meeting, on April 13, 1967, because of what he perceived as administrative duplicity. That body voted, 109 to 47, its "dismay" at both the extension of Spicerack, and the way in which the extension was negotiated, "in such a way as to deny information to the faculty and to its appropriate committees."[52] A second meeting was held on May 3, after a student sit-in had already commenced in Harnwell's office. This meeting was marked by bitter debate between Kolko committee supporters and faculty advocates of secret research. A motion was made to censure Mildvan and his associates for bringing discredit to the university in the national press. Wishner ruled the motion out-of-order on technical grounds, later commenting that "I had the hardest time ever of keeping members from bitter ad hominem attacks. All the work of two years could have come apart in personal acrimony. There would surely have been a series of motions of censure of various personalities." Wishner was equally critical of the efforts of Kolko committee members to press the moral issue to a point where "everything might have been lost," i.e. the progress that had been made on establishing university guidelines on classified research.[53]

The meeting reached a critical stage when Professor Philip Rieff (sociology) put forth a broadly-supported motion calling for condemnation of Harnwell if Spicerack was not immediately terminated. At that critical moment, Provost David Goddard pleaded that the Rieff resolution be tabled pending the trustees' deliberations the next day, May 4. Goddard argued that the trustees "had a far better chance to make a reasonable and wise solution if the faculty would trust them to act in these next few days. A majority of you in the next few days will feel the university has made a wise decision and that you will give it honor and support."[54] What underlay Goddard's plea was his awareness that the nine-member executive committee of the trustees had, that very day, unanimously voted to recommend to the full board the termination of contracts that involved any secrecy. At Goddard's request, the senate voted to table the censure proposal until after the full board of trustees meeting. Goddard issued a similar request for patience to approximately 150 students that same evening. If the board of trustees voted to retain Spicerack and Summit, Goddard claimed that he was prepared to resign, having privately opposed the research all along, and having seen the entire future of the university jeopardized by the continued presence of Summit and Spicerack.[55]

On May 4, 1967, the board of trustees assembled. The unanimous recommendation of their own executive committee to terminate all secret contracts was before them. They faced the combined pressures of faculty dissatisfaction, an on-going student sit-in at the president's office, and negative publicity in campus, local, national, and international media. Ahead of them was Kolko's pledge of sustained and growing opposition on campus. By a vote of thirty-nine to one, the trustees chose to terminate, not transfer, both Summit and Spicerack. Faced with chaos on campus, the trustees felt it unwise to continue projects held so much in disfavor by significant elements of the campus. It returned both contracts, uncompleted, to the defense department.[56]

✳   ✳   ✳

What was the significance of the CBW struggle to each of the four factions involved in the dispute?

All four agreed, in the end, that Penn acted sensibly in divesting itself of the contracts, but their views were based on varied premises. Gates argued from the trustees' viewpoint that "[y]ou can't obstinately stub your toe forever until it's broke. You have to bend with the wind a bit. The wind was blowing this way, and I think we had no choice. I regret it, however."[57] For him, ending campus divisiveness prevailed over a deeply-held patriotism. There is apparently no record of the reactions of Harnwell and the CBW scientists. Some may not have been as resigned to the outcome as Gates was, although there was little else the trustees could have done in defense of CBW short of jeopardizing the entire future of the university.

For faculty moderates, the CBW crisis had forced a resolution of the gnawing ethical dilemma of secret research versus academic freedom. Penn's senate resolved the issue in a straightforward manner which is still in force today. In the words of Robert Davies (molecular biology): "the mechanism that removed [Summit and Spicerack] from the university, removed, in all, thirty-seven classified programs. All university research programs are not in the clear. It had a major effect at the U. of P."[58]

In a retrospective article for the *American Association of University Professors Bulletin*, Wishner argued that "the discussion and resolution of the many difficult problems that arose reflected credit on the entire university community. The precedent of resolving such problems through extensive faculty participation in dialogue and discussion, particularly through the University Senate, is now hopefully well established."[59]

The secrecy issue at Penn was resolved, furthermore, without the violence and death that marred a similar controversy at the University of Wisconsin's Army Math Research Lab.

Radical faculty and students also viewed the May 1967 denouement as a victory. But the radicals claimed a different victory than did Wishner and his faculty supporters. For the radicals, the hand of the trustees was forced, so the divestiture could hardly be considered a creditable act. It was a calculated and forced choice.[60] The divestiture, moreover, probably did not substantially damage the U.S. war effort in Indochina. Spicerack was almost immediately assumed by the private research firm of Booz–Allen–Hamilton of Chicago.[61] However, for the protestors, there was more than an existential satisfaction. They saw the betterment of the American university, and the American society at large, as a result of their efforts. In a retrospective article on the Penn experience, Kolko advanced the hope that "in taking such stands, the American university community may rediscover its own essential purpose and prepare the way for its own renaissance. It may also serve as the last important institutional refuge for the preservation of civilized values and conduct in America today."[62] Kolko's belief was grounded in the political victory at Penn, where citizens, at a certain historical juncture, were able to organize, act, and achieve local, and for themselves moral, ends.

Although it is difficult to know for sure, the viewpoint of radical faculty and students on the nature of U.S. participation in the Indochina conflict may be shared by more Penn alumni today than students of 1965–1967. Many students during the mid-sixties, as indicated by the *DP* poll cited earlier, either sat on the sidelines throughout the entire CBW controversy, or tacitly supported Lyndon Johnson's policy of an "honorable peace." Since then, the Pentagon Papers, and other revelations, have documented the severe nature of the U.S. counterinsurgency campaign, which included the wide-spread use of Agent Orange and other CBW agents. Unless one still views U.S. participation in the Indochina war as a struggle in which vital U.S. interests were at stake, the Penn divestiture of its CBW contracts may be considered a positive act. No other American university, at the height of the Indochina conflict, decided to make any such clear break with classified war research.

Clifford Wilcox

Antiwar Dissent in the College Press
The Universities of Illinois and Michigan

S everal studies have dealt with the role of the media in the antiwar movement. Virtually all of them have focused on major national newspapers and television networks.[1] Even though college and university students generated some of the most articulate and sustained antiwar protest, no studies have yet examined the response of college student newspapers to the war.

Of course, the student press did not represent a unified voice—very significant differences existed among college newspapers. Nevertheless, when viewed as a single entity, the college press during the late sixties and early seventies possessed some extremely interesting characteristics. More than eighteen hundred college dailies were published during these years. They had a combined circulation of six million, which came close to 10 per cent of all U.S. dailies, and they had a readership of 96 per cent of their audience compared to 80 per cent for newspapers of general circulation.[2] The college press during the Vietnam War reached a high percentage of one of the most socially cohesive groups in American society, and campus papers had significant power to influence the people within this group.

Student newspapers have a long history at American colleges and universities. Almost a dozen college dailies have been published for over one hundred years.[3] The role of student newspapers on college campuses, however, has never been simply defined. Regents, board members, administrators, and students have repeatedly disputed the rights of campus newspapers. Most college newspapers have been funded by college administrations, student governments, or journalism departments and, consequently, have been forced to conform to the editorial standards of those providing the financial support. However, a few student newspapers have established themselves as financially independent of their host institutions. Supporting themselves through advertising and circulation revenues, these papers have been able to maintain editorial independence from administrative or state legislative censure. The college newspapers generally regarded as "the elite" among the college press, including the *Yale Daily News, Cornell Daily Sun, Harvard Crimson, Michigan Daily*, Illinois *Daily Illini*, and *Columbia Spectator*, have all been operated as independent student newspapers throughout their long histories.[4]

The handful of college dailies that enjoyed editorial independence during the 1960s dealt with many controversial issues, often providing franker and more innovative coverage than the professional press. The student press provided, in particular, pathbreaking coverage of early civil rights and anti-in loco parentis activities.[5] Of all the issues student newspapers dealt with, however, none was more controversial or significant than the Vietnam War. The following describes how two representative members of the college press "elite," the *Michigan Daily* and the *Daily Illini*, responded to the Vietnam War.

A comparison of these two papers is interesting since both emerged during the middle-to-late sixties as strong opponents of the war, but the paths they had followed in getting to this position differed dramatically. The *Michigan Daily* had long had the reputation of being a liberal newspaper. The University of Michigan had a strong tradition of student activism, and the *Daily* had often joined cause with the activists through its editorials and columns. On the other hand, the *Daily Illini*, reflecting in some ways the conservatism of the Illinois campus, had long been regarded as a conservative newspaper.[6] But by the end of the 1960s, the issue of Vietnam had transformed both newspapers, and the once dramatic differences between the *Michigan Daily* and the *Daily Illini* had all but disappeared.

Critics of the college press in the 1960s often accused student editors of turning their papers into "radical" newspapers and emulating the underground press, which had burst into popularity in the late sixties.[7] Some college papers certainly deserved this criticism. The Amherst *Student*, for example, during the 1969 Vietnam antiwar moratorium, printed on page one a picture of a decapitated man with the caption "In the Land of the Pig, the Butcher is King."[8] The *Michigan Daily* and the *Daily Illini*, however, developed strong editorial opposition to the war but never deviated from the model of mainstream journalism. The intensity of their editorial opposition to the war pushed their efforts at objective reporting to the limit. But both newspapers exercised extreme control under difficult circumstances and produced newspapers that were quite liberal, similar to the New York *Post* or *The Nation*, but were well within the bounds of establishment, rather than underground, journalism.

As early as the twenties and thirties, the *Michigan Daily* had established itself as a newspaper with a distinctly liberal slant. In the late twenties, when most college students were politically quite conservative, the *Daily* argued for the acquittal of Sacco and Vanzetti. And in the thirties, the *Daily* adopted a number of unpopular and controversial stands, most notably, siding with labor in the sit-down strikes and with the Republican forces in the Spanish Civil War.[9]

In part, the *Daily*'s historically liberal orientation was a reflection of the highly politicized environment of the University of Michigan. Student activism had reached a high point at Michigan during the 1930s, when the Michigan chapter of the Communist-sponsored American Student Union became one of the largest in the nation. During that decade of economic depression, radical Michigan students organized a labor union which bargained successfully with the university for higher wages, overtime pay, and seniority rights for student workers. However, the coming of World War II dampened the expression of dissenting opinions on the Michigan campus. After the war, repression, fueled by the politics of Joseph McCarthy, gripped American college campuses and further discouraged the expression of dissenting political viewpoints. The majority of students in the fifties withdrew quietly from the political arena into the safe pursuit of conventional careers. Political apathy characterized the decade of the fifties at Michigan as well as at virtually all American colleges and universities. [10]

The early sixties saw a re-emergence of political activism on the Michigan campus. Central to this political reawakening was the *Michigan Daily*, led by its popular and controversial editor, Tom Hayden. The civil rights movement, driven in large part by black college students in the South, combined with fledgling grass roots efforts at colleges in the North to produce a new sense of political possibilities among college students. Hayden led the *Daily* into the front lines of the newly-developing activism on the Michigan campus. He wrote forceful editorials supporting students who were picketing the Ann Arbor S. S. Kresge and F. W. Woolworth stores, which had become national symbols of white racism after the sit-in at the whites-only lunch counter by black students in Greensboro, North Carolina. Hayden also mobilized the *Daily* against the administration's policies of in loco parentis, and worked to reinvigorate the university student government that had become moribund during the fifties.

Hayden continued to exert a strong influence on the *Daily* staffers after he graduated. His prominence as one of the founders and second president of Students for a Democratic Society (SDS) provided the *Daily* editors who followed in his wake an invaluable connection with the inner circle of the New Left. [11]

One other factor strongly influenced the *Daily* editors who followed in this period: a cherished sense of intellectual elitism among the staff members. This elitism was especially important in the *Daily*'s relationship with the Michigan journalism department. Most of the *Daily*'s writers and editors majored in liberal arts or social sciences rather than journalism. And the *Daily*, riding on its prestigious seventy-five-year-old tradition, reveled in taunting the journalism department by advertising the *Daily* as the "best journalism school in the country."[12]

The *Daily*'s bravado, however, was more than mere youthful posturing. The articles and editorials from this period reflect an unusual sophistication in their writers, gained through wide reading in history, political science, and sociology. This sophistication can be seen in two ways: the awareness the editors had of news events throughout the world, and the insight they revealed in presenting and commenting on those events.

Newspaper editors have tremendous power over the presentation of news to the public, most obviously in placement of stories and in writing headlines. Most editors of college newspapers through the early-1960s followed a standard formula for the presentation of news. Campus stories were almost always given the lead. The majority of national and international news was usually relegated to a small corner of an inner page in a section of news clips pasted together from Associated Press (AP) wire stories. [13]

The editors of the *Michigan Daily* during the early-1960s distinguished themselves in their approach to presenting news to the campus community. *Daily* headlines and lead stories were usually devoted to national and international news. A comparison of the coverage by the *Michigan Daily* and the *Daily Illini* of the same or similar events reveals significant differences in perspective and emphasis. This comparison will illustrate the development of the *Daily Illini*, during the Vietnam era, from a newspaper that predominantly focused on campus events to a newspaper, like the *Michigan Daily* of the 1960s, with an international point of view. [14]

Moreover, by evaluating the responses of the two newspapers to critical developments in the Vietnam War, we can see the manner in which the editors dealt with the increasingly personal aspects of the war. For the conflict in Vietnam had started out as an extremely abstract and removed issue. But as the war escalated, the reality of personal involvement came home to American college students. The editorial changes of the *Daily* and the *Illini* over the decade of the sixties reveal the transformation of the student editors and their readers from observers to participants in the larger Vietnam War.

On the afternoon of August 4, 1964, the United States launched air strikes against North Vietnam. President Johnson claimed that these strikes were in retaliation for North Vietnamese torpedo boat attacks on the U.S. destroyer *Maddox*. The *Washington Post* praised Johnson, stating "President Johnson has earned the gratitude of the free world as well as of the nation for his careful and effective handling of the Viet-Nam crisis." With the exception of James Reston, the national press also supported Johnson's Gulf of Tonkin Resolution. [15]

The *Michigan Daily*, however, condemned the attack and urged the U.S. to take the lead in settling the conflict in Southeast Asia at the peace table rather than through military aggression. *Daily* writer Lawrence Kirshbaum called attention to the political opportunism Johnson displayed in taking the "campaign sting out of the Republican cries for a stronger military posture." *Daily* editors Ken Winter and Edward Herstein further attacked the Johnson administration, casting doubt upon the official explanation offered for the Tonkin Gulf attack and warning their readers of the possible abuse of the power Johnson had won from Congress through the Tonkin Gulf Resolution.[16]

In the fall of 1964, events in Vietnam did not affect students on campus as they would by 1966. College students were not yet being drafted by the thousands—the United States had only twenty thousand men in Vietnam in 1964, and they were there as advisers, not soldiers. But the *Daily* continued to devote front-page stories and editorials to Vietnam. Using the stories obtained through the AP, the *Daily* editors gave front-page coverage throughout 1964 and 1965 to the stories of constant toppling of South Vietnamese governments and continued escalation of America's military effort against North Vietnam. They also editorialized on the developments in Vietnam—almost always against United States involvement.[17]

Accompanying and possibly inspiring the *Daily* editors' awareness and concern over Vietnam was the concern of activist Michigan faculty members. Professors like William Gamson, Anatol Rapoport, Kenneth Boulding, and Arnold Kaufman, among others, led a group of the faculty in a sustained protest against American involvement in Vietnam. This protest achieved national attention through the March 24, 1965 all-night teach-in they conducted on the campus of the University of Michigan.[18]

The *Michigan Daily* supported the faculty organizers through in-depth reporting and editorials. The *Daily* also served as an advertising vehicle through which the faculty could communicate to the students. On the morning of the teach-ins, more than two hundred Michigan professors appealed to their students to attend the teach-in through a full-page advertisement in the *Daily*. The war in Vietnam, they urged, had grave "moral, political, and military consequences" and the faculty sponsors needed the students to participate with them in the "search for a better policy."[19]

The University of Michigan teach-in inspired similar events at universities and colleges throughout the nation. The *Michigan Daily* devoted front-page coverage to these teach-ins and, when possible, sent *Daily* reporters to cover the events. The *Daily* editors' emphasis on national coverage of teach-ins reflected their understanding of the growing importance of antiwar thought and activity in the nation.[20]

During the early years of America's involvement in Vietnam, the significant developments were mostly military and occurred overseas. The *Daily* had to rely upon the Associated Press to report these events. Beginning in 1965, however, domestic antiwar events became a significant aspect of America's involvement in Vietnam. While the *Daily* still had to rely on the AP to provide coverage of military developments, the *Daily* covered domestic Vietnam War events, such as national protest marches in Washington and New York, by sending its own reporters.[21]

While protest marches occurred in the streets of major American cities, much antiwar protest also occurred on college campuses. The University of Michigan was convulsed by a series of protests in the late sixties. The two most dramatic of these were waged over the administration's practice of releasing individual class standings of male students to local draft boards and the widespread involvement of Michigan faculty members in classified military research.

Although the fight against the policy of releasing class standings to draft boards was led primarily by the Student Government Council, the *Daily* provided extensive reporting and editorializing on the issue.[22] The *Daily* led the fight over faculty involvement in classified military research. The *Michigan Daily* was not unique in raising the issue of secret military research on American campuses. The controversy at the University of Pennsylvania had become national news by the fall of 1967.[23] (See Jonathan Goldstein's chapter, "Agent Orange on Campus: The Summit–Spicerack Controversy at the University of Pennsylvania, 1965–1967.) The *Daily* simply played the classic role of the muckraking newspaper by challenging, not the presence of secret military research at Michigan, but the hypocrisy of Michigan students, professors, and administrators who allowed the research to continue. *Daily* editor, Roger Rapoport, summed up the charge against the University of Michigan community (including the *Michigan Daily* itself) in the first of several editorials he wrote on military research at Michigan: "One thing clearly emerges from all the reports on military research at the University: for all the outward antiwar sentiment voiced by administration, faculty, and student leaders, the

University of Michigan is playing an integral role in the Vietnam War."[24] The *Daily* crusaded for months against military, especially classified, research on campus. But a year after Rapoport had initiated the campaign, *Daily* editorialist Henry Grix could state: "Despite arguments that the University's affairs with the Defense Department are immoral or at least unfortunate, researchers here are unlikely to relinquish their claims on handsome government contract offers."[25]

The *Daily* was not able to change so fundamental an aspect of the university as its financial link to the Defense Department. However, the *Daily*, which in 1964 and 1965 had been outspoken in its opposition to the war, was joined in the late sixties by most of the faculty and students in their opposition. Over two thirds of the student body attended the October 15, 1969, moratorium observance in Michigan Stadium. Even the president of the university, Robben Fleming, participated in the moratorium. The antiwar position had become mainstream at the University of Michigan by late 1969.[26]

*　　*　　*

The University of Illinois represents a contrast to the University of Michigan. Unlike the University of Michigan, Illinois has not had a strong tradition of student activism. Pacifism enjoyed some popularity during the thirties, but radicalism never attracted more than a very small number of students until the late-1960s. For most of its history, the University of Illinois has had the reputation of being a relatively conservative university.[27]

Student journalism at Illinois has reflected this conservative tradition. Although the *Daily Illini* is one of the nation's oldest independent college newspapers, the newspaper has, from its inception, maintained informal links to the university's journalism department. Several of the professors in the journalism department have served as mentors for *Illini* writers and editors. And, unlike the staff on the *Michigan Daily*, the majority of the *Illini* staff have majored in journalism.[28]

In 1964 the *Daily Illini* had a predominantly local focus. Headlines and front-page stories were devoted to the construction of an intramural sports building on campus or to athletic events rather than to developments in Vietnam, civil rights, or the Berkeley Free Speech Movement. When the *Michigan Daily* ran the story on the FBI arresting twenty men for the murders of the Mississippi civil rights workers, the *Daily Illini* ran "Illini Stun UCLA, 110–83." The editorials were similar to the reporting: the editors rarely commented on national or international issues.[29]

By early 1965, however, the *Daily Illini* editors began to run Vietnam stories, frequently on the front page. The appearance of these stories in the *Illini* often coincided with the occurrence of antiwar events on campus, such as a lecture by the outspoken Senator Ernest Gruening or the Illinois faculty teach-in on Vietnam. The editors of the *Illini* had demonstrated their growing awareness of the significance of antiwar expression by publishing a brief announcement of the teach-in at the University of Michigan. But they did not cover any of the teach-ins that followed the Michigan event at other universities until May of the same year when antiwar faculty at Illinois held their own teach-in.[30]

The *Illini*, moreover, did not play the same role in the Illinois teach-in as did the *Daily* in Michigan. The *Daily* editors praised the professors for sponsoring the teach-in and strongly encouraged students to attend. In contrast, the *Illini* editors neither endorsed the teach-in, nor encouraged attendance. The *Illini* editorial, which ran after the teach-in, reflected the lack of momentum the event had generated with the observation that the few strong opinions that had been expressed at the teach-in were blown away "in a cool, damp gust of student apathy."[31]

The *Illini* continued to devote minimal coverage to Vietnam military and antiwar events throughout 1966. By the end of that year, however, protests began to occur on the Illinois campus, and the *Illini* began to cover them in earnest. The *Illini*'s change of policy reflected the editor's increased awareness of the war that came, particularly, with the escalation of the draft and with the occurrence of significant protest incidents on the Illinois campus.[32]

The turning point in the *Daily Illini*'s approach to the Vietnam War came with the protests against recruiting on the Illinois campus by the Dow Chemical Company. The Dow protests were the first aggressive student protests at Illinois. Rather than simply rallying and making speeches against the war, the students forced their way into the building where recruiters were conducting interviews and refused entrance to virtually all interview candidates. The university administration treated the protest organizers harshly: several students were expelled without even receiving an open hearing. This action against the students polarized the university. The *Daily Illini* warned the administrators that expelling the organizers of the protests would not stop the protests; by expelling the organizers, the administration was giving the Illinois student movement martyrs. Furthermore, the *Illini* argued, the administration's harsh treatment of student activists was "giving the campus the unity and focus [the lack of which had] kept activism weak for so long."[33]

The *Daily Illini's* antiwar position became fully obvious by the 1969 moratorium. The *Illini* journalists who had initiated coverage of antiwar events in 1967 were now the controlling editors of the newspaper. The 1969 moratorium day edition of the *Illini* reflected the antiwar position of these editors. The entire front page was left respectfully blank to communicate the message of the moratorium—that all work must cease for a day to allow the nation to evaluate the direction in which it was proceeding in Vietnam.[34]

The most dramatic example of the transformation of the *Illini* from a removed observer of antiwar protests to a newspaper with a pronounced antiwar point of view was the *Illini's* coverage of the Illiac computer. The Illiac IV, designed by scientists at the University of Illinois, was the world's first supercomputer.[35] The promoters of the Illiac had introduced it to the university as a system capable of solving extremely complex problems in weather prediction, world agricultural planning, and ecology. However, the *Illini* had discovered that the Illiac was being built with twenty-four million dollars of Department of Defense (DOD) money, and actually was going to be used primarily to solve complex problems in nuclear weapons research.

In a series of exclusive stories, the *Daily Illini*, led by news editor Carl Schwartz, exposed the connection of the Illiac to the DOD. While front-page stories reported the details of the military funding, the editorial page expressed bitter opposition to installing the computer on campus. The *Illini* denounced the deceitful manner in which the university had publicized the Illiac: as a system dedicated to humanitarian projects, such as agricultural and ecological research, rather than for weapons research. More important, the editors of the *Illini* challenged the connection between military research on university campuses and increasing American involvement in such technology-intensive wars as the war in Vietnam.[36]

By 1970, the *Daily Illini* had matched the *Michigan Daily* in its antiwar position; both were committed opponents of the Vietnam War. Moreover, both newspapers had moved from simply covering the war through AP stories to uncovering the war's effects on their local campuses. The *Illini* and the *Daily* each had exposed the depth of commitment their universities had to military research and challenged the professors and administrators to renounce the connections. Most important, the process of reacting to and interpreting war developments, through editorials and columns, prompted deep personal changes in the student journalists. Perhaps most compelling is the path of John Hundley, 1969–1970 editor-in-chief of the *Daily Illini*. Hundley had come to the University of Illinois from Louisville, Illinois, a small town in the south central part of the state. He was not politically active when he came to the university; he had come to study agricultural journalism. Hundley got involved with the *Daily Illini*, though, and that proved to be his political education. Following his graduation, Hundley acted on the moral beliefs he had developed through covering the war and chose to risk going to prison as a conscientious objector, rather than be drafted into combat in Vietnam.[37]

*   *   *

As the examples of the *Michigan Daily* and the *Daily Illini* illustrate, Vietnam transformed the student press in the 1960s. Prior to the war, student newspapers could comfortably limit their news coverage to local campus events. However, as the war escalated, foreign and national developments became directly relevant to students. The draft had forced college students to confront the war. Most were either facing the draft themselves or had friends or relatives who were. College newspapers became the primary source of information and interpretation of the war for these students. High-profile campus antiwar demonstrations were covered by all members of the national press. But only the most sophisticated members of the student press pursued the deeper, more significant, campus manifestations of the war, such as faculty-military classified research and complicity between college administrators and draft boards over student deferments.

College newspapers that seriously engaged the war issue faced a choice. They could become like the underground press, with its vehemently antiwar editorial bias. Such papers often exhibited a hostility to editing; editors were "fascists" who attempted to impose their personal standards on other contributors to the newspaper. Or, they could become like the establishment press, in which editors strove to separate news reporting from editorial comment. However beleaguered this goal of objectivity had become by the 1960s, it still functioned as a working principle to provide stability and purpose to the press, in a time when virtually all institutions of the American "establishment" were being regarded by the public with increasing skepticism.[38] Unlike many college newspapers, the *Michigan Daily* and the *Daily Illini* adhered closely to the model of the mainstream press. They certainly resembled the most liberal models of the establishment press, such as the New York *Post*. But through their rigorous maintenance of standard editing practices, they remained in the establishment camp nonetheless. In the same way that the preoccupations of the New Left turned from politics to counterculture in the late sixties, the radical underground press increasingly came to feature cultural over political news. The *Daily* and the *Illini* emphasized predominantly political over countercultural concerns throughout the 1960s.[39]

Unfortunately, the intensity that the *Daily* and the *Illini* developed during the Vietnam era could not be maintained through the 1970s. Concern over the war dropped dramatically with the dismantling of the draft in the early seventies. And the Kent State and Jackson State killings brought a war weariness and protest weariness to campuses through the nation. Without an issue of the magnitude of Vietnam to pursue, college newspapers lost their central focus and drifted back to covering more parochial campus issues.[40] College newspapers, in general, declined in popularity and influence during the seventies and eighties. The *Michigan Daily* symbolized the decline as it dropped from a daily press run of 11,000 during the late sixties to a mere 3,700 in 1985.[41] However, although the college press may have slipped into a lull, student newspapers continue to be published on almost two thousand campuses in the United States. And given their history of publication over the last one hundred years, it is safe to expect them to continue publishing for decades to come. The accomplishments during the Vietnam era of a few college papers, like the *Michigan Daily* and the *Daily Illini*, stand as models for what the college press can someday become again.

Glenn W. Jones

Gentle Thursday
An SDS Circus in Austin, Texas, 1966–1969

I n the late sixties, the Austin, Texas, Students for a Democratic Society (SDS) chapter sponsored five celebrations of countercultural community and participatory politics they called Gentle Thursday. Gentle Thursday was a sixties experimental expressive form that invented and displayed multiple semiotic codes in resistance to mainstream America. Sixties expressive forms like Gentle Thursday were precursors of new social movements that are as concerned with self and group identity formation as with political transformation. The oppositional force of Gentle Thursday developed from its "relatively autonomous origins" within the Austin SDS and the countercultural bohemian community.[1]

Gentle Thursday took place on the then grass-covered expanse of the West Mall at the University of Texas campus in Austin. On November 3, 1966, and on four similar occasions over the next three years, Gentle Thursday transformed a central avenue used by everyday pedestrian traffic into a highly visable stage for a Texas version of a hippie love-in. The choice of a non-sanctioned ordinary class day and the appropriation of a mundane space provide initial clues to Gentle Thursday's oppositional agenda.

At the sixties cultural performance called Gentle Thursday, members of the community of Austin's bohemians, New Leftists, and proto-counterculturalists sat on the grass, played music, played with balloons, blew soap bubbles, drew with colored chalk, and shared food and conversation. Although sds sponsored Gentle Thursday, participation in the event was open to all. Austin sds distanced Gentle Thursday from overt political protest actions by proclaiming: "This will be no sds function but a circus for everyone." However, because it was organized by sds and was an expression of the developing Austin countercultural community, active participation was a sign of ideological solidarity with radical politics and bohemian values which were in opposition to dominant structures. Students who stepped off the sidewalks of the West Mall to join those sitting on the grass thereby became performers in a rite of separation from mainstream society.

In keeping with its theme of gentleness, peace, and love, Gentle Thursday, in contrast to many other American cultural performances, did not feature contests or competitive games. The event had a minimal script, no opening or closing ceremony, and nothing on sale. The Austin New Left and counterculture were inventing a festive form to express a new individual and group identity. In their project they had few guidelines: the performers at Gentle Thursday made it up as they went along.

At the first Gentle Thursday in 1966, bohemian dress tended toward earth tones and work clothes, with bright psychedelic colors and ethnic costume becoming increasingly popular later in the decade. Whether dressed in basic bohemian black or day-glo Indian prints, members of the counterculture used dress to set themselves apart from mainstream fashion.

Hair also functioned as a distinctive symbol of countercultural identity. Men grew their hair long and women replaced the bouffant or flip with more "natural" styles. Over twenty years later, it can be difficult to understand the shock that men with long hair had on the conformist sixties mainstream society, especially in Texas. One of Austin's bohemian musicians recalled the hazards encountered by the first longhairs in Texas: "We all knew how to fight because there were fights frequently. The town was overrun with frats and rednecks, and they hated the idea that you could parade around with long hair. I think alot of our political feelings came out of our wanting to look different and realizing how much society hated us for wanting to be different."[2]

During Gentle Thursday, local folksingers played guitars or banjos and sang folk or topical songs. In keeping with the event's participatory ethos, instruments were shared, and, often, several performances occured simultaneously. Musical diversity was added by a roaming band which played free-form tunes on flutes and kazoos while circulating among the overlapping circles of Gentle Thursday celebrants. A single bongo drummer provided a more urgent percussive undertone. The sound of energetic drumming marked Gentle Thursday's separation from the restrained everyday life of the mega-university.[3] Accomplished folk musicians made way for ad hoc performances that blurred the distinction between noise and music.

Although there was folk music, Gentle Thursday was not a folk music festival. Its primary activities were sharing food and conversation. No political speeches were made, but there were several intense debates over the rapidly escalating Vietnam War between SDS activists and members of the crowd standing on the surrounding sidewalks. These sometimes hostile, but more often puzzled, student spectators constituted Gentle Thursday's main audience. Members of the press, the university administration, and every police and intelligence agency in Central Texas were also among the interested observers.

One of the reasons the audience was puzzled was that not a great deal appeared to be going on. For most of the afternoon it resembled nothing so much as a somewhat noisy beatnik picnic. Like any picnic it emphasized sharing and casual playfulness. Yet, because of its context as an SDS circus, it was also a self-conscious act of resistance to mainstream society, opposition to the Vietnam War, and subversion of the codes of everyday life.

The use of simple childhood toys, such as soap bubbles and colored chalk, on Gentle Thursday by apprentices of the technocratic society was a quintessential counterculture ploy. Streams of soap bubbles and clusters of balloons provided a visual counterpart to the improvised tunes on flutes, kazoos, and bongo drums. Participants drew colorful designs and slogans with chalk on the sidewalks and limestone walls of university buildings that faced the mall. In their search for a form that would express and embody their alternative vision, Gentle Thursday participants recycled these childish props as markers of their separation from everyday life.

Gentle Thursday was both an enactment of New Left revolutionary aspirations and an instance of countercultural creative play. At Gentle Thursday, the Austin New Left hoped to prefigure, through performance, a postrevolutionary utopia in an actual present consciousness symbolized by streams of soap bubbles glittering in the Texas sunlight.

The use of colored chalk to inscribe countercultural and New Left slogans on university buildings also blurred the boundaries between political resistance and play. Make Love, Not War, graffiti expressed Gentle Thursday's opposition to the values of the dominant society and the Vietnam War. While they obviously lacked the basis for lasting structural change, such sixties slogans served to mobilize powerful affective forces of resistance to lockstep mainstream patrotism. The chalked graffiti of Gentle Thursday were an example of resistant nostalgias that operate by "making further inscriptions on the landscape of encoded things . . . in an effort to fragment the enclosing, already finished order and reopen cultural forms to history."[4]

The peace signs, bubbles, balloons, and flowers, as well as the music, dress, and play of Gentle Thursday, were all symbolic acts of New Left and countercultural community in Austin. The expressive forms of Gentle Thursday should be understood as symbolic acts which, rather than merely reflecting New Left and countercultural ideology, were themselves, as both formal symbols and actions, ideological acts in their own right "with the function of inventing imaginary or formal solutions to unresolvable social contradictions."[5]

From this theoretical perspective, the various expressive forms of Gentle Thursday can be seen as symbolic resolutions of fundamental social contradictions. For example, blowing bubbles on the West Mall was a symbolic act that resolved the opposition between New Left revolutionary politics and countercultural consciousness. The real contradiction between political organization and joyful community was displaced onto the symbolic act of blowing bubbles. This childish pastime was also symbolic of psychedelically induced withdrawal and transcendence. Bubble blowing at Gentle Thursday was a multivalent symbolic act that articulated impulses of psychedelic transcendence with New Left oppositional confrontation with the dominant system.

Each symbolic act contained within the Gentle Thursday festivity operated in an overarching symbolic field. For example, the V peace sign and the peace symbol were emblems of the opposition between the peace movement and the Vietnam War. They also established a symbolic field that expressed additional contradictions within the entire New Left and countercultural community in its struggle against the dominant sociopolitical order. Thus, the V-sign and the peace symbol expressed the totality of the drug-taking, antiwar, anti-establishment, and hip versus square, New Left and countercultural community.

The complexity of the counterculture's struggle against ideological closure and the real power of the dominant discourse becomes apparent in the process by which many countercultural symbolic actions and expressive forms were quickly contained and lost their oppositional values. For example, blue jeans in their sixties context symbolized the opposition between the counterculture and the dominant society and between middle-class students and the working class. Middle-class student cultural and political radicals wore the clothes of the working class, not just as an expression of solidarity with the working class as an agent of change, but also in order to "magically" exchange elect alienation for imagined preterite community.[6] However, blue jeans were adapted as part of an expanding leisure industry, where they symbolized youth and a casual outdoorsy lifestyle, instead of oppositional solidarity with a rural working class. That the oppositional nature of many countercultural expressive forms was contained within the elastic boundaries of the dominant power bloc is apparent from the rapidity with which many countercultural practices gained acceptance in the mass markets of consumer society. Other oppositional forms, such as the peace symbol and the V-sign were not so easily incorporated and continued to retain some of their counterhegemonic value even after the end of the sixties counterculture as an identifiable social formation.

The long hair, flowers, gods eyes, love beads—all the fantastic paraphernalia of the counterculture as well as its use of hallucinogenic drugs, adoption of black ethnic slang, and recourse to residual systems of traditional mysticism—were symbolic and scandalous enactments of unthinkable social contradictions. There was an ideological dimension to every aspect of the counterculture.[7] The singular subtexts of the symbolic acts of Gentle Thursday combined to form a multivocal front in a kaleidoscopic struggle between antagonistic discourses. At Gentle Thursday, white middle-class heirs to the consumer society of modern capitalist rationality embraced the primitive, the folk, and the passed over in a carnivalesque attempt to invent and construct oppositional space for an emergent and desperately contested counterhegemonic force.

Gentle Thursday employed multiple codes retrieved from the cultural debris of the participant's experience of growing up in 1950s America as well as homespun inventions from the emerging counterculture. Gentle Thursday's expressive forms were inspired by both an increasing sense of desperation on the part of SDS politcos over their failure to stop the Vietnam War and the first waves of countercultural utopian hope eminating from the Haight-Ashbury experiment in Better Living Through Chemistry.

Gentle Thursday's form was an attempt to communicate alternative, egalitarian values in a nonthreatening manner. It was influenced by SDS's search for a radical agency of change in theories of a new working class and student power. The originator of the Gentle Thursday concept was an Austin SDS member, Jeff Nightbyrd, who wanted to bring more students into SDS through a countercultural festival. Many of the Austin "praire power" faction of SDS shared the countercultural belief that resistance and even revolution could be achieved by changes in consciousness from which a structural transformation of society would follow. Over twenty years after the event, Jeff Nightbyrd recalled the immediate circumstances of the development of the Gentle Thursday idea:

> We were having an SDS meeting at the start of the fall semester in 1966. I threw out this idea for Gentle Thursday. Part of the image I had in my mind was a socialist revolution in Germany in the 1840s where they wouldn't walk on the grass. They were trying to make a revolution but they still obeyed the signs that said "keep off the grass." At UT there were these mental boundaries. People didn't step on the grass. Classrooms were rigid hierarchies. . . . The idea of Gentle Thursday was to create a counter-mentality manifested in action. We didn't just think the revolution—we lived it. When we first sat on the grass it was a big thing. The crowd was five or six deep standing on the sidewalk. They couldn't cross that cement boundary line. They were so shocked by our sitting on the grass. . . . At that SDS meeting there was a burst of energy after I made my pitch for Gentle Thursday, because it was something to do, and everybody could get behind it, and you didn't have to be a leader to be involved.[8]

Jeff Nightbyrd's account gives insight into the processes by which new cultural forms are invented. Gentle Thursday originated in response to Austin SDS's need to gain membership for its opposition to the Vietnam War. Its genesis was also informed by the perceived need of SDS members to discover a form by which to construct and express their individual and group identity in a situation of dramatic political and cultural transformation. Nightbyrd was articulating a private image that expressed the small Austin counterculture and New Left's need for an alternative oppositional expressive form. The Gentle Thursday idea sparked a debate among SDS members, but it was finally agreed to because it allowed a full range of participation. In the weeks prior to the first Gentle Thursday, the new form was very minimally described in a leaflet that proclaimed SDS's belief: that there is nothing wrong with fun.

At Gentle Thursday, Austin SDS was not calling for the overthrow of the university. However, in its immediate context, Gentle Thursday was a radical challenge to the orthodox values of the mega-university and mainstream society. And, as would become apparent in the later sixties, "fun" when advocated by the counterculture tended to take forms far beyond the acceptable limits of ordinary society—or even ordinary reality. The public celebration of Austin's bohemian underground community on the grass of the West Mall beneath the looming tower of the university's main building was a shocking and politically effective performance of transgression.[9]

Following the success of the first Gentle Thursday, Austin SDS made plans for another celebration which would be the centerpiece of a Flipped-out Week that would also feature an antiwar parade and a love-in concert at a park in downtown Austin. According to SDSer Thorne Dreyer, peace and love, New Left protest, and countercultural celebration would be combined. The planned parade against the Vietnam War "should be seen in another context as well—that of Gentle Thursday. Protest must be affirmative, creative. It is not enough to scream 'no'. . . . We must do a love thing: show that there are alternatives to the death we are asked to be a part of. We affirm life."[10]

This second Gentle Thursday, in the spring of 1967, took place during the University of Texas's Round-up festivities. Round-up was dominated by the university's active fraternity and sorority system which celebrated a stereotypical image of the Texas pioneer heritage that included various contests, exhibits, and dances with an Old West theme. Round-up week culminated in a 40-Acres Trail Drive parade of decorated

*   *   *

The civil rights movement went well beyond protesting the adjustment of the "well-adjusted slave" and translated political action into a crusade for new ways of being and becoming. When young activists formed SNCC in 1960, they consciously adapted the posture of a "beloved community" as a model for an interracial movement. Routine meetings were known as "soul sessions"; the experience of acting collectively was called a "freedom high." Later in the decade, Eldridge Cleaver (the Black Panther party's minister of information) titled an important essay on his personal and political transformation, "On Becoming."[13]

From its inception, with organizational roots in the churches of Southern black communities, the civil rights movement produced a language steeped in religion and spirituality and a political vision deeply influenced by the authority of personal identity, as well as the impact of racism on personal growth and change. Psychological questions were rooted more deeply in the historic traditions of black Christianity and church than in the postwar vocabulary of humanistic psychology because the explosion of psychological expertise—at least in the form of *voluntary* psychotherapy—was still mainly confined to the white middle class. Nevertheless, from early in the century, psychology had filtered steadily into theology and philosophy, just as it had filtered steadily into most other corners of American intellectual and cultural life. The line between religion and psychology had become less and less distinct.

Maslow, for one, thought that psychology had simply taken up where religion had left off, or more accurately, where religion had died. As far as he was concerned, psychology was the only really spiritually satisfying replacement for religion to come along in the twentieth century. Reinhold Niebuhr, Martin Buber, and Paul Tillich are only the most obvious examples of philosopher-theologians whose work inspired and was inspired by humanistic psychology, and whose influence was also strongly felt in the civil rights movement through the conduit of Martin Luther King, Jr. King's own Personalist theology and Gandhian philosophy of nonviolence brought the inner self into sharp focus and made psychological freedom an important goal of political action. "The Revolution of the Negro not only attacked the external cause of his misery, but revealed him to himself. He was *somebody*. He had a sense of *somebodiness*. He was *impatient* to be free."[14]

floats down Guadalupe Street next to the university campus. Among the spring 1967 events were a beard growing contest, a Round-up Rally with rock bands and Go-go Dancer Maggie, and a Western Dance. During Round-up week students not wearing Western clothes could be placed in a mock City Slickers jail constructed for the purpose on the West Mall.

The juxtaposition of Gentle Thursday and Flipped-out Week with Round-up enabled SDS and the local counterculture to present their oppositional and alternative programs in a dramatic fashion: "On the UT campus there is a hallowed tradition called Round-up. That's when all the cowboys get together. This year there will be Indians, too."[11]

The "Indians" of SDS soon found themselves embroiled in a dispute with the highest reaches of the University of Texas administration. Gentle Thursday was planned and took place in the panoptic space of the power structure and, therefore, required all the tactical expertise and everyday creative opportunism of the emergent counterculture. The young members of Austin's SDS outmaneuvered the UT administration by taking advantage of a "chance offerings of the moment."[12] After some negotiation, university administrators finally approved the portion of SDS's Gentle Thursday program that included "picnicking, guitar playing, poetry reading, sitting on the grass, and stump speaking." However, the UT administration objected to other parts of the Gentle Thursday program: "Grooving, kissing, mellow yellow, all these things needed clarification. I had never heard of mellow yellow before last week. I read where it was beer. Then they told me it was the inside of the banana peel. I read in *Time* that you dry it and smoke it. I don't know whether it does anything. We just couldn't approve programs advancing and promoting mellow yellow and these things."[13]

In addition to mellow yellow, the dean of student life also stated that the university "could not approve of a planned program of kissing on campus."[14] As SDS's Gentle Thursday plans continued, deans and vice-chancellors exchanged memoranda on "protecting the integrity of the University" from "undesirable beatnik . . . elements."[15] An internal debate between a soft and a hard policy was resolved when Austin city police and the Texas Department of Public Safety law enforcement authorities made it clear to the administration that they would not make illegal arrests on the orders of university officials. Only then did the administration publicly concede that the activities planned for Gentle

Thursday were "fine, as long as they don't interrupt the academic process."[16] SDS issued its own statement: "We wish to congratulate the administration on their Gentle Thursday program. SDS will also sponsor Gentle Thursday. Because of the sublime emanations generating from spontaneous acts of gentleness, the SDS program cannot be localized to time or confined to a specific locale. It is rumored that gentleness might break out in classrooms."[17]

The student newspaper reported that on the second Gentle Thursday, on April 13, 1967, there were "a few kisses" and that SDS "transformed the West Mall into a mellow mall as gentleness became the rule."[18] The second Gentle Thursday crowd wore more brightly colored clothing than did those at the first event, only a few months before, and the men had longer hair. The growing impact of the counterculture was also evident in an improvised band of guitars, bongo drums, kazoos, and harmonicas that performed the Beatle's song "Yellow Submarine."

On the Saturday following Gentle Thursday, Flipped-out Week activities continued as several hundred people marched in an antiwar peace parade, or "Gentle Thursday on foot," to a park in downtown Austin. There were antiwar speakers, and the large crowd danced to local rock bands including the Conqueroo, Shiva's Head Band, and Lord Graystoke and the Southern Flyers. On that sunny spring afternoon the electrically amplified psychedelic rock and blues music of the bands echoed from the green of the courthouse square. Austin's counterculture community reclined under the shade of live-oak trees in their newly created electric pastoral arcadia.

At the second Gentle Thursday, Austin's bohemia combined left-wing political action with a countercultural carnivalesque celebration of community. Flipped-out Week used Gentle Thursday, the antiwar march, and the concert in the park, as a coordinated ritual to oppose the dominant power structure's cowboy foreign policy in Vietnam and its traditional Round-up festivities on the UT campus. An SDS spokesman stated that the purpose of Gentle Thursday was to "prove that the campus does not have to be inhuman" and advised participants to "break down all unwritten restrictions on people having fun."[19] Another SDSer summed up the success of the second Gentle Thursday by claiming that it was a "revolutionary threat" to the establishment.

In an article in Austin's underground newspaper, *The Rag*, Gray

Thiher analyzed the university administration's attempt first to ban and then co-opt Gentle Thursday. The administration had refused to allow mellow yellow or "kissing all over campus" because such activities were "too vague." Thiher pointed out that Gentle Thursday had little or no formal program, no one had to pay to participate, and there were no event managers. According to Thiher, Gentle Thursday was "a whisper in the ear of the campus, the slight suggestion that it might be fun to have fun." The freedom of Gentle Thursday threatened the administration's bureaucratic need for control because there is a basic opposition between the "free human activity" of Gentle Thursday and the "organizational activity" of the university. For Thiher, the activities of Gentle Thursday provided a prefiguration of utopian life after the revolution: "When people do this all the time, the revolution will be a fact."[20]

In keeping with SDS's participatory-democracy ideology, anti-organizational ethos, and romantic anticapitalist worldview, Gentle Thursday participants tried to enact a theme of nonviolent opposition to the Vietnam War. Emergent countercultural symbolic codes were used at Gentle Thursday to create an aesthetic of resistance in a situation of overwhelming dominant power that had proven overt radical political action ineffectual.

Gentle Thursday was a popular success on the University of Texas campus. It expressed the social solidarity of the Austin bohemian community, brought new members into SDS, and confronted the university administration with the transgressive energy of the countercultural movement. Over the next two years, local SDS sponsored three more Gentle Thursdays with increasing participation from the student body and the growing counterculture.

The Gentle Thursday festive form did not survive the turmoil of the late sixties, but in its context it was an affectively empowering festival of resistance to the dominant power bloc. Gentle Thursday was also a cultural performance which was a precursor to the new social movements of the post-sixties, and therein lies its lasting historical significance. In the reactionary aftermath of the sixties, the University of Texas administration, exercising its usual subtlety, paved over the grass of the West Mall site of Gentle Thursday. Nevertheless, that location continues to provide a central public space for new progressive student movements and another generation of Texas bohemians.

Invented sixties festive forms like Gentle Thursday expressed and constructed an emergent counterhegemonic social movement that was as concerned with individual participation and identity as with direct political resistance. The New Left was conscious of the danger of becoming enmeshed in systemic legal-administrative organizational structures. This was why SDS preferred informal participatory organization and developed tactics of resistance through prefigurative festive forms like Gentle Thursday. At Gentle Thursday, Austin SDS was trying to avoid becoming a mirror image of the dominant hegemony.

The sixties New Left and counterculture movement's conscious choice to emphasize community over formal organization was expressed in the symbolic action of the Gentle Thursday festive event. Furthermore, that choice determined Gentle Thursday's lack of script, use of incongruity in act and agent, and overall formless quality. Gentle Thursday's New Left bohemian folk theater blurred the boundaries between cultural performance and theater, avant garde happening and political demonstration, and hegemonic reality and utopian vision. Gentle Thursday claimed a space within the mega-university for the construction of new self and group identities. As a precursor to new social movements, Gentle Thursday concentrated its action on creating and displaying new cultural codes in resistance to the dominant power bloc.

Participants in Gentle Thursday who crossed the cement boundary line of the sidewalk and sat on the grass did so in self-conscious awareness of their transgression of the accepted patterns of middle-class student life. Gentle Thursday was an early expression of new social movements that equated "self transformation with social transformation."[21] Gentle Thursday combined New Left political resistance and countercultural transcendent consciousness in a celebration of utopian hope that "cracked the mold of the dominant culture."[22]

Ellen Herman

Being and Doing
Humanistic Psychology and the Spirit of the 1960s

One of the most important transformations in recent American political culture has been the expansion of public life and political theory to encompass entire spheres of existence previously considered unquestionably private. This trend toward "personal politics," an effort not only to introduce new issues but to make political participation personally meaningful, is usually associated with the social movements of the 1960s, especially the second wave of feminism.

Recent historical analysis has begun to tie this new political consciousness to important elements in American culture and politics between 1940 and 1960: beat literature and bohemian subcultures; radical pacifist organizing during and after World War II; the enduring remnants of the Old Left, the growth of an omnivorous consumer culture (especially rock and roll) and its potentially subversive messages to youth; the meaning, to a whole generation, of being the very first to grow up under the shadow of the bomb.[1]

The direction of a booming business in psychological expertise, and its profound impact on postwar America, has yet to enter the explanatory picture.[2] Yet psychology's pervasive cultural diffusion after World War II helps to explain the appearance of social movements after 1960 and reduces the great historical divide between the 1950s, typically described as an era of apathy, and the 1960s, that period of social upheaval and national self-examination that has been made into an island in time.

Humanistic psychology, both before and after 1960, was one of the trends within the behavioral fields that oriented social movements toward a particular set of "values," not coincidentally a favorite word used by psychological professionals and political activists alike. It was a theoretical and therapeutic perspective that gained currency in the work of figures like Abraham Maslow and Carl Rogers during and after World War II. After 1960, their central ideas were transplanted from academic and clinical psychology to the very different terrain of movements for social change, including civil rights, student activism, the counterculture, and women's liberation.

∗   ∗   ∗

Within the psychological professions, the humanists defined themselves and were seen by others as a "third force," distinct from psychology's two major intellectual traditions: psychoanalysis and behaviorism. While some enthusiastic proponents went so far as to claim that the humanists' ideas were entirely original and utterly revolutionary, historically sensitive individuals, including Maslow and Rogers, were quick to trace humanistic psychology's intellectual pedigree to a variety of sources. These included the neo-Freudianism of Karen Horney, Harry Stack Sullivan, and Erich Fromm; the Gestalt psychology of Kurt Goldstein; the philosophy of John Dewey and Martin Buber; and scientific method, the connecting thread of the humanists' own professional training, which often included a healthy dose of behaviorist psychology.

Briefly summarized, humanistic psychology's core tenets included: that the most urgent human needs were to feel good about oneself, experience one's emotions directly, and grow emotionally; that "the self" was inherently healthy and contained a kind of divine spark that moved the human organism inexorably toward a process of growth and "becoming"; that "the self's" subjective experience was the highest authority; that scientific commitment to objectivity was bankrupt and useless, in need of an infusion of humanistic values; that psychotherapy with healthy individuals should be both the most fertile source of psychological data and the model for value-laden scientific enterprise.

Third force theorists shared at least one major goal with backers of the first two forces: they envisioned "a larger jurisdiction for psychology" and aimed to expand psychology's reach to include and explain absolutely everything.[3] If postwar popular psychology is any indication, they were remarkably successful. Popular psychology included everything from daily newspaper columns like "The Worry Clinic," which dispensed advice to millions of readers, to Norman Vincent Peale's bestselling *The Power of Positive Thinking,* the spiritual textbook of the Eisenhower era that promised success through old-fashioned inspirational Christianity and new-fashioned techniques like "mind-emptying at least twice a day."[4]

Although the humanists were scattered throughout the country and institutions devoted to perpetuating their ideas were not founded until the early 1960s, they operated as a self-conscious tendency within the psychological professions after 1940. For a group that was accustomed to describing itself as a band of rebels pounding on the walls of the establishment, the humanists were remarkably effective in winning conventional professional rewards as well as in spreading their gospel to the popular culture. Rogers and Maslow, for example, were each elected to the presidency of the American Psychological Association, in 1947 and 1968 respectively.

Carl Rogers was both a clinician and theorist. His institutional affiliations included the Rochester, New York, Society for the Prevention of Cruelty to Children, the University of Chicago, and the Western Behavioral Sciences Institute in La Jolla, California. Toward the end of his life, he founded the Center for Studies of the Person in La Jolla. Along with many other psychological professionals, he had worked as a guardian of military mental health during World War II, an experience that was the foundation of psychology's dramatically increased prestige and authority in the postwar decades. Rogers became famous for his work in developing, and then scientifically testing, an approach to psychotherapy first termed "non-directive," later renamed "client-centered."[5]

Abraham Maslow was an academic psychologist affiliated during most of his career with Brandeis University. He was best known for two innovations: his hierarchical theory of motivation and his descriptions of self-actualizing people and their "peak experiences."[6] He lectured widely, consulted to industry and government, and was a founder of a number of humanistic psychology's first real institutions, including the *Journal of Humanistic Psychology* in 1961 and the American Association for Humanistic Psychology in 1962.

Although they thought of themselves as scientists, Maslow and Rogers were both extremely sensitive to the political implications of their work. After World War II, they were determined to generate optimism about that unstable compound called human nature and, more originally, offer scientific evidence that democracy was possible after all. Beyond the ambitiousness of these goals, Maslow and Rogers were bucking trends that had dominated psychology since at least 1909, when Freud had crossed the Atlantic to deliver the depressing news that chaotic and destructive instincts lurked beneath the thin veneer of western civilization. Since 1909, increasingly apprehensive bulletins from the psychological frontier had confirmed not only that the mind was mysterious territory, but that human motivation—especially political motivation—was profoundly irrational and thoroughly manipulable. Throughout the 1940s and 1950s, a multitude of social critics warned Americans about the perils of emotional politics and did their best to shift the political ground away from contaminating pressures of ideological commitment and dangerously utopian notions of human perfectibility.[7]

The humanists confronted these psychological "truths" at a moment when the horrors of the World War and the dawn of the cold war seemed to offer only more encouragement to pessimism. They exhorted psychological experts to shift their attention from demolishing the dream of self-determination to shoring it up. According to humanistic psychologist Gordon Allport:

> Up to now the "behavioral sciences," including psychology, have not provided us with a picture of man capable of creating or living in a democracy. . . . But the theory of democracy requires also that man possess a measure of rationality, a portion of freedom, a generic conscience, appropriate ideals, and unique value. . . . What psychology can do is to discover whether the democratic ideal is viable. According to some of the partial truths now established and widely accepted the answer seems negative. But this answer is far from final. As we become more adept in dealing with the whole fabric of personality we discover potentialities of greater promise. Soon, we venture to predict, psychology will offer an image of man more in accord with the democratic ideals by which psychologists as individuals do in fact live.[8]

Their attempt to build confidence in a psychology of reason and an unabashed commitment to democratic values depended on severely narrowing democracy's subject to "the self." With minimal (or no) reference to the social context in which "selves" floated freely, and with maximum attention to the struggle between inner demons and peace of mind, this new unit of measure helped to breathe life into the business of explaining and controlling human beings and held out the possibility of interrupting, if only momentarily, psychology's gloom-and-doom tradition. If humanistic psychology's fondness for "the self" was a tacit concession to the impossibility of governing whatever went on outside of and between people, at least it pointed to turf that people could actually hope to control—themselves.

*　　*　　*

Psychology's success story proceeded, if anything, more dramatically during the 1960s than it had just after the war. In 1963, John Kennedy was the first American president ever to make mental health and mental retardation national priorities in an address to Congress, a clear illustration of the tremendous authority that federal support had brought to clinical versions of behavioral expertise. Aggressive federal action had begun immediately after World War II: passage of the National Mental Health Act of 1946 (which created the National Institute of Mental Health to fund behavioral research, training, and services) was followed by the work of the Joint Commission on Mental Illness and Health in the late 1950s, which paved the way for the Community Mental Health Centers Act of 1963 and the decision to build and staff two thousand community-level mental health agencies all around the country.

After 1960, humanistic psychology provided ideological ammunition to a variety of movements. Rogers, watching the political spectacle from the sidelines, sympathized with the goals of liberal and radical activists. He believed their desire for authenticity, their respect for "inner space," and their skepticism about mechanistic and value-free science were identical to his own. His understanding of movement aims tended to downplay such things as the redistribution of material wealth and the elimination of structural barriers to racial equality, in favor of the revolution in personality he saw occurring in hippies, executives who had abandoned the corporate rat race, and the period's diverse protestors. One of the last pieces of writing Rogers did concluded with the following sentiment: "I simply say with all my heart: Power to the emerging person and the revolution he carries within."[9]

In contrast, Maslow vigorously opposed any neat fit between humanistic psychology and 1960s social change movements. Disgusted by young people's rudeness, he consigned student radicals and their faculty supporters to membership in the "Spit-on-Daddy Club" and bitterly resented their use of his work to promote radical political activism. In his journal, he recorded the opinion that members of the Student Nonviolent Coordinating Committee (SNCC) and the Council of Federated Organizations were "hard-bitten revolutionaries" who should not be allowed to marry and who definitely should be prohibited from becoming parents. By 1966, he had decided: "The whole intellectual world has gone insane on the Vietnam business—essentially anti-U.S.—just the way they did during the pro-Stalin days."[10]

Maslow thought that because their parents had coddled them, young activists were caught in a psychological spiral of anger and negativity, unable to accept the responsibilities of loving America and embracing its democratic traditions. Maslow's solution was to pull the permissive rug out from under them. "You could solve the whole youth rebellion," he insisted, "by having a depression, or by cutting off their allowances."[11]

In spite of self-righteous declarations that his ideas had been abused, even Maslow recognized the kinship between his own challenge to "adjustment" and the issues raised by civil rights, antiwar, and other movement activists.

> Adjusted to what? To a bad culture? to a dominating parent? What shall we think of a well-adjusted slave? . . . Clearly what will be called personality problems depends on who is doing the calling. The slave owner? The dictator? The patriarchal father? The husband who wants his wife to remain a child? It seems quite clear that personality problems may sometimes be loud protests against the crushing of one's psychological bones, of one's true inner nature. What is sick then is *not* to protest while this crime is being committed.[12]

Over Maslow's objections, his formulation of psychological health as resistance to adjustment and conformity proved an enduring justification for all sorts of political activism.

Community activists were as or more likely than national figures to point to the movement's psychological consequences in the black community. Black psychiatrist Alvin Poussaint recalled administering large doses of tranquilizers to Southern civil rights workers who were suffering from "acute attacks of rage."[15] Mississippi Freedom Summer veteran Emma Jones Lapsansky remembered the relief involved in releasing this rage, comprehending the utter irrationality of white racism, and discovering new levels of self-acceptance. For Lapsansky, such changes in psychological awareness had moved the black community from paralyzing guilt to the mobilizing anger of the civil rights movement. She concluded: "The Movement fell short of social and political liberation, but it did move us, as black people, a long way toward psychological liberation. Can we call that failure?"[16]

At least some expert observers who watched the progress of the civil rights movement during the 1960s also saw the goal of a psychologically healthy society represented in the civil rights challenge to American society. American Psychological Association president, Arthur Brayfield, for example, had this to say when he testified before a 1960 Congressional hearing about how "deprivation and personality" effected domestic social programs oriented towards employment and education.

I believe that any inquiry into the development of human resources must focus on the black revolution. For the black revolution poses in its starkest form an overwhelming question: Can we design and develop a society—a set of social arrangements—a human environment—that will foster the sense of *personal worth* and *self-esteem* required to sustain the human spirit, give meaning to our lives, and provide the energizing force to forge our personal destinies and to insure the emergence and survival of a humane society?[17]

✳   ✳   ✳

The insight that the politics of racial justice promised a profound revolution in racial psychology was as important a legacy of the civil rights experience as its direct action tactics and the demand that America live up to its rhetoric of equality and democracy. Young white activists adapted the lessons they had learned observing or doing civil rights organizing to the requirements of the student, antiwar, women' liberation, and countercultural movements.[18] The dream of psychological transformation travelled with them wherever they went.

One of the first places they went was back to their campuses, where the slogan, Called to Be Human, had the ring of humanistic psychology as well as the feel of the Southern civil rights experience and the tone of French existentialist philosophers like Jean-Paul Sartre and Albert Camus: each had emphasized the basic unity between spirituality (or psychology) and politics and each had demanded that individuals take personal action in the name of moral responsibility and choice.

The core concepts of humanistic psychology were accorded a prominent place in "The Port Huron Statement," the founding document of Students for a Democratic Society. After a brief introduction, there is a section entitled "Values," arguably the Statement's most original contribution and clear evidence of psychology's role in shaping political activism among students during the 1960s. It echoes virtually all of the themes that were at the heart of the humanists' work. For example:

> We regard *men* as infinitely precious and possessed of unfulfilled capacities for reason, freedom, and love. In affirming these principles we are aware of countering perhaps the dominant conception of man in the twentieth century: that he is a thing to be manipulated, and that he is inherently incapable of directing his own affairs. We oppose the depersonalization that reduces human beings to the status of things. . . .
>
> Men have unrealized potential for self-cultivation, self-direction, self-understanding, and creativity. It is this potential that we regard as crucial and to which we appeal, not to the human potentiality for violence, unreason, and submission to authority. . . .
>
> We would replace power rooted in possession, privilege, or circumstance by power and uniqueness rooted in love, reflectiveness, reason, and creativity.[19]

Notice the endorsement of the benevolence of human nature, the ideals of autonomy and growth, the possibilities for comprehensive and conscious self-knowledge, even the use of the word "potential."

As early as "The Port Huron Statement," there were indications that activists would make an indelible mark of their own on psychology's legacy. For example, self-conscious references to the experience of the

Statement's authors as university students recalls humanistic psychology's reliance on subjectivity. But the Statement goes well beyond the "my experience is . . ." statements that are so characteristic of the humanists, especially Rogers. The Statement scrutinizes students' experience of higher education, not merely for descriptive purposes, but in order to mine it for clues to movement strategy and political analysis.

*   *   *

If "The Port Huron Statement" and the student activists it claimed to represent were captivated by humanistic psychology's faith in conscious, rational growth and change, the counterculture emphasized humanistic psychology's more emotional side. In many ways, countercultural rituals and institutions were humanistic theories come to life. What were hallucinogenic drugs, be-ins, communitarian living experiments, and sexual freedom if not peak experiences?

Abbie Hoffman, to take just one well known example, was an irreverent countercultural spokesperson who kept his finger on the pulse that made America tick. He had been an eager student of Maslow's at Brandeis University in the late 1950s, where he was president of the psychology club during his senior year before going on to study graduate-level psychology at the University of California at Berkeley. Hoffman counted Maslow as one of the most positive influences in his life, and remembered him with great affection. (Maslow, on the other hand, dismissed Hoffman as a clown and "pathological" publicity seeker.[20])

More important than even this important personal connection was Hoffman's conviction that "Maslovian theory laid a solid foundation for launching the optimism of the sixties. Existential, altruistic, and up-beat, his teachings became my personal code."[21] Ideas like self-actualization not only invited a generation to take a good look at itself, but promised that something positive, perhaps even perfect, could be found within.

The emphasis of humanistic psychology on subjectivity surfaced in the spontaneity of countercultural action and in the suspicion that subjectively-based action might be the only reality, that revolution might indeed exist only in one's mind. Humanistic psychology justified direct action in the name of fun, a welcome alternative to the dull tasks and hard work of building organizations and alliances from the bottom up. "*There*

*is absolutely no greater high than challenging the power structure as a
nobody, giving it your all, and winning,"* proclaimed Hoffman.[22]

The counterculture suggested reliance on drama rather than meetings, ecstacy rather than planning, and immediate sensual bombardment rather than careful political strategy. Activists like Hoffman believed that tossing dollars onto the floor of the New York Stock Exchange or levitating the Pentagon were powerful statements about capitalist greed and the horror of the Vietnam War, in part because they captured media attention, in part because these institutions were such stark illustrations of the madness and murder lurking just below the American surface. In the end, pleasure and personal happiness were elevated to the level of political ideals.

> I don't like the concept of a movement built on sacrifice, dedication, responsibility, anger, frustration and guilt. All those down things. I would say, Look, you want to have more fun, you want to get laid more, you want to turn on with your friends, you want an outlet for your creativity, then get out of school, quit your job. Come on out and help build and defend the society you want. Stop trying to organize everybody but yourself. Begin to live your vision. . . . When I say fun, I mean an experience so intense that you actualize your full potential. You become LIFE. LIFE IS FUN.[23]

How to live, how to love, and how to spend one's spare time were among the questions on a newly expanded political agenda. Politics was personal life and personal life was politics, and in this new equation, personality itself was up for grabs.

Hoffman believed that the "gimme-gimme" psychology of permissiveness that had surrounded his generation during their formative years was a resource that could push people toward direct confrontation with political and military institutions that promoted death and depersonalization. For him, psychology was neither a green light for self-indulgence nor an excuse to sit back while the inner revolution proceeded automatically. Hoffman's dedicated and good-humored activism illustrated, until his death in 1989, how persistently humanistic psychology could elicit social conscience and concerted political action in the name of personal pleasure and social justice.

*   *   *

Prefeminist rumblings also bore the mark of humanistic psychology's influence. In *The Feminine Mystique* (1963), Betty Friedan wielded the arguments of humanistic psychology to call for social change by arguing that the tragedy of the (middle-class) female condition was due to something she called "the forfeited self."[24] She used Maslow's portrait of self-actualizing individuals and the noticeable absence of women on his list of peakers (with the exception of Eleanor Roosevelt and Jane Addams) as evidence that women were doomed to a psychological hell where they were expected to renounce their natural tendencies toward growth and individuality. The sexist ideology of femininity, in other words, had to go because it directly contradicted the process of self-actualization, which the humanists had made into a veritable birthright.

When a movement for women's liberation did finally emerge out of women's experiences in civil rights and the New Left, it incorporated many of psychology's insights into demands for political and economic transformation in women's lives. Telltale traces of therapeutic practice showed up in movement techniques like consciousness-raising (C-R), which emphasized introspection, emotional self-exposure, and personal sharing in a non-judgmental context reminiscent of Rogers' client-centered approach.

> It is imperative for our understanding of ourselves and for our mental health that we maintain and deepen our contact with our feelings. Our first concern must not be with whether these feelings are good or bad, but what they are. Feelings are a reality.[25]

However, C-R was conceived as the means of developing feminist strategy and theory and that fact sharply distinguished it from psychotherapy.

> Consciousness raising is not a form of encounter group of psychotherapy. I've been involved in both and I can tell you they are very different. . . . Therapy had made me believe that I was different from other women (in this case different meant better). . . . In the women's movement and especially in consciousness raising I saw women who recognized that there was no such thing as a personal way of solving their problems so long as male supremacy in all its

formal and informal forms still existed. . . . They were not, as therapy often does, blaming women for being passive and in a rut.[26]

But C-R *was* indusputably therapeutic, and practically every woman who described the experience managed to note this fact. Even those who were most alarmed by C-R's therapy-like habit of providing a forum for women's complaints about particular men, for example, had to admit that "the rigid dichotomy between material oppression and psychological oppression fails to hold."[27] The healing character of C-R was as crucial for leading women toward political action as it was for leading them toward the humanistic goals of self-discovery and growth.

Some feminists, like Naomi Weisstein, condemned psychology as a male fantasy, a body of theory without evidence, and a convenient repository for sexist prejudices masquerading as science.[28] As an individual with the benefit of formal training in psychology as well as a developing feminist sensibility, Weisstein articulated a view that was widespread among feminists when she wrote: "Psychology has nothing to say about what women are really like, what they need and what they want, essentially because psychology does not know."[29] While feminists shared psychologists' commitment to the relevance of women's feelings, they castigated psychologists for consecrating internal realities ("inner space," in Erik Erikson's well worn phrase) when they should have been paying serious attention to the gendered social context in which women (and men) lived. Feminism, they believed, would improve on psychology's record by doing justice to both the inner *and* the outer.

Other feminists went further in extracting political lessons from psychological insights. Inspired by C-R and the gathering forces of gay liberation, they joined the chorus proclaiming pleasure and personal happiness as worthy political ends. Even when feminists accused the "sexual revolution" of being a sneaky male plot to gain more access to more women without actually revolutionizing anything, many held fast to the ultimate value of sexual freedom for women, convinced that erotophobia and patriarchy were lethal obstacles to women's emancipation.[30]

*   *   *

At their best, 1960s activists used psychology to reconnect the dots between the self and society and reattach the alienated individual to his or her social context. They honored both political protest and personal freedom and made it clear that neither would be possible, or worth much, without the other. At their worst, activists used psychology as a rationale to feel more and think less, unwittingly engendering tolerance for a program of repression dressed up in therapeutic garb.

Analysts who lament "the triumph of the therapeutic" tend to see the exploitation and depersonalization of advanced capitalism as the real problem.[31] They consider psychology to be a sophisticated bill of goods, designed to prevent rebellion by lulling people into complacency, convincing them that peace of mind is possible when it actually is not. For these critics, psychology has functioned historically to blunt the sharp edges of class conflict and keep the wheels of capital greased and turning. This mystification is no less horrifying for having been made subtle and painless, or even "therapeutic."

On the other hand, analysts who dote on psychology's blessings, in either its professional or self-help forms, offer nothing but blatant propaganda: today's current boom in recovery and co-dependency literature is just one example. Their uncritical advertisements, which have snowballed into a far more impressive industry than even the ambitious humanistic psychologists could have imagined after World War II, replace the old-fashioned bourgeois myth of hard work and social mobility with new-fashioned advice that success radiates outward from emotional labor.[32]

The impact of humanistic psychology on social movements after 1960 illustrates that psychology did push the centers of movement gravity away from conventional political agendas toward considerations of mental health and psychological survival, but the consequences were neither automatically deadening nor magically energizing. Since the mid-1970s, in a political climate characterized by right-wing resurgence, nostalgia for "traditional values," and the stigmatization of AIDS and the people who are living with it, some activists have traded in the social pursuit of personal happiness for retreat toward isolated and apolitical, even antipolitical, self-nurture. Yet for others, psychology's affirmations have provoked renewed public activism based on an unshakable belief that fortifying inner resources and controlling collective destinies are inseparable tasks.

Psychology has had a unique and formative impact on the political culture and activism of our own time. At its best, it has legitimized the concept of personal politics, encouraged the exploration of this newly politicized zone, and inspired confidence that both enlightenment, pleasure, and change can be discovered there. At its best, psychology has transformed not only that cultural mixture known as politics; it has also transformed what counts as political transformation.

Stephen J. Whitfield

The Stunt Man
Abbie Hoffman (1936–1989)

His father and mother, as well as the Federal Bureau of Investigation, called him ever-so-formally Abbott Hoffman. To the otherwise staid publisher of his 1968 manifesto, *Revolution for the Hell of It*, his nom de plume was simply "Free"—a euphonic gesture that elevated its author into an archetypal American. For giving one's self a new name tagged a new identity, a white man's monosyllable that was the equivalent of the X that Malcolm Little bestowed upon himself. Environmentalists in New York knew him as Barry Freed, a community organizer who was prominent enough to meet with Senator Daniel P. Moynihan. In E. L. Doctorow's searing novel of intergenerational radical politics among American Jews, *The Book of Daniel* (1971), he is the inspiration for the antic Artie Sternlicht, who is introduced in the presence of assorted street people, plus an interviewer from *Cosmopolitan* magazine: "He talks fast in a gravel voice that breaks appealingly on punch lines. He jumps around as he raps, gesturing, acting out his words,"[1] as though personifying Tocqueville's image of the American who cannot converse; he orates.

In Roger Simon's hip Los Angeles detective novel, *The Big Fix* (1973), Hoffman is the prototype for Howard Eppis, an outré demagogue who has disappeared in the wake of publishing *Rip It Off*. Private eye Moses Wine describes this volume as studded "with the clichés of the late and middle sixties set in an archaic psychedelic type. His prose sounded like a bad underground disc jockey on uppers." In the 1978 film version of

The Big Fix, F. Murray Abraham plays Eppis, who has assumed a new life as a highly successful advertising executive. How apt that *eppes* itself is a polysemous Yiddish term for "something," "somebody," "maybe," and "a little," which lexicographer Leo Rosten has called a "delightful, resilient word [that] has chameleon properties of a high order."[2] Yet despite the nimbus of aliases and appellations that swirled over Hoffman, almost everyone who ever encountered this eternally boyish, brash, and effervescent political activist just called him Abbie. And to those who realize that, overall, America is a slightly more open, robust, and even healthy society because of his efforts and his example, he was maybe even dear Abbie. Having hot-wired the system, he extended its contours and made it safer for diversity.

Among radicals, for whom solemnity of temperament and sobriety of purpose come with the territory, he was an oddity—a sport. Such oppositionists are usually born under the sign of Saturn. But Hoffman embodied the possibility of being at once *engagé* and engaging, and became, quite simply, the wittiest radical that the United States ever produced. Unlike the Students for a Democratic Society, whose contribution to Western political thought included the slogan, "Screw the ass of the ruling class," Hoffman enjoyed goosing it, and thus displayed the most nimble and inventive mind of any New Leftist. He was also probably the first American radical to be heavily indebted to a comedian: Lenny Bruce, to whose memory *Woodstock Nation* (1969) was dedicated.[3] Bruce seems to have taught Hoffman (or reinforced for him) the notion that everyone, including political and religious authorities, has a hustle. (Hoffman's own hustle was radicalism itself.) For Lenny Bruce show business was not marginal to society but was only its microcosm. For Hoffman show business was not the antithesis of leftism but something that could *change* and radicalize politics. No one who was funnier was ever more estranged from the orthodoxies of American democracy; no one who was radical was ever more comical in his perceptions. Nevertheless, for a comedian, Hoffman was not funny—he failed at that demanding profession, at the age of 51, doing a stand-up act in New York in 1988 that led one local critic to complain: "Comedy without laughs is just too obscure a concept for us."[4] But for a political person, Hoffman was highly unusual in concocting an identity as *homo ludens*, the stunt man.

At first, in the late 1960s, Abbie seemed to be just another self-aggrandizing citizen, clamoring to be noticed, showing his plumage. Call him a publicity hound, and he would not have been troubled, or found it a shameful accusation. Call him merely another American exhibitionist, playing to the crowd, and he would have seen nothing wrong with self-advertisements as a way of attracting attention for unpopular causes. The tradition of "the confidence man," the designer of the hoax, is a powerful one in a nation where social status is insecure, where identity is in flux; and that is the tradition to which Hoffman belonged. But he was so much of a fake that he ended up an original.

Bouncing through the late 1960s with kinetic energy, he still held "my flower in a clenched fist," as he wrote in his autobiography.[5] Inside that fist, he should have mentioned, was a joy buzzer, ready to be pressed against the body politic. The Youth International Party (Yippies) that he co-founded, at the age of 31, with Jerry Rubin, was as puckish as its high-falutin' name. "Yippies believe in the violation of every law, including the law of gravity," he proclaimed.[6] And while Hoffman was referring to the wacky effort to "levitate" the Pentagon in October 1967, during a march against military intervention in Vietnam, the Yippies also violated the law of political gravity. Their frivolity became legendary, a throwback to the *charivari* who ritually up-ended the hierarchic order of the late Middle Ages. No other "revolutionary" ever exuded as much charm as Hoffman, which is why Dustin Hoffman (who had portrayed Bruce in the 1974 film *Lenny*) should have been encouraged to play him. Though the actor did show up at the Chicago 7 conspiracy trial, learning to mimic his namesake, Cliff Gorman instead was cast as Abbie Hoffman in the CBS television re-enactment of the trial. Universal studios purchased the movie rights to Hoffman's autobiography for $200,000;[7] but *Soon To Be a Major Motion Picture* was never adapted into even a minor motion picture. He does however appear briefly, as himself, in the film adaptation of someone else's autobiography, Ron Kovic's *Born on the Fourth of July* (1976), though the book does not mention him. (The 1989 movie is dedicated, in memoriam, to Hoffman.)

He first drew attention in April 1967, by sprinkling paper money from the visitors' gallery onto the floor of the New York Stock Exchange. The dollars from heaven posed no harm, though the traders' frenzy for the cash led to pandemonium. "The sacred electronic ticker tape, the heartbeat of the Western world, stopped cold," Hoffman recalled. "Stock brokers scrambled over the floor like worried mice." He and the other mischievous visitors from the East Village thus made ridiculous, as well as contemptible, the psychological propellant of capitalism. They not only exposed one of the seven deadly sins, greed, but also highlighted what James Madison had warned against in *The Federalist Papers:* "a rage for paper money" that was among the most feverish causes of faction, making of democracies "spectacles of turbulence and contention." Two weeks later the Stock Exchange spent $20,000 on bullet-proof glass for the gallery. [8]

In October 1968, Hoffman was subpoenaed to appear before the House Committee on Un-American Activities (HUAC), those once-grand inquisitors who had intimidated and throttled assorted Communists, "progressives," and liberals in the 1950s. He was "Free," however, and showed up in a red, white, and blue shirt. Such zealous adherence to a patriotic dress code so infuriated a contingent of Capitol police that Hoffman was arrested for desecration of Old Glory. The star-spangled witness and his (second) wife resisted arrest with such ferocity that his shirt was ripped off, revealing a provocative Cuban flag that she had *painted* on her husband's back. Both Hoffmans were jailed before the witness could get a chance to desecrate the rites of HUAC itself. The next day, stripped to the waist, he stood before a judge and demanded $14.95 for the shift, marked Exhibit A. Instead the judge set bail at $3,000 and instructed the defendant to "get out of here with that Viet Cong flag. How dare you?" Hoffman corrected him: "Cuban, your honor." At the trial itself the defense invoked the First Amendment to no avail. Just before hearing the announcement of a thirty-day jail sentence for "defacing and defiling" the Stars and Stripes, Hoffman arose to proclaim: "Your honor, I regret that I have but one shirt to give for my country." The conviction was later overturned on appeal, despite the claim by the Department of Justice that "the importance of a flag in developing a sense of loyalty to a national entity has been the subject of numerous essays." The first work cited, Hoffman noticed, was a passage from Hitler's *Mein Kampf.* [9]

In 1968 the Yippies vowed to disrupt the Democratic party convention in Chicago, which would guarantee that "the whole world is watching." They mock-threatened to put LSD in the Chicago city reservoirs, which were thereupon guarded. Yippies warned of painting their automobiles yellow, to resemble taxis, in order to kidnap delegates and then dump them in Wisconsin. They promised to dress up like Viet Cong and work the streets like ordinary politicos, shaking hands and pressing the flesh. Such anarchic efforts in making "outrage contagious" helped dissuade incumbent Lyndon Johnson from attending the convention itself. Meanwhile the Yippies nominated, for president, one "Pigasus," a hog—which was also "the Carnival animal par excellence" in early modern Europe. [10]

In March 1969, Hoffman, Rubin, and six others were indicted, charged with conspiracy and with crossing state lines to incite a riot, even though an official commission under future Governor Daniel Walker later categorized much of the violence that had occurred outside the convention hall as a "police riot."[11] For twenty weeks of testimony, a Chicago courtroom became the scene of guerrilla theater, as virtually every rule of legal decorum was shattered. Making dissidence dramaturgic, Hoffman and Rubin once showed up in court black and blue, wearing judicial robes over uniforms of the Chicago Police Department.[12] By flaunting the morally tattered vestments of authority, the defendants were gleefully asserting that the emperor had no clothes. They also refused to rise when Judge Julius Hoffman entered the courtroom. Abbie dropped his own surname to protest the judge's ("I am an orphan of America"), and at one point yelled at him: "You *schtunk. Schande vor de goyim,* huh?", which he freely translated for the press as "front man for the WASP power elite."[13] This defendant relished the role of court jester. When Mayor Richard Daley himself arrived, flanked by Federal marshals as well as his own bodyguards, and sat down in the witness chair, "Abbie rose with a big grin," co-defendant Tom Hayden recalled, "and challenged him to fight it out with fists; everyone in the room, including the marshals and the mayor, burst into laughter." The Chicago 7 may well have been, in the characterization of Vice-President Spiro T. Agnew, "anarchists and social misfits."[14] But they were not, according to the jury, guilty of conspiracy. A Federal appellate court also unanimously reversed Hoffman's own convictions for riot and contempt, because the trial judge's serious errors, all biased for the prosecution, were so frequent. Though Abbie Hoffman was later re-tried and convicted on reduced contempt charges, he was released without having to serve any additional time in prison.[15]

The fun should have ended when Hoffman skipped bail after getting convicted of a 1973 attempt to sell three pounds of cocaine to undercover policemen. He went underground for six years, but no fugitive from justice was ever more flamboyant or less able to cure a sweet tooth for publicity. He went on a gastronomic tour of Europe, even posing for a celebrity photograph with Chef Paul Bocuse.[16] The stunt man personally showed up at a precinct of the New York Police Department to report himself missing, and was later arrested elsewhere on minor drug charges without getting recognized. (A friend of Hoffman's secured his release by paying off the police chief, whom the arrestee had asked: "Do you want to be rich or famous?" The chief's preference for a payoff was the answer that Hoffman had wanted.) In disguise, Hoffman de-legitimated the FBI by taking the visitors' tour of its Washington office building even as the bureau was committing itself to a manhunt to find him. "I played all authority as if it were a deranged lumbering bull," he later explained, "and I the daring matador."[17]

At a Manhattan restaurant, while still on the lam, Hoffman threw a book-publishing gala for himself. No recluse, he also appeared on television, after a production company and a magazine, New Times, paid him $3,000 for the interview. In the fall of 1979, he was again interviewed (on tape) in a Boston television studio. As the pseudonymous Barry Freed ("Free" with, or from, a past), he spoke before Rotary Clubs and gave frequent interviews to local newspapers. He also testified before a Senate subcommittee, after which he posed for photographs with Senator Moynihan. Governor Hugh Carey commended him in a letter for his "keen public spirit." In 1979, Time magazine later reported, "Freed was appointed to a Federal advisory commission on the Great Lakes."[18] When asked on television in 1979 if he could "foresee turning [him]self in," Hoffman retorted with his wall-to-wall grin: "Turning myself into what?"[19] He was so gifted a clown that he ended up worthy of being taken seriously.

It should nevertheless be admitted that the case for his political significance and effectiveness has long been problematic. Three social scientists, all by happenstance teaching in California universities, were especially alert to the limitations of his antics. In The Making of a Counter Culture, a book which boldly discerned a seismic shift in the modern mentality, historian Theodore Roszak dismissed Revolution for the Hell of It because it "conveys the foul-mouthed whimsy of hip a-politics." Sociologist Todd Gitlin charged that "Abbie and Jerry [Rubin] had to perform according to the media's standards for newsworthy stunts. . . . They had to outrage according to the censors' definition of outrage. They were trapped in a media loop, dependent on media standards, media sufferance, and goodwill. These apostles of freedom couldn't grasp that they were destined to become clichés." Historian Peter Clecak's analysis of the predicament of the American left, *Radical Paradoxes,* dismissed Hoffman as "a hollow man with a thousand faces. . . . All the confident pronouncements become tentative by virtue of his self-conscious comic pose. By disclaiming accountability for his fantasies, his thoughts, and his actions, he ultimately denies any responsibility for himself. . . . Protesting that he's 'only in it for kicks and stuff,' he nevertheless emerges as the sad butt of his own elaborate gag." His various roles were "so many unconvincing media images that fail to provide satisfying forms for the amorphous flow of energy. And so the endless cycle of expending himself continuously exposes his own emptiness."[20]

Was he then a sham? A shaman? Merely a showman? I propose that he be classified as the kid brother of Barnum, not Babeuf, and be acknowledged as the first to make anachronistic the traditional notions of revolutionary purity and integrity. "The Communists disdain to conceal their objectives," Marx and Engels had written in *The Communist Manifesto.* Hoffman disdained to conceal his interest in fame, and was less fascinated by power than by publicity. He was invariably good copy. Even his ascent from the underground was timed, with the precision of an atomic clock, to coincide with the publication of his memoirs. In fact he did a slot on Barbara Walters's show the day before (September 3, 1980) he surrendered to the police, getting to ABC before the FBI got to him.[21] Hoffman specialized not in the putsch but in the put-on. Though Norman Mailer hailed him as a "bona fide American revolutionary," James Madison was less his model than Madison Avenue. After the Yippies had helped sabotage the Democrats' hopes of retaining the White House in 1968, three advertising agencies offered Hoffman and Rubin jobs even before the Nixon administration tried to make a Federal case out of what was on their minds.[22] For "if you can make unpopular causes popular," Hoffman later explained, "you understand the communications system and the economic system on a level that very few people do."[23]

Compared to other radicals who claimed to speak for the dispossessed, he operated without a real constituency, or even a make-believe constituency. His connections to "the people" or to the proletariat or any other stigmatized class were thin, though the actuarial tables briefly granted him a certain rapport with the young. He deployed images because he had no troops. "He had a wonderful ability to attract a crowd," journalist Nicholas von Hoffman observed, "but how big the crowd would be and what it might do was as much a surprise to him as to all the different kinds of policemen spying on him"—those tails of Hoffman. "But considering he never had any cards in his hand he could count on, he was a marvelous tactician. Bluff or theatricality, call it what you will, his best strokes won recruits and spurred his opponents to stupid acts of retaliatory spite."[24]

Hoffman seemed not to care who wrote the nation's laws so long as he was free to subvert its icons. "Sacred cows make the tastiest hamburgers," he proclaimed;[25] and no one was more cleverly carnivorous. But he also gave the impression of *liking* hamburgers, and of liking American life generally, enough to believe it was worthy, not only of appreciation, but of some improvement. A son was named "america." The culture that formed him and energized him was pop, primarily in the 1950s version that seemed so immutable at the time. He wrote nostalgically in *Esquire* about yo-yos; and even after he had re-invented himself as a full-time harpooner of authority, he cherished the aborted coup d'etat that a southern California chapter of Yippies staged in Disneyland, in which a Viet Cong flag was planted atop the facsimile Mount Matterhorn.[26] (And though the Yippies' writ never ran past Fantasyland, one consolation was that not even Khrushchev, visiting the United States in 1959, had been permitted to stroll on the amusement park's Main Street U.S.A.) When Lenin had realized that chess was absorbing too much of his time, diverting him from organizing for the Revolution, he stopped playing the Russian national game. But Hoffman continued to love shooting pool, playing cards, watching sports on television, avidly following the Red Sox. Was there ever another radical's funeral, like Hoffman's in 1989, in which the mourners included a professional basketball player? On that occasion the Boston Celtics' Bill Walton insisted that "Abbie was not a fugitive from justice. Justice was a fugitive from him."[27]

No major transfer of wealth or of power occurred in the 1960s, and the systematic struggle to rearrange their distribution gained little traction. But beginning with the "underground" poster of Allen Ginsberg in his Uncle Sam outfit, values were inverted and symbols were transformed; and Abbie in his flag shirt was a walking, talking travesty of patriotic swagger. He accelerated the erosion of an earlier respect for privacy and dignity, and helped to blur further the distinction between politics as policy and politics as perception. As statecraft became stagecraft, the texture of a mass-mediated "reality" saturated with stereotypes and images became even thinner; and the news was presented as another form of entertainment. As in imperial Rome, the masses could be appeased with bread and circuses. Though Hoffman showed little interest in problems of bread, he invented the role of radical ringmaster, performing under the big top at the greatest show on earth.

To be an American is usually to make up one's culture as one goes along anyway; and, deeply influenced by Mailer's 1957 essay on "The White Negro,"[28] Hoffman yearned to be unpredictable and spontaneous and loose. Mailer may have helped validate a refusal to be rational and temperate—which is a way of measuring his distance from his more ideologically coherent contemporaries abroad, the famous ones like Danny "the Red" Cohn-Bendit, "Red" Rudi Dutschke, Tariq Ali, or Bernard-Henri Lévy. For all his smarts, Hoffman was relentlessly anti-intellectual.[29] Busily exercising his freedom of assembly and engaging in seditious libel, he did not think deeply about politics. By carefully avoiding the ear-popping altitudes of high theory, he at least deflated the historic danger of a cognitive elite imagining itself to be a revolutionary vanguard—or posing as the moral benefactors of humanity.

Instead, Hoffman invoked the sovereignty of desire, implicitly assuring the young inhabitants of Woodstock Nation that if they would unite, they would have nothing to lose but their brains. The ex-Trotskyist Leslie Fiedler once told a group of students: "We went in for Talmudic exegesis. You go in for holy rolling." Dismissing the tradition of classical Marxism, Hoffman refused to believe in the integration of theory and practice, that praxis makes perfect. He took his cues not from study but by osmosis, believing, like the German Marxist revisionist Eduard Bernstein, that movement was more important than any final goal. At one Socialist Scholars Conference in the late 1960s, Hoffman complained of seeing thousands of socialist scholars, and not one socialist.[30] He didn't want them to sympathize; he wanted them to organize. But the dream of a cooperative commonwealth had by then become a subject without an object. An orphan of America had no viable radical tradition to inherit.

On the witness stand in Chicago, Hoffman identified himself neither by ideology nor by party, neither by class nor by any particular moral heritage. His self-definition was generational: "My age is 33, I am a child of the sixties." Asked when he was born, he replied: "Psychologically, 1960." The prosecutor objected, moving to strike the answer. After some sparring, Hoffman was quizzed about what, between his actual birth in 1936 and 1960, "if anything occurred in your life?" The witness responded: "Nothing. I believe it is called an American education."[31] He mellowed by the time that he composed his autobiography, proudly recording the intellectual influence exerted on him by the 3Ms on the Brandeis faculty: philosopher Herbert Marcuse, psychologist Abraham Maslow, historian of ideas Frank Manuel.[32] Yet Hoffman joined that line of resisters seeking to wriggle out of the shackles of the "nice Jewish boy." Mailer, Bruce, Ginsberg, Rubin, Fiedler, Philip Roth, Stanley Kubrick, and Joseph Heller volunteered for the forward combat units of the *Kulturkampf* of the 1960s. Their provocative opposition to gentility and orthodoxy can be largely understood as a reclamation project, as an effort to restore the primitive life by rattling the bars of the iron cage of bureaucracy, technology, rationality.

Though Hoffman converted himself into a politicized white Negro, he refused to bleach himself into a "non-Jewish Jew." He liked to flaunt the insignia of the Jewish subculture that he flouted, and had a knack for kidding its social conventions. He became a Jewish parent's nightmare, repudiating the norms of middle-class mobility and success. Yet no radical was more eager to assert a sense of peoplehood, relishing his ethnicity in his own peculiar way, recognizing that he "came into this world acutely aware of being Jewish, and [I] am sure I'll go out that way."[33] The book that most affected him, he claimed near the end of his life, was *The Diary of Anne Frank*; and her house at 263 Prinsengracht in Amsterdam was one of the only two places where the outlaw of the 1970s signed his own name. (The other was the birthplace of the Mexican revolutionary Emiliano Zapata.)[34] Hoffman's autobiography returns to the topic of his Jewishness in an almost compulsive manner, with wry and bittersweet irony, without defensiveness or vindictiveness. He took pride in his ancestry and in the Jewish reputation for cleverness; he cherished his affiliation with the sort of intelligence that is at once subversive and sensible. "Roots, baby," he exulted to one interviewer while on the lam. "Five thousand eight hundred [expletive deleted] years. What makes the Jews so [expletive deleted] smart, man? . . . . We know when to start New Year's. It's in the fall, that's when the movie business starts, that's when school starts. What the [expletive deleted] starts January 1?"[35]

With many other Jews he shared a feeling of marginality, a spirit of dissidence and even alienation that was experienced, in the phrase of sociologist John Murray Cuddihy, as "the ordeal of civility." Hoffman rejected "the notion of 'modesty' as something invented by WASPs to keep the Jews out of the banking industry," and he "always thought the idea of postponing pleasure was something WASPs dreamed up to keep Jews out of country clubs and fancier restaurants."[36] Yet Hoffman was radicalized early in the 1960s, not by discrimination against Jews, but by the segregation imposed upon Negroes; and he worked courageously for civil rights in the Deep South, where (in Bob Dylan's phrase) "black is the color and none is the number." Such activism was hardly discredited in an American Jewish community which has often sanctioned a certain sentimental leftism. Mailer's own bar mitzvah speech in Brooklyn had acknowledged the ambition to follow in the footsteps of "great Jews like Moses Maimonides and Karl Marx"; and the eulogy that Rabbi Norman Mendell delivered at Temple Emanuel in Worcester in 1989 implanted Hoffman's career "in[to] the Jewish prophetic tradition, which is to comfort the afflicted and afflict the comfortable."[37] Because the Youth International Party was largely the creation of Hoffman, Rubin, and Paul Krassner, who edited a satirical magazine called *The Realist*, the term "Yippies" was more than an acronym or an example of onomatopoeia. It was, he claimed, really a contraction of "Yiddish hippies,"[38] the cold-sweat horror of every right-winger who has fantasized about the tentacles of an international Jewish conspiracy.

Family matters: Florence Hoffman, whose own mother had worked in a sweatshop in Clinton, Massachusetts, used clandestine couriers to send toothbrushes and dental floss to her son, the underground man. He later remembered that his mother always advised him, when he announced the next destination on his escape route, to "dress warmly." Hoffman used a scrambling device to phone home, and met his mother four or five times, including in Cuernavaca, Mexico, and even in Disneyland. "I was more scared than he was," she recalled.[39] For the Republican National Convention, held in Miami Beach in 1972, Hoffman had addressed the city council for a permit for the Yippies to sleep in the park. He mock-warned that if the permit were not granted, his father would no longer come down there for the winter. One councilman called the protester's bluff, exclaiming that Hoffman's father wouldn't dare inflict a boycott: "He'll still come down. He loves the beach!" John Hoffman, who died a few weeks after his son jumped bail in 1974, once told an interviewer: "He could have been somebody, a doctor or a professor. Now we have to read the papers to see which jail he's in." Nevertheless the son notes that John Hoffman "never (to use a gentle expression) disowned me."[40]

Hoffman called himself "a Jewish road warrior," a category that is unlisted among the enumerated occupations of the U.S. Census. On the witness stand in 1969, he answered the question about his vocation by defining himself as "a cultural revolutionary. Well, I am really a defendant . . . full time."[41] He was eventually arrested about two dozen times. His second wife complained after their 1967 wedding: "I spent my time bailing him out of jail. I'm not saying that was the greatest thrill." Such brushes with the law were echoed in the next generation. His daughter Ilya, from his first marriage, once phoned him to announce: "Dad, I got arrested!" "Great! What for?" Ilya had been caught camping in a graveyard. "Well, that's a good start," but Ilya thought to herself: "Dad, you're not supposed to say that to me!"[42] And with all due respect to E. L. Doctorow, who admired the activist's "fearless" willingness to "put his body on the line" and has compared him to a Biblical prophet, the underground man himself believed that "the person who could tell my story better than anyone was Isaac Bashevis Singer." Hoffman claimed to have "always been fascinated by Yiddish as the language of survival," with "its subtleties, its built-in irony . . . the historical road it has travelled."[43] Abbie road forked off from there too.

Like the ancient Hebrews, whose own Bible describes them as "stiff-necked" (Exodus 32:9), Hoffman's radicalism showed surprising tenacity and durability, which is anomalous in a land where faddishness and amnesia seem inevitably yoked to one another. He did not abandon his leftism, though aging radicals are supposed to join the Democratic party (like Tom Hayden or like civil rights organizers John Lewis and Julian Bond).

In Europe they can continue to immerse themselves in radical political movements (like Daniel Cohn-Bendit with the Greens in Frankfurt). But in the United States they are supposed to grow into "maturity' (like Rubin or Rennie Davis). In that sense Abbie never grew up; he was a political Peter Pan. But his irony and self-mockery saved him from freezing into a character who had outlived his historical moment, pathetically trapped in a time capsule.

Yet Hoffman operated in a country that made co-option rather than repression the chief expression of the impulse to achieve conformity. At Woodstock, for example, Hoffman tried, but failed, to politicize the rock concert, as entrepreneurs "were able to turn a historic civil clash in our society into a fad, then the fad could be sold." He was cut from the film documentary of the concert, he claimed, because "rock promoters and the rock record industry . . . always, always tried to separate the politics from culture as, of course, the movie *Woodstock* bragged about doing." On native grounds "it is possible . . . to be wanted equally badly by the FBI and Universal Pictures."[44] His books sold three million copies; and even *Steal This Book*, which had to be privately published after thirty publishers turned it down, sold over a quarter of a million copies in 1971. "It's embarrassing," he remarked. "You try to overthrow the government, and you end up on the best-seller list."[45]

But fewer and fewer of his readers were enlisted from the ranks of the young in the 1980s. He and Rubin, who were once as close as handcuffs, debated one another on the college circuit, almost fulfilling the prediction of community organizer Saul Alinsky, who had not been amused by the Chicago street theatre of 1968, that a decade later "they'll probably be in a vaudeville act someplace."[46] Their campus gigs were billed as yippie versus yuppie, as Hoffman accused his former coconspirator of subscribing to ideas that were as thin as his ties. But on the evidence of how the graduates put their values into practice in that decade, Hoffman badly lost the debate. Refusing to surrender to the materialism of the zeitgeist, he was saddened by the apolitical complacency of the young, a generation that was missing in action. "Never trust anyone under thirty," he glumly declared, making that disenchanted sound-bite into a quasi-official farewell address to a Woodstock Nation that had dispersed and disappeared. Hoffman thus jettisoned the cult of youthfulness that had so ruptured the radical legacy and had once put him closer to Ponce de Leon than to Daniel DeLeon. The 1980s were depressing: "It's like the Middle Ages. We're *willing* ourselves dumber."[47] Had he become irrelevant? After his death Dan Wasserman's editorial cartoon in the *Boston Globe* showed a child at the breakfast table, asking her newspaper-reading father: "Who was Abbie Hoffman?" He casually explains: "A radical has-been. He protested the war, pollution, White House crimes"—as the headlines in the final panel refer to the Ollie North trial, the Contras, and the Alaska oil spill—"issues of the '60s."[48]

Such continuities suggest the difficulty of recounting the story of American public culture from the 1960s—the immediate antecedents of our own time—without citing Abbie Hoffman. Despite the swing to the right that the excesses of that decade have provoked and the huge electoral victories that the GOP achieved, some of the seventeen "revolutionary" demands listed in *Revolution for the Hell of It* have been fulfilled, from the end of military intervention in Vietnam to the elimination of severe penalties for using marijuana, from the end of conscription to the passage of pro-choice laws on abortion, from the continued eclipse of censorship to the greater sensitivity to environmental destruction.[49] Of course no single individual is responsible for any of these changes. But not all consequences are unintended, and Nicholas von Hoffman speculated that "the baiting, spoofing, jeering, joking, laughing five or six years of Abbie's public ministry contributed materially to the closing down of the war and to the missteps that led to the Nixon people putting themselves out of office. The traps Abbie dared and devil danced them into setting for him, they tripped and snapped shut on themselves."[50] Hoffman's causes were a kind of sneak preview of the future. *Newsweek* recently reported that, though the biggest cash crop in California is milk and cream (over $2 billion annually), about $3 billion is derived from the sale of marijuana.[51] In economic terms the bear depicted on the official flag of the Golden State might well be replaced by the marijuana leaf on the official Yippie banner. Even Nancy Reagan, so closely associated with the antidrug campaign, hired an early champion of marijuana use to write her 1989 memoir *My Turn*.

The richest joke that Hoffman played, even as his influence waned, is that so seemingly frivolous a spirit, so artificial a concoction, turned out to be the least corrupted, the most resilient and dedicated radical of all. Mailer praised Hoffman as "probably one of the bravest . . . people I've ever met."[52] For so "empty" a clown was unselfishly committed to political action. Living in Fineview, New York, Barry Freed led the Save the River Committee that halted a dredging project on the St. Lawrence River by the U.S. Army Corps of Engineers, which intended to destroy several islands to enhance navigation. His work was so effective that, after he surfaced in 1980 to face cocaine charges, even William F. Buckley, Jr., joined other luminaries to petition for a reduction of Hoffman's sentence. (Plea bargaining reduced the time in jail to eleven months.) The last six years of Hoffman's life were spent in Bucks County, Pennsylvania, after an environmental group, New Hope River Savers, invited his help in a battle to stop the diversion of the Delaware River. The waters were to cool a nuclear reactor at Point Pleasant. In 1987 Hoffman told an interviewer that he was happy to "live and die here fighting the Philadelphia Electric Company—it's just like the '60s for me."[53] Such activism should resolve the question of whether he wasn't just goofing off, as though frisky theatricality might be incompatible with steadfast political dedication. "Though easily the zaniest of the rebels of the 1960s," Milton Viorst wrote, "Hoffman was by no means the least serious. . . . Behind Hoffman's endless capers was a sense of purpose."[54] Any doubts should have been settled by what this self-proclaimed "child of the sixties" did during the two subsequent decades.

The case for his civic virtues need not be overstated. He was guilty of saying lots of silly things (maybe more than most). He can be reproached for an incorrigible failure to realize that, as historian Marvin Meyers once asserted, "with talk begins responsibility."[55] (It was one measure of Hoffman's radicalism to impugn even the *ideal* of responsibility.) His literary legacy is now mostly unreadable—with the major exception of his little-read but very lively autobiography. "The book reads like a letter from camp," *The New Republic's* Martin Peretz complained upon its publication, a little more than two decades after they had been classmates at Brandeis. But far from being "awful," *Soon To Be a Major Motion Picture* is a piquant retrieval of a rambunctious time, written (to quote Doctorow) with "the precision of insight of a great political cartoonist."[56] The drugs that Hoffman consumed were more than just mischievous; they were dangerous. "Better living through chemistry," he had quipped in defense of such self-destructiveness. The claim was false, the indebtedness typical in ripping off an advertising slogan—as befit the former salesman of pharmaceuticals, which was the last "respectable" job he ever held before making pharmacology an extension of politics. By the end, Hoffman had learned enough to serve on the board of directors of Veritas, an organization engaged in drug and rehabilitation therapy. Nevertheless, by taking an overdose of phenobarbital in April 1989, he chose deliberately to satisfy the morbid hope that was expressed in his favorite piece of hate mail: "Dear Abby—Wait till Jesus gets his hands on you—you little bastard. —Anonymous."[57] Sometimes accused of seeking martyrdom, he yielded instead to a despair that contradicted the joie de vivre of his politics, an ebullience that he made as singular as an autograph.

Until then, Hoffman lived more or less according to his own code of honor. For example, he was not significantly associated with violence, which falsifies one journalist's analogy to the Black Panthers' Huey Newton, whose obituary notices appeared not long after Hoffman's. But Newton (Ph.D., University of California–Santa Cruz) was found dead of gunshot wounds outside an Oakland crack house.[58] Unlike SNCC's H. Rap Brown, Hoffman never sank to armed robbery—or to any other violent crime. Though the oratorical style of Stokely Carmichael influenced him, none of Hoffman's publishers imitated Random House, which put on the cover of the anthology *Stokely Speaks* (1971) a photo of the author fiercely holding up a rifle. Though the Dial Press did depict its own leaping and laughing author with a toy gun for the cover of *Revolution for the Hell of It*, Hoffman had the decency not to emulate Carmichael's habit of licking the boots of Third World tyrants.[59]

Renunciation of capitalism was also central to Hoffman's code. The introduction to a collection of his essays announces that "I own no property, stocks, bonds or anything of substantial material value." Murray Kempton recalled that Hoffman was once asked to supply bail money for a prisoner, whom he had never met. Hoffman "had just received $25,000 for a book and, without a moment of thought, he handed it over to the bail fund of a stranger. Later the prisoner, for reasons of despair, fled the jurisdiction. Abbie had lost the only comfortable stake he ever owned, and all he did was laugh and say that he was glad the man had his freedom." While reviewing *The Big Fix* from the underground, he claimed to be "the only living American . . . for whom fame does *not* equal riches." Hoffman did not cash in on his celebrity (or notoriety).[60] Having given away hundreds of thousands of dollars, he died, like Malcom X, a pauper.[61]

Political organizing was "hard, lonely work," he conceded near the end. "If I wanted to convince people that I could faith-heal them, I'd have me a jet plane by now. But I want to convince them that they have the power as people to come together and fight city hall. And this is very hard."[62] He staked his political life—that is, his life—on the proposition that freedom is not only something to be protected; it is something to be used. It is not only something to be praised; it is something to be extended. It is not only something to be defined; it is something to be tested. Those who have historically enlarged the contours of political discourse have tended to be obstreperous rather than orthodox, cantankerous rather than conciliatory. "I wanna be none-of-the-above. I want to change history, to change society," he proclaimed in one of his last interviews,[63] as though it were an epitaph. At least the friction that he generated had warmth; and his style of protest, if not his ideas, will surely be how Hoffman will be remembered. For what he bequeathed has very little to do with the policies that he championed, but rather with an ethos of liberation from the benign, civics-text assumptions that were once pervasive in America. That soothing, pre-1960s complacency Abbie Hoffman awarded himself a license to kill; and that sort of patriotism has not yet recovered from the critical buckshot that he sprayed.

Stephen A. Kent

Slogan Chanters to Mantra Chanters

A Deviance Analysis of Youth Religious Conversion in the Early 1970s

A cherubic, ice cream loving adolescent guru landed on this continent in 1971, much to the excitement of his North American followers—all six of them. By the end of 1973, the now sixteen year old "perfect master," Guru Maharaj Ji, had 40,000 American followers alone, with one of the most prominent American activists from the 1960s quite literally sitting at his "lotus" feet—sitting at them and even kissing them in homage.[1] As cultural commentators shook their heads in disbelief, many former activists seemingly abandoned their politics and converted to any number of new religious groups, and new religious centers sprang up in every major city in North America. Observing this phenomenon in the San Francisco Bay area, Robert Bellah commented that "the burned-out activist was almost as common in the early 1970s as the burned-out drug user. . . . Every one of the new religious groups, from the Zen Center to the Christian World Liberation Front, has had its share of former activists."[2]

The data on these groups from the early 1970s were a gold mine for sociologists. Some lasting contributions to sociological theory resulted from a spate of studies including theoretical work on secularization and

church-sect theory, analyses of conversion and ideology, and functional-
ist interpretations of the benefits that individuals who involved themselves in these new religious groups accrued. Analysis, however, of the
transition from "the political" era to "the religious" one has not produced
significant contributions to social movement theory, despite the intimate
conceptual connections between social movement literature and sectarian
studies.[3]

The most prominent of the politics-to-religion interpretations,
offered by Steven Tipton, asserts that "youth of the sixties have joined
alternative religious movements of the seventies and eighties basically . . . to make moral sense of their lives." In an argument that reso-
nated with the perspective of his mentor, Robert Bellah, Tipton claimed
that American culture was in crisis by the early 1970s, and people gained
a sense of moral purpose amidst this crisis by joining or participating in
new religious movements.[4]

Most of these analyses see the conversions to ideologically religious
groups in the early 1970s as providing resolutions to crises of meaning,
and in doing so have continued the widely held but disputable assumption
that religion is necessary to society because it provides a unique sense
of meaning and order to social life.[5] These studies, however, were not
designed to analyze either the politics-to-religion transitions or the
activists' religious conversions as social movement phenomena. An examination of their bibliographies shows how little they were influenced
by the literature on social movement dynamics. It is an observation and
not a criticism to say that the sources for their scholarly inspiration came
from elsewhere, and likewise their contributions lie in other areas.

In an attempt to provide a conceptual framework that establishes the
activists' conversions as a social movement process, I offer a complementary interpretation. Rather than claiming that purported crises of *meaning* caused activists to convert to religiously ideological groups in the
early 1970s, I stress the cause as being a crisis of *means* within the political counterculture. Viewing the conversions in this manner, sociologists
can analyze them as social movement phenomena, in which participants
engaged in deviant behavior along lines first identified by Robert Merton
several decades ago and subsequently clarified by other sociologists. The
conversions to the new religious groups were innovative responses to activists' appraisals of increasing costs and diminishing returns of political

action, with activists-turned-converts believing that through these religious groups they were adopting new means to the same goal. In short, I
view actors' conversions from the political protest groups of the 1960s to
the religious organizations of the 1970s as part of a shifting pattern of
deviant social exchanges whose potential rewards altered in relation to
events within the dominant culture, the prevailing subculture, and the
social movement itself.

The first step in theorizing about the activist conversions in the early
1970s is to develop a language that enables us to speak about the period
precisely and systematically. In order to do this, I will utilize concepts
from resource mobilization theory, a perspective in social movement literature that first appeared in 1966 and has gained wide acceptance in recent years. A social movement is defined as "a set of opinions and beliefs
in a population which represents preference for changing some elements
of the social structure and/or reward distribution of a society."[6] Various
late 1960s causes, such as university reform, the Vietnam War, student
representation, and community power, fit within broadly defined boundaries of a "power redistribution" movement whose goal was "the revolution," a term often used but rarely defined, and whose popular rallying
phrase was "power to the people."[7] Broadly speaking, the movement
wanted to achieve a fundamental restructuring of social and political
power. Within the power redistribution movement were a number of organizations that identified their goals "with the preferences of a social
movement or countermovement" and attempted "to implement these
goals." Among the more memorable social movement organizations
from the late 1960s were Students for a Democratic Society, Student Mobilization Committees to End the War in Vietnam, and the Youth International Party. Viewed together, these organizations that "held as their
goal the attainment of the broadest preferences of a social movement" are
called a "social movement industry." People who believe in the goals of
the movement are called "adherents," and those who provide resources
for the movement, but who need not be actual adherents, are known as
"constituents."[8]

With these concepts at our disposal, I want to focus specifically on
the power redistribution movement in the early 1970s, during which
period its overtly political nature was undergoing transition and, by most
accounts, decline. The movement's apparent decline occurred primarily

because it had both *failed* and *partially succeeded*. We can see an impressive legacy of social change that originated in the turmoil of the 1960s. Among the broad social effects attributable to the power redistribution movement are: the "humanization" and reform of education; increased public awareness of ecology and sex discrimination, of the affective rewards of interpersonal and sexual relationships, and of the creativity of religious heterodoxy; increased international dialogue between the superpowers; and even, in fundamental ways, some unsurpassed rock music.[9] Beyond these achievements, the movement's continuous antiwar activities contributed to the United States government's withdrawal of its ground troops from Vietnam in late March of 1973, two months after the end of the controversial military draft.

From the viewpoint of the participants, however, these achievements were overshadowed by a sense of profound political disappointment. The social movement theroist Anthony Oberschall commented that "the U.S. involvement in the war did not end as rapidly and as completely as the movement sought," nor did the efforts of the era's social organizations "result in a major redistribution of power in the U.S. as was hoped by some activists."[10] Indeed, movement literature from the late 1960s and early 1970s indicates how frustrated, if not despairing, many activists were with the efficacy of their political efforts. Writing in January of 1971, the Chicago 7 defendant David Dellinger already sensed the toll that seemingly ineffective protests were having on his fellow social-movement adherents. He astutely observed that the antiwar movement had been plagued by

> ideological confusion and tactical mistakes. Even more serious, it has been struggling to overcome the feelings of frustration and despair that have gripped people after they discovered that neither a million people in the streets (November 1969) nor several hundred schools and colleges on strike (May 1970) altered Washington's determination to escalate its war of aggression in Indochina."[11]

Even Cyrill Levitt spoke about the sobering effects in 1970s of the killings at Kent State and Jackson State, in the United States, and of the War Measures Act, in Canada. "The ante had been raised," Levitt concluded, and activists realized that "it was going to cost them considerably more to stay in the game."[12] Within this frustration, fear, and despair lies the key to the rapid transformation of the slogan chanters of the late 1960s, into the mantra chanters of the early 1970s. Whether the power redistribution movement actually *had* failed was not the point; activists *perceived* that it had, and they acted accordingly. In order to "stay in the game," frightened and frustrated activists simply changed the rules.

Social exchange theory suggests that "the game" involves an assessment of rewards, costs, and profits in social interactions. Individuals and groups seek a profit from their social exchanges, and they calculate profit as *rewards minus costs*.[13] Using this basic insight to view the political climate of protest in the early 1970s, many activists assessed the cost of their own political protests as potentially so great, and the rewards and profits so sparse, that continued confrontations become inadvisable, even though they still believed in the power redistribution goal that lay behind their demands. If activists relinquished political protest, they protected their physical safety, but sacrificed the aim for which they had striven so arduously. If, on the other hand, they continued their legal or extra-legal protests, they risked their freedom and their safety for a goal that still remained elusive. Caught in this dilemma, a sizable portion of the New Left suffered what I call a "crisis of feasibility" regarding the means they had been using to reach their goal. In the early 1970s, the crisis of feasibility was not one of ends ("the revolution") but of means (continued political action). The widespread involvement of former activists in new religious groups was an attempt to resolve this crisis.

From a theoretical perspective, resource mobilization insists, in classic exchange language, that a social movement organization "must have a payoff of its supporters. Aside from the joys of participation," the theory adds, a social movement organization's "major payoff is in the nature of its promise; its goals, or at least some of them, must have a reasonable chance of attainment." In language easily applicable to an entire social movement, resource mobilization theory indicates that a "failing [social movement organization] loses members because they no longer believe their goals can be achieved with that instrument."[14] In sum, a social movement will lose support when its adherents lose confidence in the feasibility of achieving its goals through its established patterns of social exchanges.

The instrument, or means, of a social movement loses its attractiveness to adherents when societal or political events render those means ineffective. Politicians, for example, may satisfy one social movement demand among many, and in so doing eliminate a major rallying point used against them by their opponents. Politically disarming events of this nature occurred in early 1973, when the United States signed a cease-fire with North Vietnam and ended the draft on January 27 and then withdrew its remaining troops from South Vietnam on March 29.[15] With these actions, the United States government removed the most contentious issues that the power redistribution organizations had used to gain support from adherents. Already slowed by activist disillusionment and fear, the power redistribution movement suffered a further blow from the realization of much of what it had been clamoring to bring about. The movement's partial success, paradoxically, was also its most dramatic failure, as America's disentanglement from South Vietnam took place without a revolution in social or political power.

According to Zald and Ash, one consequence of the failure of a social movement organization is "the search for new instruments" among the disaffected adherents. "Either they search for a more radical means to achieve their goals within the movement, decrease the importance of their goals, or change the focus of discontent." The two theorists conclude with a suggestion that "a Mertonian analysis of anomie might be relevant to this point."[16] They are suggesting that disaffected adherents might try to establish new types of social exchanges involving the use of alternative means to reach the same goals, the same means to reach lesser goals, or alternative means to reach alternative goals.

In order to consider whether the effects of a social movement organization's failure can be seen as a form of anomie, one must slightly refocus the orientation of both Merton's analysis and many of the related studies that utilized deviance schemes that addressed deviance from, and conformity to, *dominant* cultural values. Zald and Ash's suggestion that we look at anomie of adherents who are involved in a failed social movement implies that we could use a Mertonian scheme to examine anomie in a social movement context, one that might be deviant, subcultural, or countercultural to begin with.[17]

Among several qualifications to Merton's original scheme, Robert Dubin's may be the most promising. Where Merton had distinguished only between cultural goals and institutional means, Dubin distinguished between cultural goals, institutional norms, and institutional means. In order, however, to specify the importance of these categories to my study, I will define them in subcultural rather than dominant-cultural terms. Subcultural goals are purposes and interests held out as legitimate objectives for all or for diversely located members of the social movement.[18] Institutional norms are "boundaries between *pre*scribed behaviors and *pro*scribed behaviors in a particular institutional setting," and institutional means are "the specific behaviors, prescribed and potential, that lie within the limits established by institutional norms. [They are] actual behaviors of people; the things they do in carrying out functions in the institutional setting in which they are acting."[19] Institutional norms, therefore, specify the types of social exchanges that are permitted or expected, and the institutional means specify people's actual behaviors in social exchanges.

With Dubin's modified version of Merton's anomie scheme as our guide, two questions present themselves. First, what type of deviant adaptations to social exchanges did conversions to the religious groups offer to the power redistribution movement of the 1960s; and second, why did the adaptation of these exchanges take the form they did? Adherents' conversions to the religious movements of the 1970s were behaviorally innovative responses to the perceived failure of the power redistribution social movement of the counterculture, while still maintaining "revolution" as their goal. The innovations took the general forms that they did because the "defeated" adherents now were complying with the prevailing social exchange demands of the dominant culture, while at the same time they believed themselves to be utilizing these norms for the persistent goal of dramatic power restructuring.[20]

The new religious movement was a way to comply with the dominant culture's demands for power over social exchanges, while at the same time denying the authority of that power. The new religious movement changed the focus of discontent from society to the individual, and this change indicated the adoption of new means to achieve the same goal. Moreover, converts felt that their new means were more radical than the ones previously used by sixties organizations. As the recently converted Rennie Davis told reporters about his new "mission" in 1973, "Getting the knowledge [from Maharaj Ji to the people] is the central objective. . . . Then we can do what the street people sought in the sixties— abolish capitalism and other systems that oppress."[21]

Dubin's typology of deviant adaptations indicates that, as one form of behavioral innovation, persons or groups reject both the institutional norms and institutional means of goal achievement and substitute new ones while continuing to accept essentially the same (sub)cultural goal. This general scheme applies directly to the transition that occurred between the political action groups of the late 1960s and the religious action groups of the 1970s. Prior to the crisis of feasibility and perceived failure between about 1970 and 1973, the countercultural goal for the power redistribution movement was "revolution."[22] The institutional norms through which movement adherents believed the revolution would occur included proscriptions against capitalism, authority and bureaucratic structures, the work ethic, future-time orientations, deferred gratification, and, toward the end of the 1960s, traditional gender roles. The behavioral norms by which the institutional norms were actualized involved cooperative, communal living and sharing; sponteneity in interactions and general lifestyle—including drug use; minimalist, nonhassled jobs; experimentation with gender roles; free love; Marxist and neo-Marxist ideological study; hedonism; a variety of political actions; and little practical future planning.[23]

After the crisis of feasibility, the new religious movement rejected almost every one of the sixties institutional or exchange norms and behavioral or exchange means and replaced them with the norms and means that often resembled, even mimicked, those of the dominant culture. Although variations existed, the institutional and exchange norms of the new religious movement emphasized pro-capitalism, wealth, the work ethic, bureaucracy, present-future-time orientation (i.e., be here now and thereby bring about the revolution), subservience and obedience to authority, sex role traditionalism, Eastern mysticism or Western charisma, and postponed gratification.

Members of new religious movements lived cooperatively in ashrams or centers. Portions of either their shared wealth or their private incomes went to support the often wealthy gurus or their organizations' religious or business ventures instead of going to support their cohorts.[24] They worked long hours in religiously affiliated businesses and often created bureaucratic structures that were unwieldy in size, male-dominated, rampant with titleism, and inefficient. Religious adherents were devotedly obedient to their charismatic leaders and chaste in their interactions with members of the opposite sex. They studied psychology and esoteric (usually Eastern) religious philosophy and espoused millenarian or apocalyptic doctrines. Perhaps the motivation of these converts was best summarized by a new Divine Light Mission premie who had recently resigned from Tom Hayden's Indochina Peace campaign. As he explained in the autumn of 1973: "For years I have worked for peace in Vietnam and now I must turn my attention to the deepest roots of . . . imperialism, the gross qualities of the human species, and work to effect an evolution of this being, beginning with myself."[25]

The failure of the power redistribution movement's attempt to reorganize and restructure society presented its adherents with the dilemma of having to comply with dominant cultural values and exchange principles that emphasized obedience to authority, bureaucracy, and the demands of capitalism, all of which they reviled. The adherents' consequent involvement in the religious movement, therefore, was an attempt to lessen the demands of compliance by developing for themselves an alternative system of exchange rewards, which they did by adopting religious or psychotherapeutic ideologies and by affiliating with organizations that propagated the new tenets. As the social exchange theorist, Peter Blau, suggests, "[T]he more alternative sources of rewards people have, the less those providing valuable services can extract compliance."[26] The religiously ideological movement complied with most of the exchange norms and means of the dominant society, thereby rejecting the unsuccessful exchange norms and means of the 1960s power distribution movement.

Having failed to bring about the revolution by radical action against political and economic structures, adherents to the power redistribution movement in the early 1970s adopted new means to their goal by taking personalized religious or psychotherapeutic action for themselves. The revolution still would come, but its arrival would be heralded by a personal transformation of purified individuals. Moreover, its appearance would be a divinely orchestrated event, as bitter experience had taught them that it could not be a socially orchestrated event.[27] Transform the self of each adherent, the new logic went, and the heavenly sanctified revolution would immediately follow. Through religious ideology and

religious organizations, therefore, the new religious movement established an alternative system of rewards that stood in contrast to those offered by the dominant society.

One passage, written by an activist who had just heard Rennie Davis
speak in Berkeley in April 1973, dramatically captures the points made
here. Having shared with others an initial incredulousness about Davis's
religious commitment, Michael Rossman reflected that

> If Rennie was a heretic, his heresy was not one of ends, but of means;
> and it struck us where our faith is weakest. We have all been strug-
> gling for personal fulfillment and the social good in the same brutal
> climate. Few now can escape the inadequacy of the political meta-
> phor to inspire and guide even our political actions, let alone to fulfill
> them. It is not just a matter of the correct line; the problem is with
> process. All is accomplished by organizing. But was there an activist
> present who had not felt despair, simple and terrifying, at the frus-
> trations and impossibilities of working in the organizations we
> form: their outer impotence, their inner conflicts, and ego games
> and wasted energy, the impoverishment of spirit which led us to
> drop out of them again and again? Here Rennie was, proclaiming the
> perfect means to our various ends, the ideal, impossible Organiza-
> tion working in perfect inner harmony and outer accomplishment.
> Lay down your arms, your suffering, and the Master will give you
> bliss. And yet to work in the Left, to be in the Left, has meant to bear
> these arms, the suffering; we have known no other way.[28]

As the power redistribution movement searched desperately to find a successful method for achieving the ever-elusive revolution, the techniques
and the promises of the new religious groups became, for many, beacons
of hope.

From the perspective of social exchange theory, the flexibility with
which people can interpret religious ideologies and texts makes religion a
particularly useful device for adherents of a failed social movement who
are attempting to renegotiate the perceived rewards and profits resulting
from social interaction. Two sociologists of religion, Rodney Stark and
William Sims Bainbridge, have recognized the exchange value of religion
and have formulated it into a testable theoretical proposition. "In the absence of a desired reward," they propose, "[compensatory] explanations

will often be accepted which posit attainment of the reward in the distant future or in some other nonverifiable context."[29] As applied to this study, adherents in the unsuccessful power redistribution movement of the late 1960s would receive the "reward" of the social revolution, but as "compensation" in the millennial future.

Religious ideology, therefore, provided the cognitive avenues by which many former activists reduced the dissonance caused by their commitment to an apparently failed social movement; in social exchange terms, a movement in which the costs of continued participation were far higher than the rewards or profits. From the perspective of the new religious movement, the profits for participation would be reaped in the imminent millennium. Religious organization, in complementary fashion, provided the social-structural means by which former activists established alternative resource rewards in contrast to those offered by the dominant society. If we view the new religions of the early 1970s as constituting another segment of a broad, social movement industry that was striving to achieve a humanistic society, then the religious conversions of former activists simply were shifts of allegiance from a failing movement to a rising one, both of which shared the same basic goal.[30] To borrow language from deviance theory, the power redistribution movement provided the learning structures which the new religious movement supplemented through its new opportunity structures. Many of the so-called new religious conversions by former activists, therefore, perhaps should more accurately be called alterations.

By identifying the transformations in institutional norms and institutional means between the late 1960s and the early 1970s, the model used in this study may explain several disparate, but well-established, characteristics of the early new religious movements and their adherents. From various studies, we know that participation in many religious groups in the 1970s facilitated people's (re)integration into mainstream society, and at the same time "interest in radical political change and in [counterculture and personal growth] movements tend[ed] to go together."[31] On the latter point, Tipton forcefully argued against a prevalent perspective that the new religious groups had drained political energies from the activist movement. He argued that "to depict alternative religions as simply siphoning off would-be political activists or 'cooling out' the politically disaffected oversimplifies the peculiar relationship of political concern and disillusionment in these sixties youth, and, they would say, it oversimplifies the nature of social change itself."[32] As the typology offered here shows, former activist "converts" believed that they were adhering to the same goal as the 1960s power redistribution movement, but their rejection of the norms and behaviors of the period in their attempts to reach this goal aligned them with the important institutional norms of the "straight" world, and thereby facilitated their (re)entry into it.

Of interest to sociologists of religion might be the way in which the theoretical scheme developed in this study relates to earlier work on the assimilative functions served by various 1970s religious groups for former participants in the drug culture. In their study on "getting straight with Meher Baba," Thomas Robbins and Dick Anthony show how youth movements "ease[d] the tension of the familial-occupational transition . . . by constructing value orientations and normative frameworks which combine[d] elements of both familial and bureaucratic role-systems (e.g., bureaucratic universalism and familial diffuseness)."[33] As members of the drug culture encountered the disharmony between their goals and the institutional norms and institutional means or behaviors that they hoped would achieve those goals, many drug users experienced a crisis of feasibility analogous to what their politically active compatriots were about to undergo. By believing in Meher Baba as the universal, loving savior, former drug-users turned Baba-lover adherents were able to practice "selfless service" in institutionally impersonal normative settings, thereby facilitating their rapprochement with the "impersonal institutions of the larger society."[34] The strength of the theoretical model presented here is that it may provide an explanation that is sufficiently general to explain the conversion of both activists and drug users to the same religious organizations in the early 1970s.

One profitable direction for future research would be an examination of the extent to which many of the new religious organizations themselves declined as they proved unable to maintain sufficient rewards to offset both the costs of continued involvement and the allure of rewards offered by the dominant society. A crucial factor was the fragmentation of the movement caused by exclusivistic religious ideologies. This exclusivism fostered competition among groups for constituents, participants, and resources. Debates among various religious groups on these

issues were exceedingly bitter.[35] Likewise, one should examine the deple-
tion of personal resources that converts suffered as the result of irrational
capitalist ventures by some organizations and almost insatiable charismatic demands by certain leaders. In short, extended applications of exchange perspectives, especially in relation to issues of deviance and
conformity among 1970s social movement participants, would be especially fruitful, because we know that soon after the Age of Aquarius
dawned, the sun sank over the horizon. The day was short, indeed.

David Sanjek

Apocalypse Then
Apocalyptic Imagery and Documentary Reality in Films of the 1960s

I
n 1960, the year the Student Nonviolent Coordinating Committee was founded, Blake Edwards's musical comedy, *High Time*, was released.[1] It starred Bing Crosby as an aging restauranteur who returns to college to complete his degree as the capstone to his successful business career. However, the campus at which he matriculates, along with adolescent co-stars Fabian, Richard Beymer, and Tuesday Weld, is so devoid of tension that Crosby's East-Indian roommate and fellow fraternity pledge, played by Pat Adiarte, is tapped and admitted without even the mention of racism or hazing. The film's breezy implausibility is sealed by Crosby's rendition of "The Second Time Around," in which he reassures the audience "Love, like youth, is wasted on the young." As the final year of Eisenhower's second term drew to a close, before the ascension of John F. Kennedy's Camelot and the fatal bullet at Dallas, Hollywood chose to depict the campus in a manner that erased any mention of generational conflict, interracial friction, or sexual inequality. Had all the rebels without a cause become nothing more than pledges in search of a frat?

If the social world featured in many mainstream Hollywood films of the 1960s was blissfully, if not mindlessly benign, the studio system that released these films was facing the most pressing financial and structural overhaul in its history. The studio moguls were dead, their empires in the process of being engulfed by conglomerates. Their attempt to capture back the audience lost to the novelty of television through wide screen technologies, including CinemaScope and VistaVision, and big budget spectaculars was a failure, culminating in the *Cleopatra* debacle of 1963 which virtually toppled Twentieth-Century Fox. A number of the directors who embodied what we now call "classic Hollywood cinema" were no longer able to practice their craft or did so under inhibited circumstances. The Golden Age of movies was over, even if the studio system seemed oblivious to its demise and attempted to perpetuate its reign.

As the film industry floundered, American society was entering a period of substantial social, political, racial, and cultural transformation. These changes profoundly affected the youth of the United States, demographically the largest element of the filmgoing public. As the decade advanced, Hollywood began, tentatively, to document the ruptures in their world. However, acknowledging and valorizing social change are not the same process. For every *Easy Rider* (1969), there is yet another *Beach Party Bingo* (1965). The commercial cinema was quite ready to exploit countercultural modes of expression, but that did not mean it would censure the ideological presuppositions of the dominant culture. We must not forget that film is a commodity produced by an industrial system; it is dependent upon the investment of speculative capital and therefore seeks to legitimate the status quo.[2] Social tensions and contradictions are minimized if not eradicated. Any questions raised about society's vulnerabilities have to be answered; any criticisms of society have to give way before the inescapable attractions of consumer capitalism. Axel Madsen acknowledged this failure of nerve in American cinema when he wrote:

What separates Hollywood from European cinema, and constantly widens the Atlantic, is the American myth of the mechanical age that a good film is first of all a film that exhausts all its possibilities. Yet in the arts we live in Nietzschean times, the era of the charm of imperfection, where creators bequile more with what they hint at than with what they achieve. The lack of personal point of view that efficacy implies used to be the strength of American films; today this virtue seems to be a barrier to the future.[3]

Despite the applicability of Madsen's comments to most Hollywood films of the period, some produced during the 1960s possess the "charm of imperfection" of which he writes. This is particularly true of those pictures that incorporate a fictional narrative with factual documentation of environments, social movements, or events representative of the period. However, more often than not in the films I discuss here, the fictional and factual material clashes rather than coheres. Their plots, all too often melodramatic, generational conflicts, lack either the substance or the significance of the settings in which they occur. This conflict between content and context leaves the viewer free to choose where to focus attention and gives rise to what Lawrence Alloway has called "media echoes," whereby "the images on the screen are always extending to contemporaneous data off the screen, slurring into a sociological matrix."[4]

What makes many of the films of the period still worthy of our attention is just these "media echoes" that simultaneously affirm and attack the social transformation of the 1960s. Depending upon where the viewer focuses his or her attention, these films are either celebrations of social experimentation or defenses of the status quo. To examine this process I discuss five filmic modes: the grade-B exploitation feature, particularly those documenting the biker and drug subcultures; the "mondo" documentary; the road movie; the campus protest movie; the agit-prop political drama, and the work of expatriate or European directors, including Richard Lester and Michelangelo Antonioni, who bring an outsider's eye to the American scene. Each mode in turn embodies the collision between the desire to contain, if not condemn, and an often inadvertent celebration of the very forces the films undermine.

Before continuing, however, it is necessary to remember that "just as the whole use of subception techniques in advertising is blocked by the different perception capabilities of any audience, so the mass media cannot reduce everybody to one drugged faceless consumer."[5] It is all too easy to underestimate the role of the audience in determining meaning. Consumers can direct their attention to one element of a film, in this case the factual rather than the fictional material, while ignoring another, thereby deliberately recontextualizing the work by appropriating for their own uses what was designed to use them.[6] Films, like all texts, do not possess unitary meanings the audience is designed to uncover.

Meanings are produced by concrete viewers receiving images in specific cultural contexts. The spirit and the meaning of the 1960s remain alive in these films because audiences continue to maneuver their way between the tensions the films embody and to appropriate, for their own purposes, the significance of the cultural, political, and social aspirations the films document.

✳　　✳　　✳

We turn first to the commercial exploitation movie, which Tom Doherty defines as a work that incorporates controversial content, bottom-line bookkeeping, and demographic targeting, and took as an appropriate subject matter the dynamic social changes in American society occurring in the sixties.[7] Two areas of marketable interest to the exploitation filmmaker were the biker culture and the drug scene. The biker culture was first brought to public attention by the *The Wild One* (1953) and, for the more informed filmgoer, Kenneth Anger's *Scorpio Rising* (1963), in addition to journalistic reports, including Hunter Thompson's *Hell's Angels: A Strange and Terrible Saga* (1967). The drug scene was known particularly for experimentation with LSD and the corresponding changes in social relations as embodied by the Haight-Ashbury district of San Francisco.[8] The most distinctive cinematic responses to these developments were those of Roger Corman and Richard Rush. Corman, the premiere exploitation filmmaker, whose work goes back to 1955 and who had earlier examined the rock and roll scene and helped inaugurate the reinvigorated horror and science fiction genres, focuses on the countercultural revolution in his films *The Wild Angels* (1966) and *The Trip* (1967) which simultaneously salute and censure both the biker culture and the drug scene. This ambivalent perspective is shared by Richard Rush's *Hell's Angels on Wheels* (1967) and *Psych-Out* (1968).

Heavenly Blues (Peter Fonda), the leader of the Wild Angels, is a consummate antihero; while he engages in nihilistic violence, he frowns upon fellow bikers shooting heroin, attempts to constrain their most violent tendencies, and commits himself to the burial of his dead friend, the Loser. Corman's romantic validation of the Angels' antisocial behavior is illustrated stylistically by tracking shots of their riding through the mountains and desert, framing them telephotically against the landscape in a manner reminiscent of classic Western cinematic iconography. However, the predominant tone of the film is one of implicit censure, particularly in the climactic pillaging of a church by the Angels, during which the jagged hand-held photography mirrors the group's lack of control. Even if the film's final line, Blue's nihilistic statement "There's nowhere to go," uttered over the Loser's grave, romantically attempts to see the group as antiheroic, the imagery overwhelmingly validates a nihilistic depiction of the worst of human nature.

Rush's *Hell's Angels on Wheels* attempts a similarly ambivalent portrait by dividing its focus between biker leader, Buddy (Adam Roarke), and outsider, Poet (Jack Nicholson). Buddy, like Blue, is a Romantic hero who articulates his value system by quoting Milton: "It is better to rule in Hell than to serve in Heaven." Poet, despite his nickname, engages in the bikers' activities without endorsing their aggression. Splitting the narrative focus allows Rush a dual perspective, as the outsider is able to appreciate the camaraderie of the group while criticizing its deficiencies. Like Poet, Rush deplores the biker world as "distasteful," but his, perhaps unconscious, sympathies for the bikers are exhibited by the graceful images of their appropriation of mechanical technology for the expression of their personal beliefs.[9] At times, the film's plot virtually grinds to a halt to document the bikers' joie de vivre only to return to the despair of an amoral life without social sanction.

Corman's subsequent film, *The Trip*, paints a far more affirmative image of the drug culture as a force for the expansion, not retrogression, of consciousness. Perhaps as a reflection of Corman's own affirmative experience with LSD, Paul Groves (Peter Fonda), a commercial advertisement director, begins to move outside a narcissistic self-involvement as a result of dropping acid, even if the form and substance of his acid visions profoundly resemble commercial advertising imagery and style, suggesting that he has not entirely left behind the world the film rejects.[10] Nonetheless, the film's implicit endorsement of the use of drugs for the expansion of consciousness caused one reviewer to refer to it as a virtual advertisement for LSD. The film's distributor, American International Pictures, perhaps sensing the potential for such a judgement, placed a prefatory admonition against the manufacture and consumption of LSD and optically altered the film's final image by interjecting an image of shattering glass, suggesting that Paul, much as he affirms his experience with his final dialogue, has merely made a Faustian bargain with his body chemistry. Nonetheless, the predominant tone of *The Trip* undermines, if not eradicates, such a judgement. [11]

Richard Rush's *Psych-Out* (1968) presents an equally contradictory depiction of Haught-Ashbury. Its plot line, a melodramatically convoluted tale of a deaf, runaway teenager's search for her brother who is lost among the freaks of San Francisco, is interrupted by sequences documenting elements of that milieu, ranging from the Digger's Free Store, be-ins, and the communal spontaneity of the Fillmore and Avalon Ballroom. It is those sequences that most impress themselves upon the viewer's attention, as the knotty and overly dense plot is an imposition upon the playful environment. The film's final shot illustrates this conflict as a split screen incorporates an image from the film's portentously apocalyptic conclusion with an earlier idyllic image of the playfulness the Haight embodied. This confusion perhaps also reflects the fact that fifteen minutes of footage was edited from the final print. American International Pictures apparently feared being seen as an advocate of alternative social practices.

* * *

The "mondo" movies, so called by reference to the benchmark film *Mondo Cane* (1963), are documentaries that focus on shocking subject matter, the film equivalent of yellow or tabloid journalism. [12] They are clearly meant to shock and/or titillate by allowing the observer privileged access to forbidden environments or ways of life. These films often incorporate all too clearly fabricated footage, but even when they do not, their aim, through portentous and denunciatory narration, is to vitiate any meaning the subject matter might possess. Such is the case with such titles as *Mondo Bizarro* (1966), *Mondo Teeno* (1967), *Mondo Mod* (1967), and *Mondo Hollywood* (1967) which examine American and international youth subcultures. However, it is altogether possible for a spectator, particularly one appreciative of, or committed to, the way of life under attack, to ignore the narrative and appropriate the visual imagery to his or her own purposes, assuming, thereby, a belief in the primacy of the visual over the verbal as the preeminent means of communication. What the filmmaker might render banal, the spectator reanimates with a keen awareness of the "media echoes" to which the footage gives rise.

*   *   *

The road movie became an active genre in the late 1960s as the portability of lightweight camera equipment facilitated the process of taking the movies to the streets. Filmakers, like their characters, went off in search of America, but all too often they made that quest without leaving their prejudices and preconceptions behind. Their sense of the divisions within the national consciousness uncritically incorporated well worn political and social stereotypes, resulting in a propensity for knee-jerk apocalypticism. Too many sixties films reflect "the American tendency to take the national pulse all the time, . . . skepticism and anxiety tend to outpace the mastery of fact. American life [becomes] a drag strip of hotted-up crises."[13]

A choice example of the liability of uncritically exploring the national consciousness is *Easy Rider* (1969). For all the film's reputation as a historical landmark, its visual style owes a great deal to prior experimentation by its cinematographer, Laszlo Kovacs, who shot *Hell's Angels on Wheels* and *Psych-Out* among other exploitation features, and its plot reduces the characters to fashionably one-dimensional representatives of all-knowing hippies and know-nothing rednecks. Billy (Peter Fonda) and Wyatt's (Dennis Hopper) martyrdom seems undeserved, and Billy's ominous comment, "we blew it," implies a greater degree of self-consciousness than the duo's limited appreciation of their questionable behavior would allow. Stephan Farber highlights the film's deficiencies when he writes: "It's true that respectable America tends to stereotype the outsiders—hippies, radicals, blacks—and see them in conspiratorial terms; so why should we praise a hip-youth-oriented film that stereotypes its enemies just as ruthlessly, and also casts them as conspirators."[14] Too many viewers of the film, one of the most financially successful in 1969, ignored the thematic deficiencies Farber underscored and reveled instead in its heroes' self-righteousness, often acted out at the expense of others, particularly rural Americans and women.

A far more telling, better modulated, and too little known road movie is Francis Ford Coppola's *The Rain People* (1969), in which Natalie (Shirley Knight), pregnant and feeling entrapped by her marriage, leaves home and takes to the freedom of the highways only to become burdened by the care of a brain-damaged, college football player, "Killer" Kilgannon

(James Caan). Coppola, who shot the film over five months travelling from New York to Wyoming, captures the spaciousness of the landscape without losing track of the abominations brought about by our pillaging of the environment. Furthermore, he uses the road genre to tackle the issue of female liberation, although the narrative fluctuates between admiring and admonishing Natalie's quest for self-identity. Coppola cleverly highlights Natalie's habit of referring to herself in the third person and dramatizes her indecision during a series of long distance phone calls to her abandoned husband. Nonetheless, the conclusion opts for a facile tragedy and leaves Natalie cradling the now dead Killer, promising to protect him as she will likely protect the child she has deliberated over aborting earlier in the film. Coppola's film may not be politically correct, as he simultaneously promotes and discredits Natalie's liberation. Nonetheless, *The Rain People* is dramatically engrossing and too little known. By focusing on the admittedly incoherent narrative of female liberation, we can appreciate a precursor to more unified narratives.[15]

✳   ✳   ✳

The reflexive gesture toward a flip cynicism is particularly evident in the campus protest film cycle of 1970, typified by *The Strawberry Statement*, adapted from James S. Kunen's memoir of the Columbia uprising of 1968.[16] It pits noble, good-looking, white, middle-class students against the retrograde entrenched forces of the establishment in such a manner that it virtually rewrites the teenpic in quasi-political terms: they could have called it *Beach Party Barricades*. One is unable to recontextualize these films as anything other than the cynical marketing of better riots with beautiful people. Despite Motion Picture Association of America President Jack Valenti's 1967 assertion "I truly don't think the entire young audience, and surely not the old, are all of a psychedelic breed, hunkered up over their pot and acid, and lurching off on supernatural romps and trips," the campus protest cycle proves Hollywood can and will package *anything*.[17]

A representative example of this cycle is Richard Rush's *Getting Straight* (1970), one of several films released in that year starring Elliot Gould, who temporarily became an anti-authoritarian icon in the aftermath of *M*A*S*H* (1969). Set in a state institution that epitomizes the academic model of the "multiversity," designed by the University of

California's Chancellor Clark Kerr, the film details the academic failure and re-radicalization of Harry Bailey, a former activist now master's candidate and hopeful secondary-school teacher. Harry attempts to balance his libido and liberal conscience, constantly racing between the classroom and the bedroom. As his campus boils over into a full-fledged riot, Harry evades solicitations from all sides to ally himself with any number of causes, each of which he puts off with sarcastic bravado. It is only when he fails his master's oral examination, brought down by a professor's vehement denunciation of Fitzgerald as a closet homosexual, and is reunited with his girlfriend, Jan (Candace Bergen), that Harry commits himself to radical action and joins the rioting students.

However, the priorities for which the students strike in *Getting Straight* lack any substance. Even Harry realizes this, for when a campus administrator attacks their behavior, Harry responds, "It has nothing to do with politics. It's personal identity." *Getting Straight*'s characterization of politics as a matter of pique, not principle, amounts to little more than asserting that it's one step from rallying for co-ed dorms to offing the pigs. This indecisiveness is paralleled by Rush's use of a photographic technique known as "rack focus." With it one changes or "racks" focus from foreground to background, blurring one space and then the other rather than changing camera position.[18] The degree to which rack focus subverts depth in the image is comparable to Harry Bailey's inability to integrate his personal–sexual and political–social concerns. The optical lack of cohesion suggest that Rush, like his characters, cannot imagine the continual interdependence between individual and society, part and whole except through acts of unreasoning violence.[19]

A comparable tendency to programmatic simplification defeats a more illustrious example of the campus protest cycle, Michelangelo Antonioni's *Zabriskie Point* (1969). Despite the fact that the film opens with a cinema verité reproduction of a campus discussion over tactics, the participants of which include Kathleen Cleaver, this debate over revolutionary authenticity bears only the slimmest of connections to Antonioni's narrative of two young, would-be radicals who meet in the southwestern desert where they sexually and ideologically connect at the location after which the film is named. A fragment of dialogue from this sequence typifies the tenor of the film: Daria (Daria Halprin) asks Mark (Mark Frechette) "Don't you feel at home here? It's peaceful," to which

Mark answers, "It's dead." Antonioni's visualization of the American landscape, both urban and desert, devitalizes all human activity. Individuals are overwhelmed by objects, objects are overwhelmed by space. So oppressive is the environment that one can conceive of few alternatives to wiping the slate clean, albeit only by means of the imagination, not collective political action. In the celebrated final sequence, Daria imagines the destruction of her well-heeled boss's (Rod Taylor) desert mansion. As the building explodes, caught by the camera from a variety of angles, and the objects of modern capitalism drift in surrealistic slow motion, we are forced to acknowledge that this is a "bloodless bombing," the sequence is "powerful in its visceral impact and strangely disconnected from its objective correlative: it's a revolutionary image that addresses itself to the idea and sentiment of a revolution, not the fact of it."[20]

A more legitimate and coherently conceived expression of the period's revolutionary tensions is the explicit agitprop political drama epitomized by Haskell Wexler's *Medium Cool* (1968). An imperfect but compelling work, it unfortunately has borne the weight of being the period's only studio-produced piece of political cinema that attempted to incorporate a fictional narrative, detailing the recognition by television cameraman John (Robert Foster) of his co-option by the powers that be, with documentary footage of a revolutionary crisis, the riots that occurred during the Chicago demonstrations of 1968. The film seamlessly, if self-consciously, shifts between narrative and documentary modes, particularly when it features Wexler's actual footage of the police riots, used here as Eileen (Verna Bloom) searches for her missing son. However, it too often heats up into indigestible propagandizing, as in the sequence shot at a roller derby, which leadenly comments on the American propensity for indiscriminate violence. Admittedly, other sequences, particularly those shot during the convention, are undeniably effective as when, one hears Wexler's offscreen soundman cry, "Look out Haskell. It's real," after the police drop tear gas cannisters into the crowd. However, it is the quieter moments, particularly those between John and Eileen's son Harold (Harold Blankenship) and the flashbacks to Harold's childhood in West Virginia, which resonate in one's memory. Early in the film, during a discussion by a roomfull of newsmen over the scope of a reporter's responsibilities, John states, "Who wants to see someone sitting? Who wants to see someone lying down? Who wants to see someone talking peace unless they're talking loud?" While Wexler's film too often focuses on such moments of ideological aggression, the film can be recontextualized to argue for the validity and significance of recording just such quieter, domestic moments. If our political consciousness remains merely a set of self-dramatizing gestures that do not carry over to our quotidian behavior, then we are merely narcissistically engaging in self-aggrandizement.

Finally, one of the most impressive and too little known documents of the social changes in the 1960s is Richard Lester's *Petulia* (1968). Shot in San Francisco during the 1967 "summer of love," it was the first film that Lester, a native born American who has lived his adult life in England, shot in this country. It was also the occasion of his return after fifteen years abroad. Scorned upon its release, during the aftermath of Robert Kennedy's assassination, as a morally reprehensible chronicle of a set of unredeemable characters, this film makes, not only emotional, but also formal demands upon the viewer. Rather than playing to our reflexive stereotypes, Lester fragments the narrative, incorporating flashbacks and flashforwards which elicit, if not demand, the viewer's active participation in the narrative. Furthermore, while the narrative may seem only obliquely political, concerning as it does the lives of the leisure and professional class in San Francisco, *Petulia* is, nonetheless, one of the most telling documents of the period. It denies the period's predominant ethos, that love can solve all dilemmas, by dramatizing the casual violence that plagues our lives and eats away at appropriate relationships.

The leading characters in the film, surgeon Archie (George C. Scott) and Petulia (Julie Christie), struggle with their belief that individuals can provide one another a safe haven in a heartless world. "Touch it. Touch it. Make the hurt less," Petulia asks Archie as she suffers through labor at the end of the film. The image of touch, highlighted by Lester's frequent shots of Archie's surgeon's hands, is central to the film as Petulia is battered more than once by the hands of her beautiful but impotent husband, David (Richard Chamberlin). Petulia has married him because he was, she confesses, "the most perfect thing I'd ever met. . . . He must be one of those plastic gadgets the Americans make so well. But I want one." She has objectified her husband, and he has acted in kind by treating her as a beautiful accessory to his upper-class life, albeit one to be battered when it gets out of line. So too is the Mexican boy Oliver (Vincent Arias), who the couple take home with them, argue over, and then treat as an object of pity when he is injured in a car accident. These characters, rich as their material lives might be, are, as Lester states, "emotional eunuchs in a society so riddled with the cancer of its own failing that commitment is never made."[21]

However, *Petulia* does not focus on these characters alone. It mirrors their emotionally bankrupt lives by depicting San Francisco, circa 1967, as an environment in which a death wish pervades and eventually triumphs over the summer of love. Television sets are a ubiquitous presence in *Petulia*, always tuned to the news of the Vietnam War. Furthermore, random episodes of violence occupy the frame along with the major characters, creating an unsettling aura of incipient calamity. Even the young people, the denizens of the "summer of love," appear lost in a world of their own. As Petulia, battered by her husband, is carried to an ambulance, the crowd, which oddly includes members of the Grateful Dead, rubbernecks around the stretcher; "Bye, bye mama. Write if you get work," one of them sarcastically cries out.

While *Petulia* is an effective and emotionally devastating, bittersweet romance, the viewer can easily recontextualize the narrative into a prescient portrait of an eroding society. "Isn't it super. Suddenly all that love," Petulia says to Archie soon after they first meet. A comment one might read as comic, yet Lester sees the film as the farthest thing from a comedy; instead, it depicts "people [who] are aware of what's wrong and therefore not only have the problems of being, but the problems of knowing about being—the double agony."[22] *Petulia* reminds us that a film need not exhaust, but can multiply, its own possibilities by making demands upon its viewers, not predigesting its meaning or relying upon uninformed stereotypes. It fulfills Lester's aim: "I want to offer the scattershot of experience to an audience and make them work. I want to make each person sitting in a row see a different film."[23]

*   *   *

We presently live in a period where the cinema bears, not only a resemblance to the techniques of commercial advertising, but also acts as a shill for the very corporations that now own the major Hollywood studios. As Mark Crispin Miller has shown, the pervasive use of commercial films as platforms for "product placement" damages the very nature of film narrative, but more profoundly indicates a radical shift of creative power out of the hands of filmmaking professionals into those of the CEOs.[24] And the quantitative mentality of the corporate mind holds little interest in ambiguity or critique. The result is "going to the movies now is about as memorable as going to the airport. Conceived and sold as 'product,' just like the many products that it sells, so does the movie pass right through you, leaving nothing in you but the vague, angry craving for another one."[25]

Too many current films so fully exhaust their possibilities and ignore contradictions that a happy ending, devoid of irony, is a prerequisite; when and if audience research indicates displeasure with a less than buoyant conclusion which might damage a film's boxoffice potential, the narrative is modified to fulfill the spectators' demands.[26] Such practices embody what Andrew Britton has called Reaganite entertainment, which he defines as that which "refers to itself in order to persuade us that it doesn't refer outwards at all. It is, purely and simply 'entertainment'— and we all know what *that* is."[27] These films do not merely lack a personal point of view, but their producers seem more than willing to change their substance to suit an audience's needs and desires, a cynical gesture that erases the line between creation and marketing and assumes spectators to be little more than "drugged faceless consumer(s)." Yet worst of all, Britton suggests, even should a film imply that reality is intolerable, it eradicates any possibility of social transformation by asserting that reality is immutable and any desire to escape or transcend it is a flight of fantasy.

Such circumstances make the process of recontextualization ever more difficult, yet, in looking back at the films of the 1960s, one recognizes, for all their self-contradiction, potential models of alternate expression equally worthy of attention as the social movements they attempt to document.

Alexis Greene

The Arts and the Vietnam Antiwar Movement

I n the high and the popular arts, radical/undergound/avant-garde
artists, and liberal/intellectual artists, used their particular art forms
to protest the war in Vietnam. Like so many in the protest movement,
they did not know how to convey their dissent in a way that would truly
affect those in power, so they chose the method that seemed most logical
to them, and which historically had been used by artists before them,
from Aristophanes to Beaumarchais, Goya to Picasso. Whether their medium was the written word, a canvas, film, or the stage, they created art
objects through which they presented their responses to the conflict—
their ideas, their fear, their anger.

If they used their art to protest the war, they also used their status as
artists. Robert Lowell, for instance, refused to attend a White House Festival of the Arts in June 1965. Like many during the first year of Lyndon
Johnson's significant troop escalations, Lowell feared that such aggression would lead to confrontation with the Soviet Union and/or China,
and conceivably to nuclear war. He wrote Johnson that he responded to
American foreign policy "with the greatest dismay and distrust. What we
will do and what we ought to do as a sovereign nation facing other sovereign nations seem now to hang in the balance between the better and
the worse possibilities. We are in danger of imperceptibly becoming an
explosive and suddenly chauvinistic nation."[1] Lowell released his letter
to *The New York Times*. His public rebuff was soon endorsed in a telegram
sent to the White House and signed by twenty artists and intellectuals,

including Hannah Arendt, John Berryman, Mary McCarthy, Larry Rivers, and Mark Rothko.

American artists often protested the war as a group, and they were sensitive to the progress of the larger antiwar movement, with its highs and lows, its surges of enthusiasm and its disappointments. While the course of arts protest did not necessarily reflect every turn and twist of the antiwar movement, the nature and uses of antiwar art reflected the general rhythms of the movement. As the war escalated under the Johnson administration, and the frustration of trying to communicate to a stubborn government increased, the art generally became angrier, more accusatory, in an attempt to force political change. Then from 1968 until the end of the war, the uses of art gradually shifted. Some artists simply abandoned personal artistic statements in favor of participating in public protests. Others began to make artistic statements that were so private, so removed from political events, that in effect, it was clear these artists had retreated from protest and were attempting to sever their emotional connection to the on-going war.

✳　　✳　　✳

Writers were among the most critical of the American military presence in Southeast Asia. Allen Ginsberg decried the American presence in Vietnam as early as 1963. By 1968 he was asking in "Wichita Vortex Sutra"

> Has anyone looked in the eyes of the dead?
> U.S. Army recruiting service sign *Careers With A Future*
> Is anyone living to look for future forgiveness? . . .
>
> . . . .
>
> Has anyone looked in the eyes of the wounded?
> Have we seen but paper faces, Life Magazine?
> Are screaming faces made of dots,
> electric dots on Television—[2]

Indeed, as the conflict progressed, poets such as Ginsberg, Denise Levertov, Robert Duncan, and Robert Bly alternately depicted the horrible destruction of human life and satirized the American capitalist structure that could even contemplate such a war. In 1966, Robert Bly and another poet, David Ray, founded American Writers against the Vietnam War, which organized a series of read-ins. Among other poems, Bly contributed "The Teeth-Mother Naked At Last." Initially, the images juxtapose the hubris of wealthy America against the vulnerability of Vietnam:

> It's because a hospital room in the average American
>   city now costs $60 a day that we bombed hospitals
>   in the North
> It's because the aluminum window-shade business is
>   doing so well in the United States that we roll fire
>   over entire villages
> It's because the milk trains coming into New Jersey hit
>   the right switches every day that the best Vietnamese
>   men are cut in two by American bullets that follow
>   each other like freight cars[3]

Later in the poem, Bly shifts to images that are mournful and ironic in a more tragic sense:

> It is because we have so few women sobbing in back
>   rooms,
> because we have so few children's heads torn apart by
>   high-velocity bullets,
> because we have so few tears falling on our own hands
> that the Super Sabre turns and screams down toward
>   the earth[4]

In the fall of 1967, Levertov wrote the following lines in her poem "Tenebrae":

> Heavy, heavy, heavy, hand and heart.
> We are at war,
> bitterly, bitterly at war.
>
> And the buying and selling
> buzzes at our heads, a swarm
> of busy flies, a kind of innocence.
>
> Gowns of gold sequins are fitted,
> sharp-glinting. What harsh rustlings

of silver moiré there are,
to remind me of shrapnel splinters.[5]

The visual art that emerged during the Vietnam protest movement was sometimes poster art, as with an Art Workers' Coalition poster that used Ronald Haeberle's color photograph of the dead at the My Lai massacre. Superimposed in large red letters on the photograph are words from newsman Mike Wallace's interview with marine Paul Meadlo, who had participated in the slaughter: "Q: And babies? A: And babies."[6]

The gallery art that emerged to protest the war was on occasion fantastical and metaphoric in nature. Peter Saul's *Saigon* (1967), for instance, is a garish comic strip vision of whoring in Saigon, painted in psychedelic reds and blues. And Nancy Spero's *Bomb*, from her "Bombs and Helicopters Series," is a lyrical evocation of the grotesque: barely formed human figures, drawn gracefully with ink and watercolors, disgorge columns of blood from their mouths. Such metaphoric visions were the exception. Generally, the gallery art, like the posters, conveyed its messages directly, as with Peter Dean's caricaturing oil portrait of Lyndon Johnson, with blood encircling the president's mouth, entitled *No. 1 Cannibal.*

Underground filmmakers tended to be prolific creators of antiwar films. Artists like Lenny Lipton, Jerry Abrams, Peter Gessner, and David Ringo made 16mm films, often documentary in nature, that recorded peace marches and antiwar demonstrations throughout the 1960s. Usually these were shot and edited with an eye toward highlighting the communal, warm and humane nature of the marchers, as opposed to the rigid, unsmiling and often violent policemen or national guardsmen who were always present. Shots of marchers lolling in their jeans and T-shirts in the early morning sun in Washington, D.C., would suddenly be juxtaposed with shots of buttoned up, upright and uptight police, who inevitably were facing the marchers in a threatening line. Indeed, in films like *We Shall March Again* (Lenny Lipton, 1965), *Peace March* (Anthony Reveaux, 1967), and *March on the Pentagon* (David Ringo, 1968), these images soon become metaphors for victims and aggressors, Vietnamese and imperialist Americans. Such propagandistic messages were clearly in the minds of the people at Third World Newsreel when they made the film *Columbia Revolt* (1968). The filmmakers use the confrontations between the Columbia University students and the New York City police as visual metaphors that first call to mind the Gestapo assaulting the Jews of the ghettos and then, by extension, can be understood to represent attacks by goons of a fascist United States on the innocent victims of a peace-loving culture.

A similar metaphor is at work in Robert Kramer's 35mm black and white film *Ice*, a narrative film made in 1969, when the antiwar movement had grown considerably more aggressive in certain quarters. *Ice* posits a scenario in which contemporary American guerrillas attempt to infiltrate and take over sectors of an American city. Through intimidation, assassination, and the blowing up of critical buildings, these revolutionaries try to overthrow the national government for its role in continuing a war in Mexico, for which we can substitute Vietnam.

The Vietnam War also ignited a response in the theater community, although the majority of playwrights preferred to transmit their messages in indirect ways, through metaphor or parody. These protests were often aimed at depicting the danger of official power and militarism gone out of control, and the playwright left the spectator to draw his or her own analogies to the contemporary situation. Frank O'Hara's black comedy *The General Returns from One Place to Another* (1965), satirizes the American penchant for military interventionism around the world. Sam Shepard's *Icarus's Mother* (1965) creates an apparently normal American scenario, two couples enjoying themselves on the beach, that is interrupted when an airplane suddenly appears, swoops over the merrymakers and at the end of the play seems to explode in a nuclear-like flash. The cataclysmic finale is both ominous and cleansing, as though ultimate power had self-destructed. In Robert Lowell's adaptation of Aeschylus' *Prometheus Bound* (produced at Yale Drama School in 1967), Zeus came across at moments as a parody of Lyndon Johnson, although R.W.B. Lewis, professor of English and American studies at Yale, thought that this Zeus was "at once vaguer and more frightful than President Johnson."[7] As C.W.E. Bigsby writes, "Prometheus, burning in his own fire, could not easily be detached from the flames which were . . . blooming in Vietnam or from those which wrapped the bodies of protesting Buddhist priests."[8] In Kenneth Bernard's surrealistic nightmare, *The Moke-Eater* (1968), a travelling salesman's car breaks down near a New England town called Monte Waite. Monte Waite contains none of the peacefulness of its theatrical antecedent, the Grover's Corners of Thornton Wilder's play *Our Town*. Instead, Monte Waite offers violence, torture, cannibalism, and tyranny. The salesman, expecting to find that money will get him out of an unpleasant situation, discovers instead that he is a prisoner of the town and particularly of the town's leading citizen, a dictator named Alec. At night, Alec forces the salesman to watch a grotesque show, specifically an episode during which an elderly man, perhaps a vestige of an earlier civilization, is attacked by the Moke-Eater, who devours him. Whether or not violence and repression always existed beneath the surface of small-town America, we cannot know. Certainly, it exists now, Bernard implies. America has become predatory. The horrors of Monte Waite are both the guilt of American civilization's recent past and of its immediate present, and a nightmarish vision of its future. *The Moke-Eater*, like much of the art that emerged from the protest movement, projected the view that the Vietnam conflict was very much a war at home.

Few playwrights chose to express their protest through plays that were blatantly antiwar. Exceptions include Grant Duay in *Fruit Salad* (1967), in which images of three soldiers hiding out in the jungle of North Vietnam (Banana, Cherry, and Melon) alternate with the typically American image of a pretty girl in a television commercial. The girl is chopping fruit and demonstrating how to make a fruit salad. As she begins to eat her delicious creation, the three soldiers are killed by enemy gunfire. The clear, if heavy-handed, message is that the American establishment makes money while American men die in Vietnam. and perhaps because American men are dying in Vietnam. With even more directness, Barbara Garson's skit *MacBird* (1966) accuses Johnson of every crime from President Kennedy's assassination to illegal war in Vietnam. But not until the advent of David Rabe did a playwright of skill begin to launch a sustained attack on the war through his plays, beginning with his most overt antiwar drama, *The Basic Training of Pavlo Hummel* (1968).

Indeed, probably the most aggressive protests in the theater community came from avant-garde theater groups that were on the cutting edge of their art during this time, notably the Bread and Puppet Theater, the Living Theatre, the Open Theatre, and the Performance Group (with the exception of the peripatetic Living Theatre, all worked out of New

York); and the San Francisco Mime Troupe and the Teatro Campesino (both in California).

Theater is a good example of how one art form's involvement with the antiwar movement grew and then dissipated, as, increasingly, the movement itself took stage; as the street became the stage; as demonstrations became increasingly theatrical; as the very members of the counterculture, costumed self-consciously in their long hair, their beads and leather thongs, jeans and sandals, became deliberate protagonists in a drama in which, for them, the survival of America seemed to be at stake.

In theater, what began at the start of the 1960s as a revolution in content and form, aimed in a general, scattershot way at mainstream theater, eventually became part of a specific political protest aimed at the United States and its intervention in the Vietnam War. The new theater artists of the 1960s, those who worked in the lofts and coffee houses across the country, had been brought up in the shadow of a theater tradition in which they did not believe. They had been raised on a theater in which the audience sat politely on one side of the stage and the actors pretended to be in a separate world on the other side. The dramas that were performed in this theater had a clear beginning, middle, and end. Language, so far as the new theater artists could tell, was sterile. And content generally ignored the true social and political inequities that this new generation saw in American life. It was a theater that the new theater artists found unprovocative, untheatrical, un-real. "When I go uptown and see a Broadway play," wrote Joseph Chaikin, founder and director of the Open Theatre, "I go to see primarily the ushers, the box office, and the environment of the physical theatre. *This* situation has become more present than the situation being played out on the stage."9

Eager to revolutionize form and content in order to bring what they saw as a dying art form back to life and eager perhaps to atone for some guilt they assumed because of their own middle-class backgrounds, but also truly concerned about the state of the world around them, these theater artists were ripe for enlisting in a cause that would pit what they interpreted as the specious values of the American establishment against truly humanitarian values. In 1965, *Tulane Drama Review*, the journal of experimental theater in the United States, published an essay entitled "Guerrilla Theatre" by Ronny Davis, founder of the San Francisco Mime Troupe:

—America, U.S.A.—is chock full o'ennui. Distracted by superficial values, and without a sense of humanness, we let machines rule; it is easier to kill from a B-52 than to choke every Vietcong. No one feels any guilt, not even the poor fool dropping the bombs. . . .

. . . .

. . . For those who like their theatre pure of social issues, I must say—FUCK YOU! buddy, theatre IS a social entity. It can dull the minds of the citizens, it can wipe out guilt, it can teach all to accept the Great Society and the Amaaaaarican way of life (just like in the movies, Ma) or it can look to changing that society . . . and that's *political.*[10]

Indeed, between 1965 and 1970, the San Francisco Mime Troupe and other avant-garde groups took their protest into the audiences and onto the streets to direct citizens toward similar protest. As critic Theodore Shank notes, they borrowed theatrical techniques from popular entertainment, including commedia dell'arte, vaudeville, parades, the circus, comic strips. Protest theater, after all, had to be aesthetically adventuresome, and fun, at the same time that it conveyed a message. Most of all, as Shank has pointed out, this protest theater, like the protest films, like the marchers and the demonstrations, aimed to create a sense of "we" with the audience, against "them," the establishment. This protest theater aimed to posit the "good minority" against the "evil" power structure, so that there could be a feeling of community between performer and spectator. Creating this sense of community would ideally be the first step toward demonstrating that the System could really be changed.

This approach characterized Megan Terry's musical theater piece *Viet Rock*, created and produced in New York City under the aegis of the Open Theatre in the spring of 1966. *Viet Rock* satirizes America's value systems and a culture in which, in Terry's eyes, people are born to be cannon fodder. The American war machine is portrayed as a blundering, sexist operation. GIs go into battle speaking the clichés of American advertising. Grand old statesmen and women spout empty patriotic phrases. At the end of the piece, all the performers crumple to the ground amid sounds of a giant explosion, in which GIs, Vietnamese, American civilians, mothers and daughters, wives and lovers, every body and every thing are presumably blown to bits.

But then Terry introduces a kind of coda of rebirth, in which the actors rise from their tangle on the stage and flow into the audience. In the original production, each actor had to select an audience member and touch his hand, head, face, or hair. "In no way should the actors communicate superiority," Terry instructs in her script. "[The actors] must communicate the wonder and gift of being actually alive together with the audience at that moment."[11]

It was the kind of gesture experienced among marchers at a rally, among hippies at a be-in, among people at any one of a number of public events in the 1960s during which total strangers at once became friends united in a common ideological bond, were connected emotionally through a moment of hopeful, peaceful communion. Make love, not war.

But the flower-child hippie demonstration was giving way to more aggressive expressions, and artists could not help but feel this change. At the Open Theatre, Chaikin criticized Terry about the ending of *Viet Rock*, wanting an "angrier attitude" and "a tone of more dissident irony."[12] Terry did not shift.

In San Francisco, Ronny Davis and his mime troupe were asking themselves how they could actually *stop* the war, not just protest it. The troupe created a satire on their own antiwar pacifism, a piece called *L'Amant Militaire*, loosely adapted from a Goldoni comedy. The plot is intricate, but essentially the Spanish army is fighting in Italy—a parallel with the United States in Vietnam—and all the politically powerful Spaniards connive with each other to profit from the war. When the old General says the war is slowing down, the local Mayor persuades him to keep it going, so that they can both keep making money from the venture. The Mayor would like to marry his lovely daughter Rosalinda to the elderly General, but Rosalinda is in love with a handsome young lieutenant, Alonso. She convinces Alonso that love is more important than war, but when Alonso won't fight any more, he is arrested for dereliction of duty. He is about to be led off to be shot, when a deus ex machina appears in the form of a woman servant who has dressed herself up to look like the Pope; as Pope, she declares the war over and tells the audience that, "You want something done? Well, then, do it yourselves!"[13]

Some years later, Joan Holden, the adaptor of the piece, explained to an interviewer that the servant "debunks pacifism as an answer. She says that you have to fight war with war. The play called for revolution, it just didn't say who the revolutionaries should be."[14]

It was, Holden felt, an unusually militant statement for the times.

And just in case the play itself did not deliver its message clearly enough, Ronny Davis placed a puppet off stage in a puppet box, in view of the audience (the Mime Troupe usually performed *L'Amant Militaire* in the parks around San Francisco), and the actor–puppet improvised explicit antiwar and anti-establishment statements for the benefit of the audience.

Davis himself was explicit in the fall of 1967, when the troupe performed *L'Amant Militaire* at the Yale Drama School. When the performance was over, and while the audience was still applauding, Davis stepped forward and informed them that, in his view, if they wanted to end the war, they would have to take to the streets with guns.

But if the radicalization of the antiwar movement tempted Davis, it brought about the disaffection, and eventually a retreat from the barricades, of other artists in the movement. Among avant-garde theater groups, the Bread and Puppet Theatre was one company that withdrew from the streets.

Under the leadership of Peter Schumann, a sculptor and choreographer who had come to the United States from Germany in 1961, Bread and Puppet had become a rallying point for theater artists in New York City and indeed for the spectrum of protesters in New York. As critic Stefan Brecht indicates, there was hardly a rally or demonstration, from 1964 through October 1967, at which this group's huge puppets, ten feet high or more, did not create images of silent protest. Schumann created puppet parades. In one, Uncle Fatso, Schumann's version of Uncle Sam, corpulent, red-faced, dressed in black and wearing a huge ALL THE WAY WITH LBJ button, pulled a string of captives—Jesus/Vietnam and the disciples. They in turn were guarded, some slight distance back, by a platoon of dog-faced men wearing skull masks and marching in step to a drum played by their leader. They all were followed by four soldier figures, high in the air, their huge, expressionless faces towering above spindly and grotesque bodies. Behind them, one or more Gray Ladies carried gray babies in their outstretched arms.[15]

Schumann was a pacifist. He also felt that theater should be as basic as bread. In 1966, he already was expressing that the peace movement, as it was becoming more popular, was taking on a certain gloss and glamor that detracted from what he felt was its purity. By 1967 he also apparently was alienated by what he perceived as a confrontational style of resistance among the more aggressive segments of the New Left. And there is the possibility that the artistry of his street parades, his parades as artistic objects, was at least as important to him as protesting the war. As Stefan Brecht writes in his account of Bread and Puppet: "The bigger demonstrations in '67 tended to be gigantic, with no longer just tens but hundreds of thousands of participants: on that scale and given the emotional impact of such demonstrations, Schumann's puppets could no longer define or dominate them: they disappeared: the mass of the demonstrators became the overwhelmingly dominant and effective feature—and point—of the demonstrations."[16] Theater as art form in the streets retreated and was perhaps even pushed aside by demonstration as art form in the streets. Bread and Puppet, although it continued to perform certain antiwar pieces indoors, did not appear at another public antiwar march until 1971.

One question to consider here, as Bread and Puppet removed itself from the public fray, is whether Schumann and his theater, or the San Francisco Mime Troupe, or the Open Theatre, or the hundreds of other protesting artists across the country as 1967 became 1968, had succeeded in some way. Had they helped bring the movement to the point where consciousness was raised to a level that politics could leave art behind for the moment?

And if they had succeeded in raising consciousness, how had they really accomplished this? Often, certainly, many theater groups and other artists were simply preaching to the converted. Hip audiences at performances of *Viet Rock* generally responded to Megan Terry's protest in the way she intended, but the establishment reviewers who covered the production for establishment newspapers with establishment readerships thought the play a failure. Walter Kerr, for instance, writing for *The New York Times*, seemed to miss Terry's ironic intentions entirely. "None of this is comment," he wrote. It is "simple sloganeering."[17] Even less-established critics such as Richard Gilman responded that Terry was writing about Vietnam "from the headlines."[18]

Similarly, most of the antiwar protesters who trailed behind Peter Schumann's puppets would comment about how moved they were by Schumann's figures. "Peter Schumann has more to offer peace groups at this time than anyone else," wrote Keith Lampe in Dave Dellinger's *WIN Magazine*.[19] But during a march in New York City in 1965, Schumann and his troupe were attacked at one point by onlookers who took a violent dislike to the figures depicting Uncle Sam with a bloodied child on a stretcher. In December 1966, Bread and Puppet picketed St. Patrick's Cathedral, to protest a statement from Cardinal Spellman, who had called for victory in Vietnam. The members of Bread and Puppet wore black cowls and carried masks impaled on poles. Joe Flaherty, of *The Village Voice*, wrote that "The demonstration reached its high point when the girl portraying Mary tried to place the blood-stained Jesus doll on the steps. A line of cops blocked her way and told her she couldn't place the doll on the steps. 'That's littering,' one of Our Finest replied."[20]

To paraphrase Bigsby, around 1968 the time had come when personal art had indeed managed to reverberate at the public level and now had to move into the background while the political activist took stage. Art had been a tactic, in a way, like all the other tactics that had been practiced since 1963 to protest the American presence in Vietnam, and now art had to retreat before the larger picture. Vietnam had politicized poetry, the visual arts, film, and theater, and the artists who worked in these forms had tried, in different ways, to politicize their audiences. When theater and life, when art and life, resemble each other so much, perhaps one of them must disappear.

In theater, after 1968, the avant-garde artists and the liberal/ intellectual artists were still against the war, and some no doubt were deeply pained by its continuation and by the escalation of bombing raids into Cambodia and Laos. But generally their responses through their art were less and less activist. Certainly antiwar plays and productions did not disappear. But especially within the avant garde we begin to see from 1968 through 1975 that the plays, performance pieces, and productions are more fragmented, more anarchic in form, than during the middle of the 1960s. The work of the Performance Group, of playwrights like Kenneth Bernard and especially Charles Ludlam, is so fragmented, they deconstruct form and content to such an extent, that the pieces seem almost consciously chaotic. Beginning in 1968 with *Dionysus in 69*, the work of the Performance Group embraced improvisational techniques and quasi-therapeutic acting techniques so completely, that at times it seemed as if their productions were invented as they occurred. Text was embroidered upon and invented by the performers during performance, often without any concern for the elements of time or unity; the physical production of

Dionysus in 69 was often a confused, undirected grouping of bodies. The plays by Ludlam that emerged from the Ridiculous Theatrical Company seem to set out to destroy any sense of form or coherence. By making language ridiculous, for instance—not illogical, as with absurdist theater, but pointless, infantile, and compulsively repetitive—playwrights such as Ludlam were destructive of all dramatic art, their own included. "The theatre of the ridiculous," wrote Stefan Brecht, "is radical social satire & protest—anarchist . . . possibly nihilist."[21]

It is as if these artists had absorbed the violence of the times so completely that they finally could only reflect it back completely. It is as if they were acknowledging on some level that, indeed, their protest had not had the impact they intended. Alan Geyer, in *Worldview*, wrote around 1970, that "polarization is no longer an adequate word for what is happening in America these days. Try words like splintering, fragmentation, disintegration: these tell the story a little better."[22] The playwright Jean-Claude van Itallie wrote in 1970 that "the past four years have been shock after shock. It feels like the economic and social structure which is America . . . is falling apart completely; and faster and faster."[23]

Artists whose work reflected an antiwar sensibility had initially responded to violence with protests for change. As the antiwar movement itself splintered and gave rise to violent efforts to "bring the war home," many artists in the late 1960s and early 1970s responded with images of utter fragmentation in their art.

Amy Swerdlow

"Not My Son, Not Your Son, Not Their Sons"
Mothers Against the Draft for Vietnam

A s our public memory of the anti-Vietnam War movement of the 1960s is being recast in the wake of Operation Desert Storm, it becomes clear that the history of the Vietnam War has, itself, become a battlefield in which political, cultural, and gender assumptions that will shape future U.S. decisions on war and peace are being contested. There is, however, one long-held assumption about the antiwar movement of the 1960s that still goes unchallenged by either the Right or Left. It is the belief that all the significant protest came from youth under thirty. This essay challenges that assumption by examining the antidraft activity of Women Strike for Peace (WSP), a network of thousands of middle-aged mothers, who built on the female culture of the 1950s, as well as on their own long-held political commitments to peace and social justice, to organize a militant female opposition to the draft for Vietnam.[1]

Theirs was not an easy task, as only men were called on to fight in Vietnam, or to brave the risks and punishments of refusing to do so. According to sociologist Barrie Thorne, who studied two Boston area resistance groups, the young female cohorts of the draft-age men who joined the antidraft movement to make their own contribution to ending the war, found that they could not be significant players. Leslie Cagan, still a leading peace activist in the 1990s, recalled a discussion of a We Won't Go petition drive being planned by the Boston area resistance in which the young women in the room were told that they would not be allowed to speak because they did not face conscription and therefore had no right to decide the tactics of the resistance. Finding themselves barred from decision making and spokesmanship, and confined to the secondary and supportive roles characterized by the slogan Gals Say Yes to Guys Who Say No, a group of young women in the Boston area left antidraft activity to form what they called, "our own resistance."[2]

The middle-aged mothers of WSP, on the other hand, were able to find an effective, satisfying, and independent role for themselves in a political culture defined and led by men the age of their sons. The answer to why and how this was possible can be found in the political and gender consciousness of these women of liberal to left-wing political backgrounds who had taken to the streets in the fall of 1961, after a decade of cold war consensus and profamily antifeminism, to conduct a widely publicized and highly effective campaign for a nuclear test ban treaty.[3]

At a time when antimilitarists were dismissed by the press, the public, and political leaders as either "commies" or "kooks," the image projected by WSP of respectable middle-class, middle-aged mothers picketing the White House to save the children helped to legitimize their radical critique of the cold war and the nuclear arms race. The movement's defeat of the House Committee on Un-American Activities' (HUAC) attempt to brand it as a communist front was accomplished through humor, evasion, irony, and scornful moral superiority; manifestations of the creativity, playfulness, and potential power of the politics of motherhood.[4]

By mid-decade WSP had moved from antinuclear politics to militant protest against the United States intervention in Vietnam. The key women, many of whom were mothers of draft-age sons and in touch with thousands of other mothers in the same predicament, sensed that conscription was the weakest link in the interventionist chain and that sabotaging the draft would undermine the war. They were also convinced that antidraft activity, particularly draft counseling, would be a vehicle for attracting "ordinary women" whose concern for the fate of their sons would open their ears to the deeper moral and political arguments against the war.

What was different about these middle-aged women of WSP that made it possible for them to achieve a sense of personal and social purpose, and also work effectively, in a political culture not of their making? One answer is that the WSPers' socialization in the postsuffrage, antifeminist 1930s and 1940s and their experience as mothers and housewives in the 1950s had predisposed them to identify the needs of their sons as their own. They valued and enjoyed acting as political mothers to the young men who "refused to kill or be killed in an immoral war." And the response from the draft resisters was appropriately filial and grateful—not sexual; making it both possible and comfortable for the WSPers to cross gender, age, race, and class barriers to counsel, and later to aid and abet, thousands of young men to avoid or resist the draft. It is also important to note that the married, white, middle-class women of WSP, with their recognized social standing in the community and their access to family discretionary funds, possessed the social respectability and the material resources to conduct a struggle against the draft on their own terms. The young unmarried women in the resistance did not enjoy this kind of community acceptance or command of resources.

A letter to WSP, from Gary Rader, a former Marine who had become an antidraft organizer, communicated the kind of message WSPers found irresistible. Rader described himself as: "woefully young and powerless . . . a twenty-three year-old facing eleven or so years in prison, working in my first movement ever, being trailed by the FBI and harassed by the police." He asked for support for those men who were "putting their lives on the line," and called on WSP to provide bail and legal defense funds as well as living space and financial support for resistance organizers.[5] The *Sacramento Women for Peace Newsletter* responded to this kind of appeal by declaring: "It would seem that Women for Peace, if we are worthy of our name, should get behind this fine group of young idealists, working not for themselves but for the future of the race."[6]

A call to the women in Oakland, California, to swell the ranks of a weekly WSP picket line at the local induction center stated:

We know that we are effective because we can see it; we often escort young men directly from the busses to Draft Help to be counseled before they enter the induction center—this in spite of the attempt by induction officials to herd them quickly into the building. We are often thanked for being there. We are even told we are beautiful.[7]

There was little traditional female vanity here. To the WSPers the word beautiful meant moral, brave, selfless, politically on the ball. The Los Angeles GI Civil Liberties Defense Committee, thanking the women for financial contributions and the provision of office space for GI resistance work, wrote to WSP, "The help that each of you has offered, and given us, in our day-to-day work has been beyond what anyone could really expect."[8]

What WSP gave; money, space, time, and emotional support, was typically parental. It was a personal offering, far beyond that which was expected from male political allies. While the WSPers did not underestimate the value of providing money, clothing, hot food, and emotional support to resisters and deserters awaiting arrest; neither they nor the young men would have expected these services from the older male activists. From pacifists like Dave Dellinger, Dave McReynolds, and Sidney Lens they expected leadership, not comfort.

Accordingly, the WSPers were rarely consulted when national antidraft policies or tactics were determined, nor were they treated without condescension when they disagreed with movement decisions. This disdain frustrated and angered the WSPers, but it never drove them out of antidraft work. Their staying power can be attributed, in large measure, to the fact that they never sought to be integrated into the draft resistance movement on an equal basis. They had their own separatist movement where they felt appreciated and important, and in which they shaped their own policies. WSP decided on its own terms which issues, which groups, and what kind of rhetoric and tactics it would initiate or support. The Philadelphia group, for instance, reported that it had "adopted" a number of young antidraft organizers and resisters, was providing them with funds for housing and office expenses, and *criticizing* them as well as encouraging, and listening to them. (Emphasis added.)[9] This prerogative, to influence the sons, an ambiguous privilege of motherhood, mollified those who were frustrated by generational and cultural conflicts, even as it obfuscated WSP's real lack of power and influence in the decision-making bodies of the larger antiwar movement.

By late 1966, as Vietnam casualty figures rose, WSP's fifth national conference decided to make opposition to the draft a central focus of its antiwar work. This meant developing a policy statement against the draft, a series of pressure tactics that could appeal to the mythical average woman, the creation of photogenic demonstrations that would dramatize the personal cost of the draft to mothers and sons, testimony at congressional and party platform hearings, and newsworthy mass lobbies of Congress for repeal of conscription and for withdrawal from Vietnam.[10] When Congress voted to renew the Universal Military Training Act in 1967, despite an active peace movement campaign for repeal, WSP determined to undermine the draft by counseling those who chose to evade it, and supporting those who refused to be inducted. Jumping in, WSP set up new centers, conducted counselor training workshops, and developed educational materials for the movement activists as well as the community at large. Much of WSP's draft counseling was conducted in coalition with other groups, but the women were usually the mainstay of counseling centers, as they were free from full-time paid employment or the care of young children.

Very early in its campaign WSP raised the slogan, Not Our Sons, Not Your Sons, Not Their Sons. But movement literature demonstrates that the WSP women were aware that their sons were benefitting from the race and class inequities built into the selective service system. These benefits included student and teacher deferments as well as conscientious objector (CO) status, granted only to those who had sufficient education to articulate their religious or ethical beliefs in a manner acceptable to their draft boards. *La Wisp*, the Los Angeles WSP newsletter, declared that counseling those who can avoid the draft is, "simply a promulgation of the racism and dollar discrimination that has caused the war. . . . Who takes the place of the middle-class student with a 2-S deferment," *La Wisp* asked, "or the C.O., or the emigrant to another country?" The WSP literature made it clear that the women understood that the deferred student, or the conscientious objector, would soon be replaced by a poor or minority youth, "who probably was totally ignorant of his rights, and who might come home in a coffin."[11] A pamphlet, "Your Draft-Age Son: A Message for Peaceful Parents," published by Berkeley-Oakland Women for Peace, a WSP chapter, pointed out that the draftee for Vietnam is "young, often working-class, often black; while his [draft] board, statistics show, is overwhelmingly old, middle-class and white."[12]

The WSP women took advantage of their role as community leaders, PTA activists, and mothers of high-school students to create pressure on the schools to provide all graduating seniors of all classes and races with alternative information on conscription, particularly when Army and Navy recruiters were present in the schools. Los Angeles WSP filed suit against Major General Lewis Hershey and several California educational authorities for failing to provide high-school students with information about all the draft law's options as was required by the Selective Service regulations.[13] The organization also objected to tax monies being spent on ROTC and military assemblies while schools refused to provide peace assemblies or time for antiwar speakers.[14] These appeals were seldom successful. Failing to win their battle for draft counseling in most high schools, WSP, along with other peace groups, organized end-the-draft caravans that travelled into blue-collar and minority neighborhoods to counsel young men who had no access to information on legal alternatives. Many WSP women worked full time on these projects, as they were free from economic constraints, and their children were old enough not to require parental supervision.

On the Upper West Side of New York City, WSP's draft counseling was housed in a storefront in a black and Puerto Rican urban renewal area, which also contained middle-income housing projects. This center advertised its services in a Spanish language newspaper, worked with reform Democratic clubs, and reported that it was hoping to train some black counselors to work in the streets.

The extent of WSP draft counseling is revealed in a report from Nassau County, Long Island, where the organizers of the service claimed that one hundred thousand young men were counseled in an off-the-street facility administered and staffed by volunteers. These volunteers often included doctors, lawyers, and psychiatrists who were, for the most part, the husbands and male friends of the WSP women. As a result of stories in the local press, word-of-mouth recommendations, and a sign on the headquarters advertising Free Draft Counseling Sponsored by Women Strike for Peace, the Long Island service attracted blue collar workers, black youth, school dropouts, and working-class apprentices. When, in a 1979 interview, I questioned the claim of Irma Zigas, WSP's national antidraft coordinator, that as many as one hundred thousand men were counseled by the Long Island Draft Information and Counseling Service, she insisted that her estimate was fair.[15] She admitted that "in the beginning WSP provided only ten counselors working twice a week from 7:00 P.M. until midnight, but that in the end there were thirty-five to forty counselors working five days and nights a week, often staying on until one or two in the morning." She explained that at the height of the operation in 1968, 1969 and 1970 "the center opened at 10:00 A.M., and was staffed by as many as fifteen reception people." Zigas, who is now a business executive, recalled with pride that "not one person was paid, not even a receptionist."[16] If one were to estimate that at least two hours were spent counseling each individual, and if this service were given a cash value of ten dollar per hour, the WSP draft counselors in Nassau County alone contributed over a million dollars in volunteer labor.

In the early stages of the Long Island draft-counseling service the majority of the counselors were men, but the men were interviewed and appointed by WSP women. According to Zigas, the men in the Long Island center were as devoted and faithful as the women, giving as many evenings and weekends as the women, which she recognized as a greater sacrifice on their part, as the men, unlike most of the women, worked at full-time paying jobs and professions. The number of male counselors fell off when Irma Zigas, the center's director, and Bernice Crane, its political mentor, insisted that no lawyers be used as draft counselors because they could have exploited the draftees to build their own practices. This meant that the women who ran the center had to acquaint themselves with the draft law, which was chaotic and changed frequently by new regulations and court decisions. The nonprofessional, "housewife" counselors met this problem by subscribing to the *Selective Service Law Reporter* and studying it carefully. According to Zigas, the women became so well informed on the changes in the law, that they had no problem giving lawyers the third degree regarding their knowledge and motivations. This did not sit well with the men. Zigas recalled with a good deal of bitterness: "Many men left. They felt that the women came on too strong, that they were too bossy. . . . It took a lot of commitment for those who stayed because most wanted the women to act as hostesses and secretaries; not to take charge or rock the boat."[17]

Resentment toward the women came mainly from the counselors, according to Zigas, not from the draft-age men. They "thought we were the greatest thing that ever happened," she recalled. "Many asked, 'Why don't you talk to my mother and show my mother what you're doing?'" And that is just what WSP did. As the sons were being counseled the WSPers spoke with the mothers and fathers—mostly about the war and why it was immoral, illegal, and unjust. Zigas maintains that it was the admiration and appreciation they received from the young men that kept the WSP draft counselors and receptionists working far into the night five days a week.[18]

Those young men who decided to refuse the draft, after exhausting all avenues of appeal, usually called upon WSP to support their decision to refuse induction. The WSP women found such appeals hard to deny. Women who might have been leery of civil disobedience found themselves leaving home at five or six o'clock in the morning and driving long distances to stand at induction centers with placards supporting, as Zigas put it, "the kid who was going to say no that day." The Nashville, Tennessee, newsletter urged women to go to induction refusal demonstrations "because an adult on a picket line does wonders for young people and for their press image." The Nashville WSPers were also urged to telephone or visit the parents of draft refusers as, "a friendly call is a big help not only to their morale, but it usually effects the way the parents treat their sons."[19]

The next step for WSP was to be present at the arraignments and trials of those who refused induction. Their purpose was to create a climate of sympathy and understanding by showing that respectable mothers considered these young men to be exemplary citizens in the best traditions of the nation. The WSP communications network also provided long lists of prisoners-of-conscience in jails and stockades all over the country and urged the women to write, especially during the Christmas season. Some WSPers even took long, lonely trips to visit jailed draft resisters and GIs who refused to fight. They returned home saddened, but strengthened in their commitment to fight the draft. One Los Angeles woman made weekly visits to fifteen young men in the federal prison at Lompoc, California. She reported in La Wisp: "We talk, drink coffee, read things I bring up, and laugh a lot for three hours. Then they go back to be stripped naked for searching and I drive back to my family in Santa Monica." The WSP women raised funds to buy books and subscriptions to periodicals for the young prisoners.[20] They also picketed draft boards, and the homes of board members, where they read aloud the names of the war dead in an attempt to remind draft board officials that each number they dealt with was a live human being, too young to die.

Despite their militance and persistent antidraft activity, the WSPers (pronounced Wispers) were very careful not to speak for the sons, or to seem to lead or control them. The women were evidently intimidated by the antifeminism and antimomism of the 1940s and 1950s that blamed assertive mothers for "sissy" sons, and attacked political women as dissatisfied, castrating neurotics. On the other hand, they took credit for the proper moral upbringing of their sons. Accordingly, in October 1966, when Charlotte Keyes, a leading WSP activist from Champaign-Urbana, Illinois, published an article in *McCall's* on her son's decision to resist the draft, she explained: "We have tried to find the seeds of his present way of life and have more than once been taken aback to realize that we ourselves had planted some of them. . . . Well, we parents don't realize—do we— when we inculcate our moral standards, that the children may try to really live by them."[21] Keyes's conclusion: "We stand by our son, and we learn from him," could have been the credo for WSP in relation to the Resistance.

The problems involved in directing a son's response to the draft are illustrated in the case of Evelyn Whitehorn of Palo Alto, California. She is described in press reports as a middle-class, graying, forty-seven-year-old, devoted mother of four boys who had never belonged to anything more controversial than the PTA and the Committee to Save Walden Pond. Whitehorn, who decided to seek a restraining order preventing the induction of her eighteen-year-old son, Erik, contended that his pacifist convictions were due, in large part, to her efforts to bring him up with good moral character.

East Bay California Women for Peace saw the Whitehorn case as a conflict between the rights of mothers and the power of the state, but as it turned out, it was not much of a contest. Erik was arrested, indicted, convicted, and eventually imprisoned for refusing to register. In court the judge belittled his mother; suggesting that her tears were false, and making much of the fact that Mrs. Whitehorn was five years older than the husband from whom she was divorced.

The "Young World" section of *This Week* magazine reported that Whitehorn had received hundreds of letters supporting her stand, including many from servicemen who wanted to borrow her for a while. An air force reserve officer sent Erik his reserve paycheck, and one little boy taped his allowance of five pennies to a letter, "to help because of my older brother." A grandmother in Long Island sent five dollar bills, one for each of her five grandsons. The Whitehorn mail was about five hundred to fourteen in favor of their action, but *Plain Rapper*, the publication of the Palo Alto Resistance, noted growing tension between mother and son brought about by governmental pressure. *Plain Rapper* commented "it is tough for an 18-year-old male to let his mother stand up for him, even if that is the best legal strategy available."[22] "To make matters worse," according to the men of the Palo Alto Resistance, "mother and son are extremely articulate and sometimes find themselves competing."[23]

By the end of the summer of 1969 the Whitehorns had lost their case, their confidence in their cause, and their family unity. Erik eventually went into the army to get out of jail. In a statement to the press which was filled with regret and anger, Evelyn Whitehorn stated that she had decided not to appeal her son's imprisonment because "the draft law doesn't give any consideration to the . . . earnest desire of parents to interpose themselves between their offspring and injustice." She concluded that, in the future, "whatever I can do, or contribute, will be done only as me, not with the use of any member of my family."[24] Whitehorn had been defeated, not only by the law, but by a gender ideology that found her to be presumptuous and deviant.

Because WSP was reluctant to act in the name of the sons, the women felt that they had to find a way to resist on their own terms. Civil disobedience had been a problem for WSP, not because the women were timid, but because they believed that the average woman would not sympathize with a mother who broke the law or went to jail, thus neglecting her own children for her principles. However, as the war escalated, the horrors of death and destruction pushed them beyond these scruples. They, like other sections of the peace constituency, became convinced that civil disobedience in the face of illegitimate authority was a social responsibility. The question for WSP was only where and how to do it, in a motherly fashion.

In mid 1967, the National Consultative Committee began to compose a women's statement of conscience and complicity with draft resisters, and to solicit signators who would vow to aid and abet, in defiance of the Selective Service Act and the Pentagon, all those young men who refused to fight in Vietnam. The response within WSP was not uniformly positive. Some women felt that they could not endanger all the individuals in the movement by undertaking illegal action in its name. Others felt it unwise to risk the jailing of the entire leadership, thus paralyzing the movement. But there were a sufficient number of women who were enthusiastic about building a woman's resistance. Because WSP followed a do-everything policy, those who wanted to act in their own names, to take risks, and to write their own scenarios did just that. What they hoped to accomplish was to provoke the government into taking legal action against hundreds of moral mothers who, they believed, would win public sympathy, tie up the courts, intensify the debate over the war, and escalate the struggle to end it. They stated clearly:

> We believe that support of those who resist the war and the draft is both moral and legal. We believe that it is not we, but those who send our sons to kill and be killed who are committing crimes. We do, however, recognize that there may be legal risks involved, but because we believe that these young men are courageous and morally justified in rejecting the war regardless of consequences, we can do no less. [25]

To publicize the Woman's Statement of Conscience, and gain adherents, WSP organized the first "adult," and the only women's, demonstration in support of draft refusal. It was planned as a triple header: a rally to launch a women's resistance, a march to the office of General Lewis Hershey, director of the Selective Service System, to deliver the statement of complicity, and a picket line at the White House to demand that the president stop listening to the generals and begin to hear the mothers. [26]

After WSP had issued its call for the September 20 rally and march, the Department of Interior announced a new ruling limiting the number of persons permitted to picket at the White House gate to one hundred. The WSP organizers would not accept this new restriction on peace protest and refused to cancel their march on the White House. They appealed to sympathetic Senators and Representatives, the American Civil Liberties Union, and the Washington, D.C., police in the hope of persuading President Johnson to waive the restriction; but it was not revoked. They bought space in the New York Times to publish an open letter to President Johnson that asked, "What Must We Mothers Do To Reach the Ear, To Reach the Heart of Our President?" The letter declared: "We women gave you our sons, lovingly raised to live, to learn, and to create a better world. . . . You used them to kill and you returned 12,269 caskets and 74,818 casualties to heartbroken mothers." Warning Johnson that he must stop accepting the disastrous advice of his generals, the letter concluded: "We will walk where you can see us. We will walk where you can hear us. . . . A mother in defense of her family is not easily turned aside."[27]

The rally and march to challenge the draft calls drew close to one thousand women from the eastern seaboard. After an emotional meeting and addresses by two resisters, the women were determined to reach the White House. First, they marched to the office of General Hershey carrying a coffin covered with a black shawl bearing the slogan, Not My Son, Nor Your Son, Not Their Sons—Support Those Who Say No. The police were particularly cooperative; allowing the women to march in the road, even though the organizers had applied only for a sidewalk permit. At the White House, however, the atmosphere changed abruptly. The women were met by a solid line of Park Police standing shoulder to shoulder behind a green fence barrier that blocked their access to the White House. Incensed at the denial of their rights as mothers and citizens, the women trampled the fence, pushed through the police line, most narrowly avoiding police clubs, and dashed into the road in front of the White House. Victory was within reach, but another solid wall of police suddenly materialized, also brandishing clubs. The WSPers then felt they had no alternative but to hold their ground by sitting down in the road in front of the White House. There they sat singing and chanting, blocking traffic, and refusing to move despite threats of arrest. Bella Abzug, WSP's national legislative coordinator, arranged a compromise with the police that would allow all the women to picket at the White House, if only one hundred at a time were directly in front of the gate, and if they agreed to get out of the road and move back behind the police barriers. The women still refused, but Abzug and Dagmar Wilson, WSP's national spokesperson, finally convinced them that they had made their point, that their case would be taken to the courts, and that forcing the arrest of the WSP leadership would make it necessary to cancel a national conference for which women had arrived from all over the country. At that point, the women reluctantly gave up the space, claiming that they had, in effect, won their fight as all the women were actually allowed to march at the White House in a revolving line. The police pretended that they were counting to see that only one hundred were in front of the gate, but it was clear that they were looking the other way.

A front-page UPI story in the *New York Times* carried the headline "WOMEN FIGHT POLICE NEAR WHITE HOUSE." At the height of the fracas, according to the *Times* report, about ten women were seen lying on the ground, and one had blood on her head.[28] *The Sun* (Baltimore) carried a photo of a bedraggled women's head pushing through a solid wall of police standing with arms locked. This wire service picture was published across the country with the caption: "Coming through—A Women Strike for Peace demonstrator maneuvers a blockade." *The Sun* reported that there were more police on the scene than women, but that the women were apparently not intimidated. "The women screamed at the police and jeered at them," according to *The Sun*, "when they announced that the WSP picketing permit had been revoked."[29] At the national conference, which met that evening, it was noted that the two young resisters, who had joined the women, were treated much more brutally than were the women. They were dragged, beaten, and arrested, which only affirmed the WSP conviction that middle-aged mothers could get away with more militancy than radical young men, and that WSP had to do more in its own name.[30]

This confrontation with the police did not fit the image WSP had carefully nurtured for almost six years, and the Washington, D.C., media was outraged. The *Washington Post*, which had defended WSP in the confrontation with HUAC, called the action at the White House "Strike Three," and declared the women's attempt to break through the police barricade by force as open to serious reproach. "Such conduct diminishes any influence the group might have;"[31] WSP was not contrite. The sixth national conference applauded "the spirit of determination displayed by the hundreds of women who challenged the arbitrary restriction of their right to demonstrate." A press release from the national body explained: "The women broke through the police lines, strengthened by their conviction they were fighting for the lives of their sons, the survival of the people of Vietnam, and the right to petition the President. Neither billy clubs nor bruises will deter us. 'We will not be stopped.'"[32] WSP continued its campaign against the draft until after the U.S. withdrew from Vietnam. It was also one of the organizations most active in the movement for total amnesty for deserters as well as resisters.

Throughout the struggle, WSP leadership displayed a high level of political acumen; a sense of the strategic moment for pressure, a talent for research, self-education, and public relations unexpected from non-professional women. Without setting out to do so, the WSP women challenged the 1950s image of motherhood. The good mother was no longer passive, but militant; no longer silent, but eloquent; no longer private, but public. Testing themselves in public battles with the Pentagon, learning the loopholes in the draft law, providing assistance to deserters in Canada and Sweden, speaking in public, confronting draft board officials and army officers at induction lines, counseling working-class and minority sons and mothers, the WSPers became conscious of their powers and the ways in which they had been prevented from using them. The WSPers realized that although many of them had become full-time political activists, community leaders, and notable citizens, they were still rushing home to make dinner and apologizing for lapses in housework or domestic management "due to the emergency." When the rhetoric of the rising feminist movement reached them, most of the WSPers were ready to recognize the connection between their secondary role in the family and their powerlessness and invisibility in the peace movement and in the state. The WSP experience fighting the draft for Vietnam demonstrated that mothers confronting the military state soon learn that they are fighting against male dominance over foreign policy. For many of the key women of WSP the recognition and abhorrence of gender dominance and inequality in the political arena gave rise to an examination of all manifestations of gender inequality. For many there was no turning back to gender blindness.

Gerald Gill

From Maternal Pacifism to Revolutionary Solidarity
African-American Women's Opposition to the Vietnam War

S peaking before an audience of twenty-five thousand people at a November 1965 antiwar demonstration in Washington, D.C., Coretta Scott King stated: "Freedom and destiny in America are bound together with freedom and justice in Vietnam. I am here as a mother who is concerned about all the children of the world."[1] Almost two years later, Karen, a St. Louis teenager, told a researcher: "I wish the war in Vietnam would stop because what they are fighting for doesn't seem right. Most people—like relatives—they go over there and get shot and it causes a whole lot of crying. There shouldn't be a war over something that doesn't hardly make sense."[2] And, in a 1969 interview in the party's newspaper, an unidentified female member of the Black Panther party stated that the Vietnamese woman

> is a prime example of the role women can play in the revolution. The Vietnamese women are out there fighting with their brothers, fighting against American imperialism, with its advanced technology. They can shoot. They're out there with their babies on their backs . . . and they're participating in the revolution wholeheartedly just as the Vietnamese men are participating in the revolution, in the national liberation struggle. The success of their national

liberation struggle is just as much dependent upon the women continuing the struggle as it is dependent on the Vietnamese men.[3]

These three statements, although coming at different stages in the American military involvement in the Vietnam War, represent, both individually and collectively, concurrent aspects of African-American women's opposition to that war. Scott King's comment represents the beliefs often voiced by maternal pacifists—women, black and white, who came to oppose the Vietnam War largely out of what many activists then viewed as the gender-specific instincts of women as the givers and nurturers of life. That is, their pacifism resulted from their biological abhorance of violence and the wanton destruction of life, particularly that brought about by war. Karen's comments, while not gender-specific, were more indicative of those voiced by African-Americans of both sexes who viewed the war as a waste of young men's lives in a conflict few could understand. The comments of the unidentified Black Panther party member were markedly different in tone and in emphasis. Identifying completely with the struggles of the Vietnamese people, particularly the Vietnamese women, against American oppression, women in the Black Panther party viewed Vietnamese women as "sisters in the international struggle" who were most worthy of emulation.

These perspectives, from maternal pacifism to revolutionary solidarity, were expressed in several of the critiques raised by African-American women against the war in Southeast Asia from 1964 to 1973. While contemporary pollsters of that era, and later, students of American public opinion, have found that African-Americans of both sexes, as well as white women, were among those groups most opposed to American military involvement in Southeast Asia, there has been little detailed or systematic examination of how race *and* gender converged in fashioning the way that African-American women viewed the war. Public opinion polls conducted during the war consistently reported that black women were *the* segment of the populace that believed most strongly that the United States had "made a mistake sending troops to fight in Vietnam." And, after the beginning of troop withdrawals in 1970, black women were found to be *the* group most supportive of speedier withdrawals.[4] Yet, the opinions, sentiments, and activities of African-American women opposed to the Vietnam War have been little noted in the growing literature on the antiwar movement or in the burgeoning historical and theoretical literature on feminist politics and peace.[5]

Among the earliest of the African-American female dissidents were several women active in either radical pacifist organizations or the two traditional female pacifist groups, the Women's International League for Peace and Freedom (WILPF) and Women Strike for Peace (WSP). For black women such as Juanita Nelson and Eroseanna Robinson, opposition to war was long-standing and not necessarily rooted in gender considerations. As members of Peacemakers, a radical pacifist organization that espoused nonviolence as the means of settling disputes among nations and supported worldwide disarmament campaigns, Nelson and Robinson were tax resisters. Each refused to file federal tax forms or pay withholding taxes as ongoing protests against the allocation of federal revenues for war purposes and human destruction. Nelson was arrested in 1959 but was released within days as the charges were dropped; Robinson was sentenced to a one-year jail term in 1960 but was released after engaging in a three-month fast which led to her being force-fed.[6]

While prominent African-American clubwomen and educators had been affiliated with WILPF since 1919, the organization made a more concerted effort to reach out to black women who were active in local civil rights campaigns in the early 1960s, such as Virginia Collins of New Orleans and Amelia Boynton of Selma, Alabama.[7]

Women Strike for Peace was established in 1961 to protest continued nuclear testing and to call for an end to the arms race. Among those taking part in its earliest protests was Frances Mary Albrier, a longtime civil rights stalwart from the San Francisco Bay area. Albrier was one of the two spokespersons who led a demonstration of Berkeley housewives into the home office of their congressional representative, thereby asking him to support "a world crusade for disarmament and peace."[8] While an organization principally composed of white women, usually college-educated and middle-class, WSP sought to broaden its concerns and constituency in the early 1960s by linking the issues of peace and civil rights.[9]

Among the women attracted to both WILPF and WSP was Coretta Scott King, the wife of Dr. Martin Luther King, Jr., the president of the Southern Christian Leadership Conference (SCLC), and a distinguished peace activist in her own right. As early as 1962, Scott King was a WSP delegate to a conference in Geneva, Switzerland, calling for the continuation of talks between the United States and the Soviet Union on limiting the use of nuclear weapons. In November of 1963, she was part of a group of wSP demonstrators in front of the United Nations, holding aloft a banner that read, Let's Make Our Planet a Nuclear Free Zone. Moreover, by early 1965, Scott King, in the words of one early biographer of Dr. King, held "sharper, more finely honed opinions" on foreign policy matters than her husband. As more overt criticism of the war in Southeast Asia emerged in 1965, she became a featured speaker, one of the few blacks and one of the few women, at antiwar rallies sponsored by the National Committee for a Sane Nuclear Policy (SANE).[10]

Initially, Scott King, citing her roles as wife and mother, placed her opposition to the war in the context of maternal pacifism. However, in appearances at antiwar rallies and demonstrations from 1967 on, she shifted her focus to the war's impact on stateside reforms. In comments delivered in a March 1968 press conference held by WILPF officers, Scott King stated:

> As long as we kill men, women and children in Vietnam, millions of poor people face unnecessary death and suffering in America. As long as we lay waste to the beautiful countryside and communities of Vietnam, we shall see destruction and chaos in the ugly ghettoes of America. As long as we are poisoned by hatred of a freedom-seeking people in Asia, the sickness of racism will exploit our own minorities and corrupt the American majority.[11]

After the assassination of her husband, she became even more prominent in antiwar activities. Employing more of the arguments her husband had used in his speeches against the war, Scott King became more and more critical of the geopolitical underpinnings of the war. In a speech given less than a month after King's death, Scott King denounced continued American military support for a corrupt and unpopular regime. While assuming more of a public role, Scott King still couched many of her appeals in gender-specific terms. Seeking to rally women opposed to the war behind her 1968 Campaign of Conscience and its slogan of Woman Power, she exclaimed, "Women must realize that the war in Viet Nam is the most crucial and evil war in the history of mankind." Calling for the organization and mobilization of women's groups across the country, she asserted that, "the women of our country have been called at this hour to furnish the kind of forthright, honest, dedicated and creative leadership necessary to bring about positive solutions to the difficult problems we face."[12]

Yet, as the war dragged on, Scott King became less inclined to appeal to an especial role for women to bring about an end to the war. She was a featured speaker at the Vietnam Moratorium Day protest in Washington, D.C., in October of 1969 where she described the ongoing American involvement as a "godless cause" to which "[n]early 40,000 of our men have given their lives as sacrificial lambs." In a 1971 speech before an audience of 175,000 at a demonstration sponsored by the National Peace Action Coalition, she called for the immediate end "to this inhumane and insane war," that, in a veiled reference to the upcoming trial of Lt. William Calley, allowed far too many Americans to equate the wanton killing of Vietnamese people with heroism.[13]

While Scott King's opposition emerged from a "political femininity" that defined women's protest activities within the traditional sphere of motherhood or wifely status, concurrent forms of opposition to the war by other African-American women were more directly rooted in the male-dominated public sphere of political protest.[14] Initially, these women dissidents, several of whom were active in organizations on the political left, did not attribute their opposition to war to specific gender concerns but to ideological differences with the prevailing cold war consensus. In the early 1960s, Eslanda Goode Robeson, wife of singer-activist Paul Robeson and a longtime activist in campaigns against European colonialism and American neocolonialism in African and Asia, began to criticize the presence of American military advisers in Southeast Asia. As in the case of her earlier opposition to the Korean War, Goode Robeson criticized the military escalation in Vietnam as "a war against a colored people engaged in a long valiant struggle for freedom and self-determination." Her views were echoed by writer-activist Lorraine Hansberry. Described by a contemporary as a "Pan-Africanist with a socialist perspective," throughout the 1950s and early 1960s, Hansberry was committed to the liberation struggles of oppressed people in Asia and Africa. In a June 17, 1964, public presentation in New York City, Hansberry lambasted the federal government for its inability to protect Southern black activists while committing itself to "fighting a war for a bunch of other colored people, several thousand miles away."[15]

Hansberry's critique was similar to those voiced by local and national activists. At the height of the 1965 Selma, Alabama, campaign for voting rights, an irate Fannie Lou Hamer of the Mississippi Freedom Democratic party (MFDP) sent a telegram to President Lyndon Johnson demanding that American troops be withdrawn immediately from South Vietnam and sent to protect Southern blacks. As the fighting intensified so did Hamer's opposition. By early 1967 she was still critical of the rationale for the American presence in Vietnam—to bring democracy to the region—when her state's two senators were among those most opposed to civil rights for blacks. Yet, her opposition to the war transcended the views and actions of John Stennis or James Eastland. Hamer's worldview had broadened from one initially shaped by life in rural Mississippi to a more expansive domestic and internationalist perspective that criticized American elected officials for their willful failure to eradicate hunger and poverty within the nation's borders while waging a most costly war abroad. In addition, she came to criticize the federal government for not taking stronger measures against the white minority's 1965 usurpation of power in Southern Rhodesia. The Johnson administration "wasn't worried about it," she noted caustically, "cause it was all black folk."[16]

Signs of heightened international consciousness were evident throughout the early- to mid-1960s in a growing number of women active in freedom movement struggles. Some women, such as Diane Nash of SNCC (Student Nonviolent Coordinating Committee), came to note similarities in struggles being waged in the American South and in South Africa as early as 1961; other SNCC women took part in Fair Play for Cuba rallies in 1962. Male and female SNCC members had the opportunity to meet African dignitaries traveling in the United States. In 1964, a group of SNCC workers visited several West African nations where they were advised to compare the nature of SNCC's work in the American South with liberation efforts and independence movements across the African continent. For Diane Nash, a trip to the Bahamas in the early 1960s showed her the similarities in the conditions and treatment of black Bahamian workers and black southerners.[17]

While individual members of SNCC had paid some attention to events in Southeast Asia in the early 1960s, it was not until 1964 that increasing numbers of women and men in both SNCC and MFDP begin to make connections between the disfranchisement of Southern rural blacks and the disempowerment of Vietnamese peasants. As its members continued to assess and analyze the war in Vietnam and the ongoing, but changing, nature of the freedom struggle in the South, SNCC became the first civil rights organization to come out against the war. For Gloria House, one of the drafters of SNCC's January 1966 declaration of opposition to the war in Vietnam, dissent stemmed from her growing awareness of other liberation struggles around the world. "We saw ourselves as black people, a nation within a nation, a people colonized, warred upon—and the Vietnamese were, too," House has recalled. "So it made sense to say, Stop this war!"[18]

During 1966–1967, SNCC's opposition to the war became more pronounced and more anti-imperialist. In late 1966 and early 1967, Diane Nash, a veteran of the sit-in and freedom-ride campaigns conducted by SNCC before she joined the staff of SCLC, was one of four American women invited to visit North Vietnam. Perhaps the first black woman to visit Hanoi, Nash came away from meetings with Ho Chi Minh and other National Liberation Front (NLF) leaders permanently impressed with the struggle being waged by the North Vietnamese. Nash, formerly one of the pacifists within SNCC, had initially described herself as an opponent of war because "I am against using murder as a solution to human problems." In interviews in black publications after her return, she stated: "Sweethearts, mothers and other relatives of black soldiers fighting in Viet Nam can forget any notions that the Vietnamese people will give in to American aggression. The only way white America will defeat the people of Viet Nam is to murder each and every one of them."[19]

While expressing a definitively anti-imperialist perspective that equated "oppression and exploitation by the white West" to conditions faced by African-Americans, Nash was particularly impressed by the resolve and determination of the North Vietnamese women. As a mother, she expressed empathy for those women who buried their children. "The death and destruction I witnessed was far worse than any picture could communicate." Yet, in spite of the destruction of their country, Nash maintained, North Vietnamese women had expressed their "unyielding dedication to Vietnamese independence and freedom from foreign domination."[20]

Nash's comments in 1967 helped to mark the beginnings of an ideological transformation in the public political critiques of activist women.

No longer was the war seen in the context of a political femininity or even in the context of traditional freedom-struggle activism. The opposition of a growing number of young black women, women described by political scientist Inez Smith Reid as "together black women," emerged from more revolutionary organizations that called for the destruction, if not the radical transformation, of the American political, economic, and social order. Unlike a goodly number of white women who would leave white male-dominated organizations, such as Students for a Democratic Society (SDS), and would be among the early proponents of radical feminism, most black female activists remained within or aligned with existing black organizations. For example, several women in SNCC formed the Black Women's Liberation Committee and its successor group, Third World Women's Alliance. Formally affiliated with SNCC, the Third World Women's Alliance involved itself in antiracist, anti-imperialist, and antisexist organizing campaigns.[21]

In 1966, the newly established Black Panther party embraced a revolutionary nationalist ideology that emphatically stated that male members of the party would "not fight and kill other people of color in the world who, like black people, are being victimized by the white racist government of America." However, the party's early nationalist ideology consigned female members to what several contended was the subordinate role of Pantherettes. With the exception of Kathleen Cleaver, communications secretary of the Black Panther party, few women emerged as spokespersons before 1969. In speeches and in writings throughout 1968, Cleaver was unstinting in her criticism of Lyndon Johnson. The president, Cleaver intoned, was a "murderous dictator perpetrating the most barbarous war in human history." In addition, Cleaver, like Nash, was effusive in her praise for the Vietnamese people who "refuse to be controlled by the capitalist racist American government, and are fighting to retain control of their own country."[22]

By 1969, as the Black Panther party's ideology more firmly embraced both Marxist and Third World ideologies, women other than Kathleen Cleaver came to the fore. Whether in the *Black Panther* or speeches at antiwar conferences, more women began to make direct references to the role of revolutionary women in recent liberation struggles. In a July 1969 speech at the United Front against Fascism Women's Panel, party member Roberta Alexander asserted:

The sisters are more and more taking a leadership role. We have sisters who can shoot, who shoot as well as brothers. They're not sitting home with the babies . . . and the sisters in the Black Panther Party . . . follow the example of the Vietnamese women (applause). This is the example we're going to follow. We're going to go on the offensive and we're going to take an advanced position. We're going to fight backwardness, and the Right On, Vietnamese Sisters, we're with you. Right on. [23]

Alexander's comments were staples in the critiques offered by women in the party. Seeking to challenge the still-prevailing sexism of the party's male leadership, female members pointed to their Vietnamese counterparts as warriors in the proletarian revolution. Their roles would make it all too apparent that, in the words of one woman member, "the success of the revolution depends upon the women." Thus, in the struggle for gender equality within revolutionary organizations, women in the Black Panther party pointed to the struggle of Vietnamese women as being worthy of emulation. Indeed, for Assata Shakur, a member of the New York City chapter of the party, the struggles waged by Vietnamese women caused her to think seriously about guerrilla warfare within the United States. [24]

At the same time that women within the Black Panther party began to focus on the commonalities of liberation struggles in the United States and throughout the world, individual African-American women in the Communist party began to speak out against the war. In 1968, Charlene Mitchell, co-chair of the Black Liberation Commission of the Communist party, stated that the war was "not just a bloody and unjust war but it is a war by the U.S. to maintain the status quo and refuse people the right of self-determination." Mitchell's assertions would be echoed repeatedly by Angela Davis, the party's most prominent and most visible African American. Davis's opposition to the war was part of her ongoing political education and consciousness from the early- to mid-1960s. As an exchange student in France in 1963–1964, the Brandeis University junior had met North Vietnamese students and South Vietnamese students opposed to the government in Saigon and had begun to understand the nature of their opposition to the American military presence in South Vietnam. As a graduate student in philosophy at the University of

Frankfurt from 1965–1967, she had taken part in "increasingly militant demonstrations against U.S. imperialism, its aggression in Vietnam, [and] its flunkies in West Germany."[25]

Imbued with such an ethos, Davis returned to the United States even more committed to the applicability of Marxist-Leninist thought in the struggle of oppressed people for liberation. As a graduate student at the University of California at San Diego and as a member of the Che-Lumumba Club, an all-black division in the Los Angeles chapter of the Communist party, Davis became more involved in antiwar activities. Linking her studies abroad, her meeting with representatives from the National Liberation Front, and her organizing work in Los Angeles, Davis stressed the "relation between aggression in Vietnam and racism and repression at home." She called for African Americans "to look towards Vietnam because they are really on the front lines of the battlefield in the fight against repression." In spite of her arrest in 1970, Davis remained an outspoken opponent of the war. In published interviews held before her trial, Davis repeatedly stressed the similarities in revolutionary struggles for self-determination throughout the world. And, like several of the female members of the Black Panther party, Davis, by 1970, began placing more emphasis on the role of women in revolutionary movements. The struggle of Vietnamese women was "part and parcel of a total revolution" and its lessons would be "especially critical with respect to the effort to build an effective black liberation movement."[26]

Davis's later statements demonstrate how she, as well as women in the Black Panther party, had become more forthright in demanding gender equality in revolutionary movements. Whether they had embraced orthodox Marxist-Leninist views or more internationalist perspectives on revolutionary struggles, these women had moved beyond calling for the military defeat of the United States. They had espoused a critique that, while in part socialist feminist, was also fully immersed in African feminism, a feminism more expressive of the historic values and struggles of women of African descent. Indeed, by challenging institutional as well as intraracial forms of oppression, women activists in the Communist party and the Black Panther party were continuing, in the words of sociologist Patricia Hill Collins, the "Black women's activist tradition."[27]

Yet, if more radical voices, particularly revolutionary voices, came to represent the stated views of more militant black women in the late 1960s–1970s, other voices came to light as well, voices from either a liberal feminist perspective or from a radical feminist perspective. The liberal feminist critique often had much in common with political femininity and was more rooted in the newly emergent National Organization for Women (NOW) than in traditional women's peace reform groups. However, in 1967, NOW leaders were averse to suggestions that the organization come out against the war. Such narrowness, according to activist-lawyer Flo Kennedy, would be one of the reasons for her departure from the organization. Only after NOW, still composed largely of white middle-class, college-educated women, came out against the war in Vietnam and broadened its programmatic agenda to include issues of importance to women of color did liberal feminism make more than isolated inroads to African-American women.[28]

Perhaps the most noticeable liberal feminist voice among African-American women was Representative Shirley A. Chisholm from Brooklyn. From her initial run for Congress in 1968 through the American defeat in Vietnam, Chisholm would be one of the staunchest congressional critics of continued American involvement in Southeast Asia. Chisholm, like Coretta Scott King after 1968, would repeatedly criticize the billions of dollars spent yearly on an "immoral war." Calling for the massive reordering of the nation's priorities, Chisholm vowed to vote against every bill introduced in Congress to provide funds for the Defense Department. While maintaining that she was not a pacifist, Chisholm stated that "I could not vote for money for war while funds were being denied to feed, house, and school Americans." And as the war dragged on into 1972, her exasperation grew. In a 1972 speech lamenting government lies and coverups about the war, Chisholm angrily charged: "What conceivable gain can be worth all this? Is there no end to this insanity? This grotesque absorption in war and all its offshoots has virtually destroyed the ability of our government to function effectively at home, and to respond to the process of change and evolution which our society is undergoing today."[29] Rejecting the Nixon administration's call for peace with honor, Chisholm, then seeking the Democratic party's nomination for president, contended: "This vile tragedy continues in Indochina because this Administration is now trapped by its own overweening self-obsession, self-delusion, and its moral and intellectual poverty into an endless, violent and blundering search for a settlement on its own ludicrously unrealistic terms."[30] Chisholm called for Congress to terminate immediately all funding for the war.[31]

Yet, while Chisholm's critique was that of an African-American woman policymaker, one who was critical of the war but was still willing to work within the existing American political framework, several black women used a radical feminist argument to criticize both the patriarchal system and the war. Several of the African-American radical feminists had emerged from the Poor Black Women's Group, organized in suburban New York in the late 1960s. Initially employing a revolutionary nationalist argument that sought to infuse race and gender issues into international concerns, by 1969 they had established a working relationship with white radical feminists and had come to reject the teachings of black male cultural nationalists. Embracing a critique against the war that damned partriarchy and capitalism, radical feminists Patricia Haden, Donna Middleton, and Patricia Robinson wrote: "One-half of these courageous South Vietnamese NLF fighters are women and children, and they have proved that no U.S. male, black or white, got what it takes to destroy a people who have decided in their guts to own themselves and their land. That is power U.S. males have forgotten, but not black women, especially those of us who are poor."[32]

Articulate voices, whether encompassing pacifist, reformist, orthodox Marxist, revolutionary nationalist, or any of the several strands of feminist thought were concurrent voices that ranged across the political spectrum of African-American women's opposition to the Vietnam War. Yet, these voices could not and did not represent all of the dissenting perspectives recurrent during the war. For countless black women, none of the perspectives discussed above could fully or adequately represent their views. Their opposition to the war, perhaps expressed in not so eloquent or consistent a manner, often centered around who was fighting and who was dying in a war they did not understand. While similar to the arguments of maternal pacifists, the perspectives of the majority of black female opponents were not so easily categorized. Public opinion polls conducted in 1965 and 1966 by the traditional polling services suggest that a large percentage of African-American women polled may have opposed, then supported, the Johnson administration's early handling of the war. However, polls conducted by black publications found more opposition than support among black women. Throughout 1965, a clear majority of women polled by the Pan-African Research Associates were opposed to the escalation of American involvement in Vietnam. According to M. Thomas, a Chicago secretary, "Johnson is spending billions of dollars of taxpayers' money in Vietnam and the Dominican Republic when this money could be used to help persons at home who are not working and need aid." When asked in late 1965 about the war in Vietnam, Chicago waitress Irene Brandberry replied: "[N]o one seems to know why we are over there in the first place. I certainly don't. There must be some shady reason, or it seems they would level with us and explain the whole thing. I'm sure no one believes those notions about saving Viet Nam for democracy and such."[33] In a similar vein, Vernell Boyd, of San Francisco, commented in early 1966, "I think it's wrong. We go there and fight for the white people's war, then come back here and are treated bad."[34]

From early 1966 until the end of the war, what most galvanized many black women to oppose the war was the escalating number of black troops killed in Vietnam. For many of those who lost husbands, sons, other loved ones, friends and neighbors, the continued fighting was both painful and galling. According to Christine McCullough of Chicago, whose Army son was killed in 1966, "black boys are giving their lives in a war they don't understand and can't win." Lamenting her spouse's death, Juanita Butcher of Queens, New York, stated: "My husband told me before he died that the war is useless." And, expressing her grief at the news of the death, in 1969, of a neighbor's son in Viet Nam, Mollie Reid of Brooklyn exclaimed: "Now he's dead. In a place we don't know—can't even pronounce the names—and for reasons we don't understand at all." McCullough's, Butcher's, and Reid's anguish was similar to that expressed by others who lost relatives and friends over the course of the war. While countless families grieved silently, others became more demonstrative in their opposition to the war. Louise Ransom, whose son was killed in combat, returned the medals posthumously awarded to her son. In a protest staged before the South Vietnamese embassy in Washington, D.C., in early 1969, Ransom stated that the South Vietnamese government was "suppressing the freedom of [its] people."[35]

Indeed, the mounting deaths of black military personnel stationed in South Vietnam firmly and unalterably changed the thinking of many African-American women throughout the nation and caused them to oppose the continued fighting in Vietnam by late 1966–1967. Although traditional polls began to monitor the shift, few pollsters asked why. The discontent and dissatisfaction of increasing numbers of African-American women was now coupled with their negative perceptions of the war's worsening impact upon domestic conditions. Thus, their opposition heightened. To a Chicago mother of four, "Why should we worry about Communism over there when we have poverty over here? What's the sense of fighting over there when there's so much to fight for here?"[36]

If any event signaled the rising discontent of African-American women, it may have been L'Affaire Kitt. On January 18, 1968, singer-entertainer Eartha Kitt was one of a group of women, black and white, who were invited to a White House luncheon, hosted by Lady Bird Johnson, to discuss ways of combating juvenile delinquency. When asked to speak, Kitt stated, to the astonishment of those assembled: "You send the best of this country off to be shot and maimed. They rebel in the street. . . . They don't want to go to school because they're going to be snatched off from their mothers to be shot in Vietnam. . . . You have children of your own, Mrs. Johnson—we raise children and send them to war!"[37]

The surrounding uproar would have a negative effect on Kitt's career, but she was instantly praised for her courage by opponents of the war. Across the country African-American women rallied to Kitt's defense. In letters-to-the-editors, particularly in black newspapers, support for Kitt was nearly unanimous. From her hometown of Los Angeles, women wrote:

I thought it was great because she told the truth.

Someone should have done it sooner. . . . Miss Kitt was definitely in her right.

I think she was very courageous. She was the first to get the opportunity to say what she had to say to people who are partly responsible for the war.

I think it was appropriate. She was not out of place; she was exercising her freedom of speech.[38]

Yet, the comments made by Kitt only suggested the burgeoning opposition to the war. African-American women, not just elites or activists, become more prominent in antiwar activities. While Coretta Scott

King, Fannie Lou Hamer, Ella Baker, and Angela Davis would often appear as platform speakers at antiwar rallies and demonstrations, many other black women would be in the audiences. In rallies held in Chicago, New York City, Washington, and Boston, in 1966 and 1967, African-American women would be in attendance holding signs reading: Black Men Should Fight White Racism, Not Vietnamese Freedom Fighters; Children Are Not Born to Burn; No Vietnamese Ever Called Me Nigger; and Black People: 53% of the Dead, 2% of the Bread . . . Why? Other women, such as a group of black Women Strike for Peace demonstrators, chanted in a 1967 demonstration: "Should they die? We say why" and "Support the boys who will not go." While a small number of these demonstrators were members of traditional peace groups, many were high school and college students, working women, and self-described welfare mothers who often participated in all-black contingents.[39] Recalling her participation in the April 15, 1967, antiwar demonstration, Laura Moorehead, then a high school student, remembered: "I stood right there and saw Martin Luther King speak. That was a big thrill for me because I had waited so long for him to come out against the war and I became so excited when he actually did. That was one of the main reasons I came—because I knew King was going to speak and publicly identify himself with the demonstration, and I hoped that would help win my parents over."[40] Describing the reason she and a contingent of black students came to Washington from Detroit to take part in the march on the Pentagon, Owen Walter stated that their purpose was "to show the country that black people are concerned with the international issue of colored peoples all over the world."[41]

As rallies and demonstrations became more routine after Richard Nixon took office in 1969, black participation, while limited, became more evident. Hospital workers in New York City, many of whom were African-American women, took part in the October 15, 1969, moratorium there. Howard University students, male and female, were among those assembled for the November 15, 1969, antiwar demonstration in Washington, D.C.[42]

In the rallies and demonstrations held nationwide in the spring of 1970 to protest the invasion of Cambodia and the killings at Kent State and Jackson State Universities, black female students, women from union locals, and from the National Welfare Rights Organization (NWRO) were in attendance. Union activists and workers bemoaned the continuing violence at home and abroad and the war's impact upon their salaries. According to one New York City waitress, "I don't make that much to begin with but when the inflation caused by this tragic war takes its bite, I'm really behind the eight-ball." Welfare rights supporters and proponents attended national moratoria and local demonstrations, often carrying signs reading, Stop the War, Feed the Poor. The involvement of NWRO women in antiwar demonstrations allowed, according to Frances Fox Piven and Richard A. Cloward, "anti-war groups to link the issues of imperialism and war abroad with the government's failure to deal with poverty and injustices at home."[43]

The activities of African-American women were not limited to their involvement in antiwar protests and demonstrations. Over the course of the war, black women of varying ages became involved in protests against the draft. As early as the summer of 1965, activists in the MFDP strongly considered initiating campaigns to have black women in rural Mississippi advise their sons to resist the draft. In 1966, a Harlem organization, Black Women Enraged (BWE), openly picketed in front of local recruiting stations. Urging black males of draft age to "stay here and fight for your manhood," members of the organization strongly encouraged black women to support the stands of black draft resisters. In leaflets directed expressly to black women, BWE stressed: "If we, their Black mothers, from whose wombs they sprang, who love them as only we can, can't help him to be a man, how then can the army, run by *white* men, who have nothing in common with them and who feel nothing but contempt for them, put manhood in them?"[44] Moreover, BWE stressed the anti-imperialist and racial aspects of the war, while calling for black men to "protect" the vulnerable. According to another broadside:

> Whitey's war in Vietnam *is not our fight*! Whitey would rather see our men dead in Vietnam, than men in the street. If our men must fight, let it be here for their dignity as Black men, and let it be to protect us, their women and children from the murder and rape of the White racist.
>
> Black women, we must have the courage to back our men when they choose jail rather than die in Vietnam!!![45]

While BWE had minimal success in eliciting acts of draft resistance in 1966 and 1967, its message, calling for a direct role for African-American women in inculcating an antidraft consciousness, spread to other organizations. A New York City branch of CORE (Congress of Racial Equality), for example, sought to arrange a demonstration in which women from Harlem would burn the draft cards of their male relatives and boyfriends. Other women were adamantly opposed to the draft or openly supportive of draft resisters. In New York City in early 1967, black pollsters found young women in particular answering "No" to the question, "Do you think black youths should go to Viet Nam?" And, across the country, black women were starting to express support, verbally and in writing, for the antiwar stance of Muhammad Ali. Expressing her support to her co-religionist, Sister Patricia X wrote: "Many a black man is refusing to go now because of the incentive you gave."[46]

By late 1967, antidraft activities were more apparent in black neighborhoods. Unlike accounts of SDS's involvement in draft resistance which often describe gender demarcation in assigned roles, there was more equality between the sexes in several of the antidraft organizations in urban black centers. Indeed, African-American women, such as Gwen Patton and Pat Berg, played prominent, if not leading, roles in organizations such as the National Black Anti-War Anti-Draft Union (NBAWADU) and the National Black Draft Counselors (NBDC) respectively. Patton, former student body president of Tuskegee Institute and later chair of SNCC's Black Women's Liberation Committee, took a leading role in formulating antidraft strategies for SNCC. Active as an undergraduate in anti-ROTC protests, Patton, by late 1967, hoped to see an organization created that would aid black antiwar and antidraft resisters.[47]

Thus in 1967, male and female members of SNCC joined with black members of the Socialist Workers party, the Communist party, the Progressive Labor party, and members of locally based nationalist groups across the country to form NBAWADU. This organization sought to conduct draft resistance work while taking "an anti-imperialist stand against the racist, aggressive American government." For NBAWADU, women members' role went beyond the simplistic Women Say Yes to Men Who Say No slogan. In a leaflet calling for draft resistance by men *and* by women, NBAWADU organizers stated:

> Women are going to have to move to stop this system from drafting their sons. We have an obligation to our people first. . . . Black women need black men at home now!

The next time your son receives a "greetings" letter you go to the Draft Board in his place . . . tell the Board that you will go in his place. We must at all times urge our sons to resist the draft. We cannot afford to permit this system to continue this type of genocide.[48]

This NBAWADU's statement was not a rhetorical boast. Female relatives and friends of black would-be draftees and war resisters staged dramatic and defiant acts of protest. To prevent her son from being inducted, Sister Lily Jones, the head of a small Detroit religious sect, led chanting members of her congregation into the induction center and took her son home. Mothers of imprisoned war resisters worked tirelessly on behalf of their sons. Explaining her longtime efforts to seek freedom for her resister son, Virginia Collins, formerly a member of WILPF and later a member of the Republic of New Africa, emphatically stated that war resisters "are some of the most courageous, intelligent, and morally responsible people that this country has produced. They must be freed from jail and returned from exile so they can help us build a society free of racism, war, and poverty."[49]

The arguments of and activities undertaken by African-American female opponents of the Vietnam War varied in tone and in intent. While more public figures expressed divergent points of view about the war, they were nearly unanimous in their calls for an immediate end to the war. The continuing struggle in the United States, whether viewed as the ongoing struggle for civil rights reform or as the overthrow of an oppressive, capitalist, and as some did argue, patriarchal, system took precedence over the waging of a war nearly all viewed as unjust and immoral. Whether they called for a negotiated withdrawal in 1965–1966, an immediate withdrawal after 1967, or a military victory for the National Liberation Front, women dissidents often put forth a critique of the war that was different from that articulated by black male dissidents. Consciously, gender concerns affected the critiques. While the traditional argument of maternal pacifism, given shape by Jane Addams and other members of the Women's Peace Party during World War One and adhered to by successive generations of female peace activists, cannot explain the full range of dissenting activities in which African-American women engaged, there is still some validity to the construct. For, even some radical black women, whether in oratory or in antidraft work, would appeal to the professed nurturing urges of women. Still, whether the origins of antiwar expression lay in nurture, in socialization, or in political ideology, African-American women responded to the war in terms clearly defined by race, gender, and class. Thus, whether expressed by Angela Davis, Coretta Scott King, or welfare rights activists, many spoke against the war so that their voices would have to be heard and heeded.

Barbara L. Tischler

Voices of Protest
Women and the GI Antiwar Press

N ew scholarship on American culture and society in the 1960s is beginning to eschew the "top down" focus on personalities that has been the mainstay of many popular works. Studies of "great men," "great women," or even "great movements" have been only partially successful in portraying and analyzing the decentralized and loosely-structured opposition to United States involvement in Southeast Asia. Antiwar activism was not a product of any single ideological perspective or group sensibility, but was the product of coalition-building on college campuses, in local communities, and, increasingly after 1968, on military bases in the United States and abroad.

GI antiwar activity was the product of many political perspectives. The movement espoused resistance, not only to the war and American foreign policy, but to the military ethos itself. The idea of challenging United States policy from within the military took shape in the late 1960s and early 1970s as antiwar soldiers began to see themselves in the front ranks of a struggle against American foreign policy and a broad range of injustices at home.[1] GI coffeehouses, counseling centers, and "alternative" newspapers gave voice to antiwar sentiment and to demands for First Amendment rights for military personnel. These demands included equality for African Americans and an end to pervasive sexism in American society in general and the military in particular.

African-American soldiers spoke proudly, often defiantly, of their opposition to fighting in the name of an American government that they regarded as racist and imperialist. They could rely, however tentatively, on a body of nationalist political theory developed within the Black Power movement. A rhetoric of empowerment and separatism which articulated a clear mistrust of the established government, society, and culture characterized the militant civil rights movement after 1966. Stokely Carmichael articulated his opposition to the Vietnam War in terms of his identity as a black man in 1966:

> A mercenary is a hired killer and any black man serving in this man's army is a mercenary, nothing else. A mercenary fights for a price but does not enjoy the rights of the country for which he is fighting. A mercenary will go to Viet Nam to fight for free elections for the Vietnamese but doesn't have free elections in Alabama, Mississippi, Georgia, Texas, Louisiana, South Carolina, and Washington, D.C. A mercenary goes to Viet Nam and gets shot fighting for his country and they won't even bury him in his own home town. He's a mercenary, that's all. We must find the strength so that when they start grabbing us to fight their war we say, "Hell, no."[2]

In contrast to African-American soldiers, women GIs in the late 1960s and early 1970s were only beginning to develop a vocabulary with which to articulate their opposition to the war and to their treatment in the service. These women were generally less connected than their counterparts in college to emerging "new feminist" groups whose first principles were often grounded in the personal experiences of their members and whose leaders were engaged in a serious effort to create and employ a viable political theory. Female volunteers for military service were wary of attaching a "feminist" label to their own ideas about a woman's place in the world. Like their counterparts in the civilian women's movement, they often began their feminist analysis with an iteration of personal grievances. An understanding of the importance of the personal enabled military women to relate their problems to the more general condition of women in American society and to the repressive conditions under which both male and female soldiers served their country.

* * *

Challenges to military authority that ranged, even in wartime, from grumbling comments on latrine walls to draft riots and refusals to fight, were not new in the 1960s and early 1970s. American soldiers had long complained about the oppressive nature of military bureaucracy and the meaningless nature of its regulations, the degree to which advancement was based less on merit than on favoritism, and the fact that the institution saw no need to grant its citizens in uniform the basic constitutional rights of free speech and assembly. But expressions of dissatisfaction did not necessarity connote resistance or rebellion. Prior to the Vietnam War, GIs generally accepted the legitimacy of military authority and the capacity of superiors to make a dissenter's life unbearable.

Why did soldiers who served during the Vietnam War presume that they had rights protected by the First Amendment when their predecessors had resented, but essentially accepted, the authority of the brass and the Uniform Code of Military Justice? Clues can be found in the nature of the conflict, the profile of the antiwar GI, and the emergence of protest as a significant aspect of American culture by the late 1960s. The fighting in Vietnam was part of an undeclared "non-war" against unseen enemies. It exacted a high cost in American and Vietnamese lives with few tangible signs of victory. Even soldiers who enlisted with the idea of saving the world from the "Communist menace" often became disillusioned because they were fighting a war they could not win. Army nurse Jeanne Rivera expressed the frustration of many women and men who had volunteered for duty in Vietnam. Years after the end of the fighting, Rivera reflected that she had been

> a very patriotic person. I thought that whatever we were doing, we were doing because it was right. . . . I believed that these people were being invaded by an enemy that they didn't want. And I believed we were supporting the right government in Vietnam. And then, once I went there, I saw what a catastrophe the government was, and that the government was really lying to the people in the United States. . . . And then when I found out we were getting out of Vietnam, and all those people had died—died for nothing. . . . I don't believe half, not even half of what the government tells me now.[3]

Such a transition from faith to unbelief was not uncommon among Vietnam veterans.

Resistance to the war was part of a larger oppositional culture that flourished as the Vietnam War intensified after the 1968 Tet offensive. This culture can be analyzed both in terms of the challenges it posed to traditional authority and the demands it made for a better and more just American community. The seemingly endless war in Southeast Asia became, for many Americans, a symbol of misguided policy and outright betrayal, and the slogan, No More Vietnams, connoted resistance to what many in the antiwar movement, both in and outside of the military, saw as an imperialist venture by an undemocratic government. In alternative newspapers throughout the United States and in Germany, Japan, and the Philippines, citizen soldiers criticized the war, not as an isolated phenomenon, but as part of a larger matrix of social ills.

In the late 1960s, GI antiwar newspapers emerged to fill a gap in the mainstream coverage of news that GIs thought was important. Until 1968, the majority of American newspapers accepted government assertions of the validity of United States policy in Southeast Asia and military claims of victory. After the Tet offensive, however, reporters in greater numbers began to question the information that was fed to them in the daily Saigon military briefings known derisively as the "five o'clock follies." Even as major newspapers and television networks began to take notice of the student–civilian antiwar movement, resistance in the military went largely undocumented. Military papers like *Stars and Stripes* could offer no outlet for expressions of protest. For many, the need for an alternative was obvious.

The protection of the First Amendment rights to free speech and a free press was a major issue in many GI antiwar papers. Clearly, editors were vitally concerned about their right to publish unpopular views about the military, but the notion of freedom of expression evoked a broad range of rights that enlisted personnel began to demand from their military employers. The first issue of *Fun, Travel, and Adventure* (known by its initials FTA, seen more commonly as an abbreviation for the popular slogan, "Fuck the Army") identified the paper as "Published Underground for and by the GI's at Fort Knox. Dedicated to free speech and the Struggle for Our Rights."[4]

Throughout the history of the movement against the war in Vietnam, the demands articulated in the GI papers included:

∗ Freedom from harrassment for attending antiwar demonstrations off base

* The right to produce, distribute, and possess antiwar newspapers and other antiwar and antimiliatry documents

* The right to wear peace signs, long hair, African unity bands, etc. while in uniform

* An end to the institutionalized miliatry racism

* An end to sexism in the military

* The right to refuse an order to fight that a soldier considered unlawful or immoral

* An end to the war in Vietnam

That this generation of soldiers spoke in terms of rights reflects the extent to which broader challenges to authority fueled opposition to American foreign policy. Women and men in the military could not have struggled for their rights without support from the culture of protest that influenced American political life late in the 1960s.

It was in the context of a culture of protest that women's voices within the GI antiwar movement began to be heard through the alternative press. Women's letters and articles reveal a growing awareness of their oppression in the larger culture, dissatisfaction with their treatment within the enlisted ranks, and a sense of futility about their ability to bring the war to an end. Antiwar activists who organized women on or near military bases realized that enlisted women and military wives who may have opposed the war did not "see themselves in a direct relationship to the war effort as guys do. . . . [N]o one seems to see herself as able to do anything to stop it."[5]

Women who were dissatisfied with military life could not help being ambivalent about their new-found urge to speak out. They were, after all, volunteers, who had entered the service with the expectation that the military would enhance their career options, or social status, and would also value their contribution to the war effort. They did not generally identify themselves as "feminists," even though, as women workers in a military man's world, they often had to transcend occupational and social barriers based on gender. Recent collections of GI women's narratives reflect this ambivalence, as they reveal a strong, nurturing, care-giving impulse among women whose jobs were generally more difficult and stressful than those of civilian women. According to Renny Christopher, who has analyzed oral histories of both male and female veterans,

Women often felt that they were supporters of the men, and not participants in their own right. Women in the military often felt that what they were doing was not as important as what the men were doing, and that in addition to their own jobs they also had the responsibility of acting as mother, sister, and girlfriend to male soldiers. Having absorbed the gender role stereotypes of the larger American society, these women expected to submerge their own needs, and to take care of the men, whose role as combat soldiers was valued more highly than that of nurses or "support" personnel.[6]

Despite a commonly held feeling of powerlessness, many women began to speak out in the GI alternative papers about the conditions of military life, institutionalized sexism, and what they, like women in the emerging civilian feminist movement, saw as the objectification of women. They did so in a language and style that lacked the theoretical clarity and intellectual polish of academic feminists, but their views mirrored those of women in the civil rights and antiwar movements and, increasingly but slowly, in American society at large.[7]

The GI antiwar newspapers were not necessarily a logical forum for women writers. One important subtext in many of these papers is a close, personal, male bonding. In military training, this bonding is achieved in part as a result of the high value placed on aggression and the fear of being labeled a woman. Mark Gerzon has argued that the fear of man's feminine side,

> the "anima" in Jungian terms, seems inextricably involved in triggering our capacity for destructiveness. It is as if war provides men with a periodic exorcism of the anima—a ritual cleansing and purification of masculinity. The anima is banished from the Soldier's consciousness because it disturbs, in Emma Jung's words, "a man's established ideal image of himself."[8]

The male soldiers who rejected the war and who, in many cases, struggled to distance themselves from the most destructive aspects of the aggressive "male" military ethos, nevertheless often developed their own bonds that excluded women. Ritual handshakes which emulated those of African-American GIs, calling each other "brother," and a vernacular peppered with expletives and military jargon often excluded women from group participation on an equal or comfortable footing. Military women proved themselves capable of "getting along" in a male environment, but as they struggled on the job to survive among "the guys," they often wrote in the GI papers of their frustrations and anxieties as women.

The mainstream press of this period portrayed military women as patriotic but essentially ancillary to the war effort. Female GIs, almost always referred to as "girls," were often described as having volunteered because their husbands or sweethearts were serving in Vietnam. Articles in major newspapers compared these women favorably to those who joined the services or worked in defense plants during World War II, although no character comparable to the famous Rosie the Riveter appears in Vietnam iconography.

Female GIs were often presented in the press as ornaments whose presence made life more "bearable" for male soldiers. Under the headline, "41 WACs are First to Serve in Vietnam: 3,000 GIs in Area Suddenly Spruce Up," United Press International ran a story in January of 1967 that described life in Vietnam for a group of clerk-typists, not from the women's point of view, but from that of the male soldiers who surrounded them:

> After their arrival this month, the WACs appeared on the parade ground for a command formation. When the GIs marched onto the field, there was chaos as more than a few got out of step while watching the girls. . . . After the girls' arrival, one company of GIs which has been exercising each evening in dirty fatigue uniforms and T-shirts suddenly appeared in sharp-looking track uniforms. . . . [One soldier commented] "Take that first sergeant, for instance, . . . [f]irst sergeants are supposed to mean and nasty. But she's the cutest one in the bunch."[9]

A few months later, the *Philadelphia Bulletin* printed an article about women in the service called "Our Soldiers in Skirts Go Off to War" that focused on the patriotism of the women and their eagerness to go to Vietnam. Most of the women interviewed, including "a petite, pretty brunette with short cropped hair" and "the head of the nation's lady Leathernecks," were officers.[10]

An analysis of women's protest against the conditions of military life during the Vietnam War is better informed by an understanding of the demography of the women who served. The 197,513 women who volunteered for all branches of the military during active American involvement in Southeast Asia represented only 2.1 percent of the entire military force, and 83.5 percent of these women were nurses who were low-ranking officers. The majority of nurses did not engage in active protest against the war or the military during their tours of duty, although many have spoken out on these issues in the years since the end of the fighting. Non-nursing military women were mainly in the enlisted ranks and were mainly working class, according to the United States Servicemen's Fund, a GI antiwar organization:

> They are in the Army for many of the same reasons as lifers (with economics being an even more compelling factor for women in a time of depression). For many, it's the first time they don't have to worry about housing, medical attention, etc. . . . Many WACs like the Army. As women, they can be on their own WITHOUT men—something very unusual for women of their class.[11]

Rank was not the only factor that separated those women who protested both the war and their subordinate status in the military from those who were less vocal. The all-consuming professionalism required of a nurse in or near a combat zone also helps account for a relative absence of overt resistance or rebellion by women in Vietnam. While male antiwar soldiers wore peace signs, planted their bayonets in the ground as a signal to the enemy (and their own officers) that they would not initiate combat, or simply refused orders to fight, women nurses performed their jobs under extreme stress and with a high degree of competence. Their shifts were long, and their working conditions terrible, but nurses have spoken with overwhelmingly positive feelings about the quality of the work itself. Nurses were unlikely to refuse to obey orders, as their job was to heal rather than to kill.

Many returning nurses noted the let-down of civilian jobs in which they merely followed a doctor's orders. Normal hospital life paled in comparison to the high many felt in assuming life-and-death responsibilities under fire. Major General Jeanne Holm described the special working conditions in Vietnam, in which nurses assumed authority and performed medical procedures generally restricted to doctors:

Almost any case [on a medical evacuation] could turn into an emergency in flight. When that happened, the nurse could declare a "Medical Emergency"—air evac's equivalent of "Mayday"—and in effect assume command of the aircraft. She could instruct the pilot to change altitude or cabin pressure, turn back, or make an unscheduled landing at the nearest medical facility. Despite the dangers and responsibilities, or maybe because of them, nurses considered flight duty the most prestigious in the Air Force.[12]

In spite of the high level of job satisfaction during the war, former military nurses have, in recent years, been among those to decry the human cost of American involvement in Southeast Asia. The ravages of war in the form of post-traumatic stress disorder, drug and alcohol abuse, and a host of other psychological difficulties have affected these women dramatically in the years since the end of the fighting. Their stories are only now being told in oral histories and personal narratives.[13]

Enlisted women, wives of service personnel, and civilian antiwar organizers often marched in demonstrations, conducted consciousness-raising groups off base, and took part in other symbolic acts of resistance. Women at Fort Bragg, North Carolina, organized a small group to study American history, which they defined as "worker's history, third world history, and women's history." The Fort Bragg women also instituted courses in such "essential" skills as emergency first aid, basic auto mechanics, self-defense, and carpentry.[14] When women contributed to the GI antiwar press, they wrote for existing papers rather than starting new ones, although one women's paper, *Whack!*, did appear briefly at Fort McClellan, Alabama, in 1971. In a few cases, such as *Left Face*, also published at Fort McClellan, a paper's masthead might read "Published by GIs and WACs Against the War."

The presence of women's concerns in the male-dominated GI antiwar press reflects a growing awareness of the emerging women's liberation movement as well as the depth of military women's dissatisfaction with the war and with their own lives in uniform. The issues raised in the alternative press were the emerging "women's issues" of the late 1960s and early 1970s, including equality of opportunity and liberation from the traditional and subordinate role as the "weaker sex." Many letters and articles written by women and supportive men stressed that women were treated as inferior soldiers because of pervasive sexism in all branches of the service emanating from the top down. Women also complained of sexual harassment and an inability to gain promotions. One medical technician, sp/4, wrote to *Fragging Action* about the special problems faced by military women, citing frequent weight checks, the lack of weapons training because, "as the story goes, one very hip sister threatened to do in her c.o.," and the difficulty in attaining higher rank: "Well, where do the promotions come in? The hard part about being a woman in the green machine is if you don't kiss the right ass or fuck the right people, forget about any more rank."[15]

Military women who voiced their grievances often were subjected to surveillance, restrictions, transfers and undesirable job assignments, and charges filed against them for minor infractions. In general, these women had only minimal connections to feminist or left political groups that could provide theoretical sustenance, emotional support, or legal counsel. In spite of the organizing efforts of antiwar activists, women's groups in and around the military were especially fragile. Like their counterparts in new feminist groups, military women who met to discuss their grievances often had no common political perspective. Such groups often disintegrated after only a few months, not over disagreements about the validity of their complaints, but over strategic and tactical debates about how to organize women and for what purpose.

Military women could be haunted by the issue of lesbianism. Homosexuality was cause for less-than-honorable discharge, and many gay women feared being too outspoken on political issues. According to ussf (United States Serviceman's Fund) women organizers, gay women "don't relate to fta politics because the army is basically pretty good for them and our relationship to them was much more essentially political: we talked about class, the war, women. The problem . . . is that they are not in a position to move politically—they don't want to get kicked out of the army."[16] Women who were not gay feared charges and innuendo that they could neither accept nor refute. It was not surprising that women in the military were wary of organizing.

Many women used the existing gi press to express individual grievances and to describe their living and working conditions. For example, women who distributed *Broken Arrow* at Selfridge Air Force Base in Michigan described their interrogation by the fbi as well as military authorities. Fort Bragg WACs wrote in *Bragg Briefs* of being questioned and intimidated by the brass who wanted them to "name names" and substantiate "charges" of drug use, homosexuality, or subversive behavior. One WAC wrote that the tactic of publicly dragging people off their jobs to be questioned was working: "WAC company has got us WACs so uptight and paranoid about being reported to the CID as gay, that we avoid sitting together in the dining room or buses. It gets pretty lonely here when you can't even be close friends with other WACs for fear of being labeled gay. Don't let them scare you from relating to your WAC sisters."[17]

Women faced major obstacles in the male military culture in which women traditionally served men. *Helping Hand,* the GI antiwar paper at Mountain Home Air Force Base in Idaho, described lectures on sex that were presented to new female recruits. The easy availability of oral contraceptives, often without a medical examination or warnings about the risks of their use, and the fact that a pregnancy could be "handled with discretion by the Air Force" were among the subjects of these talks to new WAFs. The paper wondered why the Air Force was not more candid about its "true" purpose for recruiting women:

> If WAFs are on this or any other base entirely for the purpose of servicing GIs, then there should be some kind of warning that recruiters give to potential WAFs. Each girl who is thinking of joining the service with the intent of serving her country should know that the recruiter she is talking to is really a pimp for the United States Air Force. The eighteen-year-old girl, fresh out of high school and patriotically motivated should be made aware of how the military is planning to use her.[18]

Enlisted women, many of whom began their military service as self-described flag-wavers, often felt a sense of disillusionment at the reality of their military lives. Unfulfilled promises of education, travel, and other benefits convinced many women that the military did not offer as good a deal as it promised. One Asian-American veteran commented that "when the recruiter said that women never got sent to Vietnam unless they volunteered, I believed her. That was the first—but not the last—time the Army lied to me."[19] Angered at being treated simply as adjuncts to the male military power structure and increasingly aware of the harassment they faced, both as soldiers and as women, female GIs demanded to be taken seriously.

The GI antiwar press provided practically the only forum for discussing women's issues. Often, male writers wrote supportively of the women's situation, as in the following excerpt from *AFB* (*A Four-Year Bummer*), the American Servicemen's Union paper at Chanute Air Force Base in Illinois:

> The WAFS stationed at Chanute are continually oppressed and discriminated against by the brass. They are referred to, and treated in, materialistic ways, as decorations for the "dreary" offices of the brass, and a release for the airmen on Friday night. The brass refer to WAFS as prostitutes and sex objects, and cannot seem to think of women as normal human beings.

The author also pointed to the absence of recreational facilities for women, a hostile atmosphere for women at the servicemen's clubs, movies shown on base that portrayed women as "the main character's playthings, or sex toys," and unrealistic curfews and regulations that prohibited women from being out of the barracks after dark without a male escort. With a sharper analytical perspective than most GI papers, *AFB* argued that military sexism had its roots in "the capitalist economy of this country" and that unequal treatment "dehumanizes men and women." *AFB* took the position that "anything that divides people serves only the pigs, whether it's racism or male chauvinism or inter-squadron rivalry."[20]

Some papers described more than the usual harassment of military women. At Strategic Air Command headquarters at Offut Air Force Base in Omaha, the antiwar paper, *Offul Times*, reported that a WAF unit that had failed a general inspection was assigned a variety of unusual duties:

> Working with little, if any, supplies, our sisters at war have been cleaning in places never touched by civilian janitors. Stripping wax off the floors on their hands and knees until early hours of the morning; scraping paint off windows with razor blades; cleaning vents that haven't been cleaned in a number of years; dusting the inside of BX candy machines; painting over furniture marks on walls; and cleaning stairways with toothbrushes, are only a few examples of

the outrageous "duties" that our sisters in the WAF squadron have been doing.

The article ended with the assertion that no Air Force enlisted person should have to tolerate such excesses of "military discipline." The writer suggested that individual GIs should file grievances against harassing sergeants or officers under Article 138 of the Uniform Code of Military Justice, advice that appeared frequently in GI papers throughout the country.[21]

Occasionally, GI alternative papers reported individual acts of resistance by women, such as the refusal of a WAF at Travis Air Force Base, California, to accept a transfer to the Philippines because of her opposition to this country's presence and investment in third world countries.[22] Many papers also attacked sexism in advertising and editorialized about the importance of legalized abortion as a women's issue.[23] These papers contributed to a process of consciousness raising for military men and women and helped women in particular to make connections between the difficulties in their own lives and debates on women's issues that were taking place in the mainstream culture.

Resistance to the military ethos and demands for an end to officially-sanctioned sexism helped to broaden the base of the GI antiwar movement. By using the only forum available to them, the women who contributed articles and letters to their local base antiwar papers helped to connect the movement for both civil liberties for citizens in uniform and for an end to the war to a call for an end to sexism in the armed forces. Military women, like their enlisted male counterparts, demanded changes in the way this major institution organized itself. Like their civilian counterparts, they began with an understanding of their own oppression and came to realize the extent to which the personal often does represent the political.

Gerald R. Gioglio

In the Belly of the Beast
Conscientious Objectors in the
Military during the Vietnam War

I n 1789 James Madison attempted to include a conscientious objector
clause as part of what ultimately became the Second Amendment
to the Constitution.[1] Madison's proposal did not succeed, and the
struggle between the government's desire to raise troops by force of law,
and the right of the individual to refuse to participate in the military, began. During the Vietnam era, the struggle between state power and individual conscience rose to a fever pitch as both civilians and members of
the armed forces resisted the war.

This paper focuses on a select group within the resistance, in-service
conscientious objectors. These were men who either entered the service
after receiving noncombatant status from their draft boards or who applied for such status, or for discharge, *after* serving some time in the military. Their formal status as conscientious objectors (cos) and their
perceptions of the war offer us a unique perspective, one that is just starting to be explored in the literature.

This project was originally conceived as an analytical study of in-
service conscientious objectors. However, since military personnel and
draft counselor records are confidential, there were no lists of cos from
which to draw a representative random sample. Because respondents had
to be found, I moved from a quantitative to a qualitative approach.

To locate respondents, I made a concerted effort to contact five fellow
cos I had met at Fort Lewis, Washington, in 1968; and on the hunch that

many COs were politicized by their military and antiwar experiences, I placed a number of classified advertisements in several liberal journals. I also informed a number of major veterans organizations and peace groups of this work. Given the size of the sample and the method of selection, those who responded to my search do not necessarily represent all in-service COs from that time. Rather, their views on the war represent a distinctive range of perspectives that is unique—a collective voice that, until recently, has been missing from most discussions of that era. The testimonies collected for this project were published as oral history in *Days of Decision*.[2] This paper utilizes material from that oral history in combination with demographic and attitudinal data not previously published.

The twenty-four individuals who contacted me completed a comprehensive questionnaire which was subsequently used to structure face-to-face and, in a few cases, telephone interviews. The men were asked about their lives prior to entering military service, about important influences that led them to become COs, and about the treatment accorded them by draft board members and military personnel. Those sent overseas were questioned on their experiences in Southeast Asia. All were asked to describe their involvement in antiwar activities and experiences involving court-martial or imprisonment. They were also asked to discuss their postmilitary experiences, especially those related to being a conscientious objector and a veteran.

In-service resistance took many forms, violent and nonviolent, individual and organizational, antimilitary and antiwar.[3] Frequently, participants were returned combat veterans who had become disillusioned and angry over what they had been sent to do, and what they had seen and done. Opposition to the war occurred stateside as well as in Vietnam. Newspapers were published by GIs who also joined GI–civilian organizations, wrote to Congress, participated in demonstrations, formed underground networks to help one another, went AWOL, deserted, refused orders, fragged their superiors, and committed innumerable acts of sabotage against equipment and standard operating procedures. There was even an attempt to organize GIS into a trade union, the American Servicemen's Union.[4]

In 1980, Louis Harris, using an extremely narrow definition of "antiwar activities" concluded that 9 percent of all Vietnam era servicemen (over 900,000 men) did one or more of the following: attended an antiwar rally or a demonstration, wrote letters critical of the war to officials or newspapers, or helped someone avoid the draft.[5]

Harris, however, ignored most of the military-specific forms of resistance, like disobeying orders and similar actions. Thus, the true percentage of Vietnam era GIS involved in such forms of antiwar activity remains unknown. Nevertheless, even though the Harris estimate is conservative, it does point to a high degree of disaffection, much more than any organization can handle without experiencing serious disruptions in standard operating procedures.

Conscientious objection was the legal remedy for men who, by reason of religious training and belief, were opposed to participation in warfare. There were two classifications, those who would agree to perform noncombatant military service (1-A-0) and those who would allow themselves to be drafted *only* into alternative civilian service (1-0). Neither status was easy to obtain. Indeed, local draft board members often considered those who applied for either status as cast from the same mold as nonregistrants or draft evaders.

Many CO applicants had to appear before local boards to be quizzed on their objections. One CO described his hearing as follows:

> A group of old men questioned me about my ethics and my morals. It was a sleazy situation at best—horrendous. It reminded me of being—"backroom down and dirty." I knew I had no chance of getting alternative service. The board was very specific in saying I was qualified for noncombatant military duty.

During the Vietnam era, approximately 172,000 men received 1-0 (alternative service) status from local draft boards.[6] These men were usually assigned to two years alternative civilian service in hospitals, government agencies, or nonprofit organizations. Some local boards were apparently more lenient with 1-A-0 requests, because unlike 1-0 civilian inductees, the induction of noncombatants counted toward fulfillment of military manpower quotas. One CO described it this way:

> Getting a 1-A-O was a piece of cake, because you were saying to them, "I'll go, however, I would like to serve in this capacity." Well, that's no hassle for them, because they're still getting you in the service.

We simply do not know the number of young men who were inducted as 1-A-O conscientious objectors; the Selective Service System never published accurate statistics. For whatever procedural, or more likely political, reasons classifications 1-A-O and 1-A were combined and published only as "available for military service."

Once inducted, most 1-A-O conscientious objectors were trained as medics at Fort Sam Houston, Texas. The COs received regular basic training, minus weapons handling. According to draft literature of the time these trainees were more likely than draftees in general to be sent into combat.[7]

In this study, all eight of the men who entered the military as noncombatants became medics; seven of the eight were sent to Vietnam. An observation from one of the respondents underscores this point:

> There were four platoons in my company. The regular Army went to Germany, the Reserves, and the National Guard went home, all the COs went to Vietnam. It was that clean-cut; we were the cannon fodder.

Data are incomplete on those who filed CO applications while in the military prior to 1965; however, approximately 18,000 applications for discharge or noncombatant status were processed by the various branches of the military between 1965 and 1973.[8] Fourteen of the men in this study applied for CO status *after* having been exposed to military life, or in two cases, to Vietnam. The time between induction and filing for CO status ranged from one to thirty-six months, with an average of twelve months active service.

The relatively small number of GI applications for CO status reported by the military is not surprising for a number of reasons. First, the troops were not told that conscientious objector status could be obtained while in the military. In addition, members of the cadre were often unfamiliar with procedures to be used in processing claims. Further, potential applicants needed good writing and speaking skills to complete the complex CO forms and to detail their objections during interviews, no small chore for the average 18-year-old inductee. Also, as would be expected, men who expressed interest in CO status were discouraged from applying for it by both officers *and* chaplains.

Those who did apply and those who were inducted as noncombatants often reported being harassed and discredited by higher ranking members of the chain of command. In this study, 73 percent of the COs reported harassment—mostly from superiors—that ranged from occasional to most of the time. The reception center experiences of two COs graphically depict this treatment. One reported this event:

> I'm sitting there all by myself and I'm greeted with a yell down the stairs, "Conscientious objector, come out!" They call me out to the parade ground and in front of the whole shebang . . . the sergeant says, "This, gentlemen, is a conscientious objector." They lined the whole company up on bleachers; then the lieutenant walked in front of this company. They started jeering at me, you know— obscenities—everything was just pouring down on me. It was like, "We're going to get you, fella, we're going to take care of you." I was getting scared. There was intense anger coming out of those bleachers. The Army was essentially telling hundreds of men that I was fair game.

And another:

> The sergeant told the group, "See this guy right here? He's not going to have to go through the hell you guys are going to go through. . . . We're going to send him to a little country club in Texas. He won't carry a weapon . . . because he's a conscientious chicken-shit." Later, when they shaved our heads, the barber shaved a couple of furrows right down the middle of my head . . . dry-shaved off my moustache and had me sit in the middle of the room. They told the trainees, "This is the guy who's going to the country club."

In-service claims were reviewed by each applicant's company and base commander, a chaplain, and a psychiatrist before being forwarded to the Department of Defense for final review. This process often took several months. In the meantime, COs were usually placed in holding status and were exempt from military training, weapons handling, and combat. Between 1965 and 1969, only 19 percent of the CO applications filed by active Army personnel were approved. Toward the end of the war, however, as the Army cleaned house of its malcontents, over 80 percent of all applications were affirmed. Approval rates for the services as a whole were comparable: 28 percent approved in 1967, 77 percent in 1972.[9] Of the respondents to this study, eight (47%) of the in-service applicants were discharged, two (12%) were reassigned as noncombatants, and the remainder had their applications denied.

If a CO application was denied, applicants were expected to return to duty. No longer protected by restrictions on training, weapons handling, or in some cases, shipment to Vietnam, these young men had to decide whether to cooperate or to disobey orders. Those who refused to obey were usually court-martialed and sentenced to military stockades or to the United States Disciplinary Barracks at Fort Leavenworth, Kansas. Life in a military prison included experiences some of us might consider surreal. From this study's group of respondents, one of the four COs who was imprisoned for disobeying orders put this in perspective:

> Look at it, if recruits were almost invisible to the caste system of the service, you can imagine how prisoners in the stockade were viewed, something on the order of inventory, something to be kicked, counted, and fed. . . . I saw men being harassed, driven to suicide attempts, insanity, and to odd acts of beauty and kindness. I heard men being beaten, screaming through the walls of . . . maximum security.

Another, who refused to wear his uniform in the stockade, described his personal horror this way:

> They threatened me saying, 'If you take that uniform off we'll break your arm.' I reached up to unbutton it and found myself face down. They put restraining straps on me, wrist cuffs, and a strap to hog-tie me. They carried me to my cell and began to swing me, 'one-two.' And Lord have mercy, I landed on the bunk."

For the most part the respondents were remarkably ordinary individuals, neither saints nor soldiers, who accomplished extraordinary deeds while part of an organization in which they were anathema. They were a heterogeneous group, except that all were white and none were from the more traditional peace church groups, as the Quakers. For the most part, they came from fairly typical social environments and mainstream religions. All but two were raised as Christians, mostly Protestant. Two men were Jewish. None, however, were overtly religious. Many of the COs came from rather conservative backgrounds, and most had parents or close relatives who had been in the military.

The level of support a CO received from family members and non-military friends varied tremendously. It ranged from near total support from wives and girlfriends, to some degree of disapproval, from 55 percent of their fathers and 41 percent of their mothers. An Air Force officer, who filed for CO status after he returned from Vietnam, recalled this reaction from his family:

> I came from a real conservative background . . . my stepfather said he'd never forgive me and my mother said, "James you'll never be able to get a job."

When asked about influences that led to the decision to file as a conscientious objector, the following items were ranked as "very" or "extremely" important:

70% Personal reading/study
45% Religious training
38% What learned from parents
32% Participation in social movements

The questionnaire did not ask specifically about involvement in the youth culture of the 1960s. When interviewed, however, most discussed the power of the counterculture and the music scene in raising their consciousness about the war and other social issues. Said one:

> I don't think you could have believed in the music and . . . the kinds of noises the sixties were making . . . and still have thought about going to Vietnam to defend the "sanctity" of the South Vietnamese political system.

Only a handful of these men had been exposed to radical politics, although about one-third had experience in social movements, usually the civil rights movement. A number, however, had been involved in some form of antiwar activity before being inducted. This antiwar activity ranged from joining an antiwar organization and providing draft counseling to writing letters to newspapers or politicians and attending antiwar seminars.

As young civilians waiting to be drafted, some felt obligated to be in the military, but at the same time, were opposed to killing. Several wanted the best of both worlds in meeting perceived obligations of citizenship while obeying the dictates of conscience. Others, overwhelmed by the prospect of military service, not wishing to expatriate, and unsure of their convictions, enlisted or let themselves be drafted without filing for CO status. Once exposed to the military program, however, beliefs crystallized and several applied for discharge as COs. One, who became a CO as a result of exposure to the military, said:

> It got to the point where the fundamental fact of boot camp became more and more apparent, more and more precisely insane. I was no longer willing to be a medic, the whole thing was fucked at the root, and I would not be part of it.

Another CO, who was eventually discharged, said this:

> Taking bayonet training and watching a movie on escape turned me toward conscientious objection. I realized I was being led by a bunch of maniacs. It came to me that these people had no conception at all of human life. I thought, "how could they make murderers out of people?" I realized it wasn't just what they were doing to the Vietnamese people, but also what they were doing to us.

One stopped cooperating while in Vietnam, saying:

> I felt like part of the chain. . . . No matter what job I did . . . I was contributing to an organization that believed in solving problems by going in and, with force, trying to subdue an entire population.

Comparing those who filed for CO status after some exposure to military life with those who came to the military as noncombatants shows that the former were more likely to have been disciplined because of their

stand. They were more likely to have received nonjudicial punishment
(29% to 13%), and to have been court-martialed (39% to 13%).

All of the COs knew their actions could lead them to prison, and
many prepared themselves psychologically for that possibility. For them,
jail became a viable alternative to further cooperation with the military
system. As several COs pointed out, coming to such a position was no easy
task. Desertion and expatriation were considered by some; but for these
men, such thoughts seemed to be part of the process of arriving at the
decision to be jailed.

Many of the tactics used by the COs were rooted in the classic techniques of nonviolent resistance. Several mentioned reading Ghandi,
Thoreau, and Martin Luther King Jr.. They translated this knowledge of
nonviolent resistance and of the fundamental rights of free speech and
association into personal, and sometimes collective, action. Some of these
actions included: instituting a petition drive among sailors to stop a ship
from returning to Vietnam; distributing GI underground newspapers; attempting to organize chaplains to speak out against the war; taking the
military to court when CO applications were disapproved; refusing to
train; and participating with civilian groups in the larger movement
against the war. In effect, given levels of pre-service activism among this
group, many of these COs acquired "on the job training" in organizing and
resistance while they were GIS.

The presence of COs in the military environment and their model of
personal resistance made it possible for others to question the war and to
look for alternatives to what they were being asked to do. By design and
circumstance, they were engaged by peers and cadre who were interested
in their convictions, and by those seeking advice for a variety of military
and personal problems. Said one:

> I would rap with the new guys and tell them about their options.
> I'd explain conscientious objection . . . and stuff like that. In every
> cycle there would be three or four guys who would put in an applica-
> tion [for discharge].

In-service COs were seen as eccentric, and for many their message
seemed unusual, but virtually all reported that peers respected their positions, even if most disapproved of their stand. One noncombatant reported these in-country conversations:

We'd talk about the war lots of times. You know, what was our State Department's objective, and how were we going to accomplish it? These guys just couldn't picture themselves saying no to the war. It went against their whole concept of family and country. We'd sit and discuss it; yet, for them to stand up against the war, was beyond them. We always had respect for each other, but right up to the last day I was there they'd ask if I wanted to sign out a weapon.

Measures of disapproval reaffirm this, showing lower levels of disapproval from nonconscientious-objector peers than from various levels of the cadre.

A few COs were challenged over issues of patriotism and courage, but those who were were challenged by the cadre. One such incident involved a CO combat medic in Vietnam who said he was accosted by a sergeant,

armed to the teeth, bulging with protective gear, looking at me in my fatigues, going, "You coward!"

Another, who actively organized against the war, said:

Once in awhile someone would say, "you're anti-American," and want to fight with us. We didn't challenge anybody. We just tried to get them to think and to question things.

Then again, the very presence of COs promoted the idea that, under those historical conditions, activities as disrupting the military and working for peace were quite valid expressions of patriotism. "I am *the* patriot," responded one CO, when questioned by grade schoolers during a presentation he gave after the war.

As healers, the daily routine of the noncombatants ranged from the predictable and gentle tasks of ministering to the troops to the random and spontaneous horror experienced in the field. One CO remembered his initial assignment this way:

I was a nineteen-year-old kid with a bag of medicine—and they called me "doc"—and it was real wild.

Another medic described his role as follows:

It was like being a father, confessor, psychologist, everything. Sometimes it was really easy, sometimes . . . really hard, like deciding when somebody was dead, and just moving on.

And another said:

> I was what they needed me to be at the time. If they needed a brain
> surgeon, that's what I was; if they needed a chest surgeon, that's
> what I was. I wasn't those things and I was scared to death that I
> wouldn't be able to cope with serious wounds. So, a lot of what I did
> was automatic.

In addition to detailing their daily struggles to keep men healthy and
alive the COs provide some valuable insights into the problems the military had in conducting this unpopular war. They report on the manipula-
tion of casualty statistics to lessen the impact back home; about soldiers
refusing to go out on patrols; about armed guards monitoring U.S. troops
being shipped to Vietnam to keep them from deserting en route; and
about armed marines assigned to protect aircraft carriers from sabotage
by U.S. sailors.

One CO reports being part of an infantry unit that regularly attempted to avoid contact with the enemy.

> We'd hump until about nine o'clock. That's all we did. We'd lay low
> during the day and [the North Vietnamese and the Viet Cong would]
> lay low. We were not going out there searching and destroying at
> this stage in the game.

Many of the men reported that others in their units were skeptical of
them, of their commitment to conscientious objection, and of their ability
to perform their jobs. That faded as the COs held fast to their positions and
performed their assigned duties. One medic, described it this way:

> To be a medic in Vietnam and to have said, "Okay, I'm going to take
> care of you, and I'm not gonna' carry a gun" was a very personal
> thing that the guys accepted, if you proved your worth in the field. It
> was like, "Either this mother fucker is crazy or he's into some deep,
> heavy, personal shit," and the guys accepted that.

Another, who was sent home after being wounded, said this:

> After the first couple of operations, the guys protected me. These
> were guys who were really skeptical about me at first, but I became
> something special to them, I became *their* medic. That kind of baffled
> me, because I felt like I was not actively involved in the war. I felt like

it was their war, not mine. I was mad and frustrated that there was nothing I could do to stop this idiocy—this lunacy. It wasn't a war, it was just goddamned stupid.

As COs and medics these men were recognized as healers and confidants. Frequently, they were a voice of reason in an atmosphere that often reeked of confusion, meanness, and violence. One reported this incident:

> One day we had a suspected VC in custody. My lieutenant told one of the younger guys to take him out and kill him. He came back all upset, just shaking. He said, "Doc, I don't think I'll be able to do that again." I said, "You don't have to do it again, that's ridiculous. Tell him you're not going to do it."

And another:

> I did intervene to stop senseless violence against Vietnamese civilians. Once a guy . . . was roughin' up mama san. I said, "Back off. If you hit her again, I'm gonna' cut your fuckin' head off." . . . that's how crazy you could get over there. He said, "Okay, doc. Okay."

Field medics were highly respected, but there was a limit to what they could do. Their training was geared mainly toward stabilizing the sick and wounded and shipping them back to medical professionals. In doing so, some saw more than their share of injury and death. One medic worked at a MASH (Mobil Army Surgical Hospital, or triage) unit; because of the number of dead he saw he was called a walking war memorial by other Vietnam veterans. From his perspective:

> The best way to know about war is to ask a medic. . . . mass death, death on a grand scale . . . to me it was so dark, so evil. There was no value to life. If parents only knew how valueless their children's lives were; we really didn't care. You can't care, mass death is just that.

Vietnam era veterans who chose to separate themselves from the military program, either by becoming antiwar GIs or by drawing the line at participating in certain actions, often suffered as much self-doubt and guilt as those combat veterans who later came to question what they had been sent to do. Two of the cos in this study became "trip-wire GIs," retreating from society, traveling and living in isolation, in one case for years. Experiences of post-traumatic stress disorder were reported by six of the seven in-country medics; overall, 57 percent of the respondents reported having trouble adapting to civilian life. Many of the classic symptoms were there: night terrors, guilt, escapism, and rage. As one expressed it:

> I would sweat through my bedding, mattress and everything. I'd do it night, after night, after night. These were horrific, awful, black dreams. I'd wake up, stark awake, at any sound, and I'd just be drenched with sweat. This carried on for quite a few years; it was my penalty for going, I think.

And another:

> When I got back to the States, I didn't recognize my emotions anymore. It was like I didn't have any. About eight years down the road I started feeling again, but I didn't understand what I was feeling. I actively contemplated suicide. I felt like I was being tortured and I didn't know what I had done to deserve it.

And another:

> During those first few years I was scared, walking the streets at night. I was giving blood downtown, giving blood to make money, hanging out at bus stations, shit like that.

We have grown accustomed to hearing these reports from those who did the fighting, but it was surprising to find that even those who resisted the war felt the pain. It is suggested that whether one opposed the war or actively participated in it, whether one served as a healer or got caught up in unnecessary killing, the moral and ethical dilemmas raised by the very fact of America's presence in Vietnam were often overwhelming. Vietnam was Vietnam, and being caught up in it, on any level, hurt.

The respondents were asked whether or not they agreed or disagreed with a series of statements concerning their experiences. Detail on their responses demonstrates that, for most, the co experience ranks as the critical life event which led many to involvement in other social causes. Further, these men wanted to be known as conscientious objectors *and* as veterans, even though a significant minority had trouble thinking of themselves as veterans. Virtually all expressed concern over the postwar problems of those who fought the war. One CO summed up these feelings nicely by saying:

> The Vietnam era is not necessarily something people are proud of, but I am proud of having been discharged as a conscientious objector. I stood up for myself, declared what I valued, what I wanted, and I got my way. That experience also made me more inclined to speak out against things I don't think are fair, and to support things I think should be done.

Indeed, a large number of these men continued to be active in the antiwar movement after discharge and even into the mid-1980s when these interviews were conducted.

The statistics alone do not tell the whole story. Many have made peacemaking a way of life, becoming "lifers" in the war against war. Some are very active, working with peace and antiwar veterans groups. Others make peacemaking part of their daily lives, attempting to raise consciousness on their jobs or in their communities. One of these described his role this way:

> I tell people of my experiences and compare what happened to me then, with what is happening now. I talk about peace, weapons spending, and nuclear power. I'm effective in informal, one-on-one situations, just talking and bringing these things into casual conversation. My role, these days, is just to share what I've learned.

One CO, who spent eighteen months in Fort Leavenworth prison, told me, "I was made in America;" a revealing insight, one that is significant in understanding GI opposition to the Vietnam War. Indeed, resistance to the war can be viewed as a natural product of the political, cultural, and moral socialization of the young in American society. Ultimately, that training came smack up against the reality of the Vietnam War, the result being that masses of young men could not jibe what they were taught with what they were being asked to do. Many, falling back on what they learned, became resisters in the military. The COs may have occupied the moral and spiritual center of the in-service resistance, but masses of others registered their opposition in a variety of other important ways, from the personal to the political.

Despite the popular view, these decisions to act or to refuse to act did not reflect an absence of patriotism. Rather, those who opposed the war, like those who supported it, were attempting to put into practice the very same values of truth and justice learned from the major socializing institutions that shaped their lives. These were acts of defiance that are deeply rooted in the American spirit, a form of patriotism that demands resistance to intolerable laws or behavior. As servicemen rising up in resistance, this generation of citizen-soldiers seized history. Together with other antiwar GIs and civilians they not only helped to put an end to conscription, but forced an end to the war.

One last observation. In the 1980s we finally began to listen to Vietnam veterans and to let them come home. And return they have, flooding the literature and art of this nation with their memories and their tears. Most recently, films as *Casualties of War* and *Born on the Fourth of July* have gone a step further in exploring issues of conscience and morality in warfare. Perhaps now the nation is ready to examine the legacy of America's antiwar veterans. Perhaps, as a people, we are ready to consider the contributions these veterans made to ending the killing of Americans and Vietnamese. Perhaps, finally, we have reached a point where we can celebrate their commitment to peace and human dignity. And perhaps, as the healing continues, the 1990s will be the time when we welcome them home, too.

Barbara Ehrenreich

Legacies of the 1960s
New Rights and New Lefts

We have come to think of the 1960s as a period of a great left upsurge, but it was also a time when the groundwork for much of contemporary *right wing* ideology and analysis was developed.[1] This occurred principally in reaction to the student Left and was the intellectual product of men and women who had, to greater or lesser degrees, considered themselves to be *on the Left*, at least until the late 1960s. There were the intellectuals who became known in the 1970s as neoconservatives.

This essay will reflect on the period as a time of critical rupture within American liberalism and will examine what it was about the politics of the New Left that helped inspire this rupture, that is, what was distinctive about the New Left as compared to the Old. Given the global crisis of the socialist Left as the twentieth century draws to a close, there is a special urgency to rediscovering the politics of the New Left.

The conventional story of what happened to American politics in the 1960s is that the New Left and the civil rights movement inspired a blue-collar blacklash that became the basis of an ascendant right-wing populism from the period of Nixon and Agnew to that of Reagan and Bush. There is some truth to this analysis, but it overestimates the extent of the blue-collar backlash. First, the American working class was more opposed to the Vietnam War than has generally been acknowledged in most histories of the period. The latter part of the decade also saw an upsurge in working-class militance in the form of strikes and job actions, an aspect of 1960s history that awaits serious attention. Second, the conventional wisdom leaves out the intellectual or academic backlash that was a response especially to the student movement (more than to the civil rights movement) and was critical to the development of the Right.

The breadth and fury of the intellectual–academic backlash were startling, as was the diversity in background and intellectual orientation of its spokespersons.[2] Psychiatrist Bruno Bettelheim likened student rebels to Nazis.[3] Then-liberal Professor John Silber, later the conservative president of Boston University, called them "the new fascisti."[4] Nathan Glazer compared student New Leftists not only to Hitler, but to Lenin and Stalin,[5] and Daniel Bell described the students at Columbia University as "impelled not to innovation, but to destruction."[6] Critic Irving Kristol, not yet a conservative, called them "rebels without a cause—and without a hope of accomplishing anything except mischief and ruin."[7]

Nor were the howls of outrage only from the liberal center of the political spectrum. Marxist Eugene Genovese attacked the "nihilist perversions" of the student Left.[8] Socialist Irving Howe dismissed the student movement as "romantic primitivism," motivated by a "quasi-religious impulse."[9] Philosopher and former Marxist Sidney Hook organized faculty members on ninety-seven campuses into a Coordinating Center for Democratic Opinion in order to combat the student insurgency.[10] And leftist William Appleman Williams, whose critiques of United States foreign policy were deeply influential within the New Left, had this to say of the movement that included so many of his young fans: "They are the most selfish people I know. They just terrify me. They are acting out a society I'd like to live in as an orangutan."[11]

I remember that academic backlash and how hurt many of us on the New Left were to be attacked by people we had admired or imagined to be roughly on our side. We have often been criticized since for our intransigence, our hostility to liberals and older people, but the truth is, *they turned on us first.*

The single thing about the student Left that most appalled and fascinated its adult intellectual antagonists, especially those intellectuals who had come from the Marxist Left, was that it was comprised of relatively affluent young people. This fact became central to their efforts to discredit the student Left. According to simplistic versions of Marxist theory, the affluent should not rebel; revolution was a prerogative of the economically oppressed, preferably the industrial working class. The fact that many college students were relatively affluent led to both psychological and sociological theories of the New Left, neither of them the least bit flattering.

The psychological theory emerged first, around 1968. Put simply, this theory posited that student rebels were spoiled brats: they had everything, and yet they were still complaining. Put more eloquently, the theory analyzed student rebellion as a tragic error in middle-class child rearing, usually referred to as "permissiveness." David Truman, the administrator who had unleashed the police on the Columbia University students in 1968, blamed campus unrest on "the permissive doctrines of Dr. Benjamin Spock.[12] Among the academics, Edward Shils described the students as "a uniquely indulged generation," led astray by "parents who were . . . persuaded of the merits of hedonism."[13] Looking back from the 1970s, sociologist Robert Nisbet fulsomely indicted "[the] massive doses of affection, adulation, devotion, permissiveness [bestowed on the youth by their parents and] a whole national mood not only of indulgence but of almost awed, perhaps guilt-ridden, adoration of the young."[14] Dr. Bruno Bettelheim added the weight of medical respectability to the outcry against "permissiveness": "I have known mothers of extreme campus activists who, when the children were infants, fed them goodies against inner resistance because that is what good mothers were supposed to do."[15] In his view, the students had lost that indispensable middle-class virtue, the capacity for "delayed gratification." As babies, they had been given the bottle whenever they wanted, so that as adolescents they had no "inner controls" and readily resorted to "violence" to get their way.

Thus went the first establishment explanation of the New Left, that it was a prolonged tantrum on the part of over-fed, over-indulged, affluent young people. This became the theme of Spiro Agnew's 1968 campaign, in which he blamed the student movement on "affluent, permissive, upper-middle-class parents who learned their Dr. Spock and threw discipline out the window." Agnew's recommended remedy was "a good spanking."[16]

The sociological theory of the New Left came into prominence a bit later, in the early 1970s, a time when the New Left was largely dead, but still the subject of obsessive interest on the part of the intellectuals associated with the backlash. In brief, this theory argues that student rebels were the shock troops of a New Class, an affluent class of white-collar "mental workers" that was bent on taking power in the United States and turning it into a Soviet-style bureaucratic dictatorship.

The idea of a New Class was very much an idea *from the Left*, the Old Left, in fact, the old Trotskyist Left, and had emerged as part of the explanation for what had gone wrong with Soviet socialism. The theory, which grew out of anarchist as well as Trotskyist thinking, was that communist societies really represented not a "dictatorship of the proletariat," but a victory for a new class of intellectuals and bureaucrats who had become the ruling class. From there, it was only a small intellectual leap to seeing the New Left as the advance guard of a New Class takeover in this country. As Norman Podhoretz speculated, "the New Class was using its own young people as commandos, sending them into the streets to clash with the enemy's troops (the police and the National Guard) while the "elders" directed the grand strategy from behind the lines and engaged in less dangerous forms of political warfare against the established power."[17]

It remained for the New Right that arose in the mid-1970s to take these theories of the student movement and synthesize them into a single theory of what is wrong with American society. Ironically, given the provenance of these backlash theories, what was wrong, from the New Right's point of view, was liberalism. Essentially, the New Right thinkers of the 1980s—including Michael Novak, Tom Wolfe, Pat Buchanan, and many others—extrapolated from the sociological explanation of the New Left to argue that America had *already* been taken over by the New Class, which they refer to colloquially as the liberal elite. Thus the right effectively utilized a rhetorical weapon that had been fashioned by liberals for use against the New Left, against the former liberals themselves. In New Right theory, the New Class controls the media, the universities, the foundations, and much of the government, at the very least. This New Class theory provided the blunt, all-purpose way of discrediting the ideological enemy. Anything that liberals or leftists do can be dismissed as another cunning scheme to advance their own class power.

Here, for example, is Michael Novak, in a 1972 article in *Commentary*, arguing that the student Left's moral causes could all be reduced to an effort to advance its own class interests:

> The New Class covers its political campaigns . . . with an aura of morality so thick it would make the righteous Anglo-Saxons of a century ago envious. Because two of its chief causes—civil rights

(including poverty) and resistance to the Indochinese war—are morally sound, it has been able to conceal its own lust for power and its own class interests, at least from itself.[18]

Liberal goals could now be discredited as cover-ups for New Class ambitions: supposedly generous impulses could be exposed as self-serving strategies. Above all, any efforts on behalf of the poor could now be understood as a scheme to fatten the public sector and expand the career opportunities of its New Class operatives. As Podhoretz summed up this insight, the New Class represented itself as "concerned only with . . . the good of others (especially the poor and the blacks), but what it really wanted was to aggrandize its own power."[19]

This leads to the Orwellian insistence by many neoconservatives that any effort to bring about greater *equality* is actually a camouflage for the schemes of a power-hungry elite. Take, for instance, Pat Buchanan's attacks on Mario Cuomo for his "incessant" invocation of the poor and downtrodden, which Buchanan characterizes as an attempt to augment the power of his own class, the "Welfare Statists." But probably the most important effect of this right-wing formulation, which goes back to the backlash against the student movement in the 1960s, has been to discredit the concept of liberalism, simply by its repeated association with the word "elite." One need only recall candidate George Bush's pseudopopulist attacks on Michael Dukakis and the "L word" in 1988.

The psychological theory of the student Left also came to play a key role in right-wing thought. As we have seen, "permissiveness" in the 1960s referred to the childraising practices that supposedly explained the absence of "middle-class values," such as hard work and delayed gratification, among student rebels. By the 1980s, "permissiveness" connoted a general moral laxity, characterized by both indulgence toward others (such as criminals, the poor, and the young) and *self*-indulgence. Permissiveness became the central problem with liberalism, liberals, or any policy or idea that could be vaguely imagined as liberal. In fact, by the 1980s, permissiveness became a code word for the moral breakdown that supposedly pervaded American society, as this observation from the *Conservative Digest* suggests: "George Washington was not a permissive individual. He did not come from a permissive family. So the United States did not begin as a permissive society. Is it too late to go back to our beginnings?[20]

This pervasive permissiveness is localized as a form of personal decadence in the New Class or Liberal Elite. For example, an article by New Right theorist Samuel T. Francis contrasts the liberal elite's "cosmopolitan ethic" with the "domestic ethic" supposedly upheld by the white working class. Conveniently, from an employer's point of view, the workers still uphold "the duty of work . . . the social and human necessity of sacrifice and deferral of gratification." The New Class's "cosmopolitan ethic," on the other hand, "idealizes material indulgence, the glorification of the self, and the transcendence of conventional values, loyalties, and social bonds." What kind of person exemplifies this self-serving "ethic," and hence the spirit of the entire New Class? Francis suggests Mick Jagger.[21]

It is worth noting that, by the 1980s, the New Right was not using these notions of permissiveness and the New Class to attack student rebels, or even liberals. Their principal target was the *poor*, and their reasoning went as follows:

❋ Anti-poverty efforts and programs represent New Class permissiveness toward the poor.

❋ Permissiveness spoils children, and it also "spoils" the poor, undermining their morale and work ethic and, in effect, making them poorer. Or, in Charles Murray's stunningly Orwellian formulation, "Welfare causes poverty."

❋ The best thing to do for the poor is to cut all those vicious, indulgent, permissive programs, which is what Ronald Reagan attempted as president and almost succeeded in doing.

Arising, as it did, in response to the student Left these right-wing views have to be seen as another legacy of the great upheaval and rupture within the broad Left—Old and New, old and young, liberal and radical—in the 1960s. To return to the political legacy of the New Left itself: Why did this rupture occur? Why was there such a furious response to the New Left on the part of people who often agreed, more or less, on the issues of Vietnam and civil rights? Why was there an intellectual–academic backlash that created the new intelligentsia of the Right? Of course, neoconservatism and the rightward turn of America's intellectuals during and after the 1960s also reflected concerns that had little to do with the student movement—for Israel, for example, and against black urban demands for "community control." There were also *ad hominem* explanations, e.g., the backlash reflected the affluence, not of students, but of their adult critics, who may have been Marxists in their youth, but had become comfortably ensconced in their positions, particularly in the university. The student Left, for better or for worse, had made the academy one of its targets. I remember the argument of some older Marxists critical of the New Left: We have a toe-hold in the academy—don't screw up!

But neoconservatism, and hence so much of current right-wing ideology, was also a response to the *politics* of the New Left, especially the ideas that represented the most decisive break from the traditional politics of the Left, both Trotskyist and communist. It is important to understand how much the New Left represented, not just an upsurge of "the Left," but a radical break from the socialist and communist traditions that had for so long defined Leftism. Consider the New Left's definition of democracy. Probably nothing appalled and terrified most older left-wing intellectuals more than the radical anti-hierarchical positions of the New Left, which rejected both hierarchical and representative forms of governance in favor of a "participatory democracy" in which each person was assumed to have an equally valuable contribution to make to the decision-making process. Participatory democracy was consistent with New Left attacks on forms of social authority vested in professionalism, claims of "expertise," and bureaucratic position.

This amounted to a direct attack on the power and privileges of the professoriate. By and large, the student Left did not say that their knowledge was useless or irrelevant (although some said that too!) but that it was not, in principle, superior to the knowledge that other people gained through life experience, for example, the experience of poverty and oppression. They said, "Why should we listen to you? If the issue is poverty, why not listen to a woman on welfare? Or, if the subject is foreign policy, to a Vietnamese peasant?" Nothing was more threatening to the men who led the academic backlash and who, in fact, wrote copious defenses of professionalism and hierarchies of expertise. Thus, in contrast to the New Right's theories, it was really the student Left that attacked New Class privilege, and it was the academic backlash that represented a *defense* of New Class power. In this respect, the New Left represented a direct break from the Old Left tradition that did indeed often see socialism as something that would be "engineered" by cadres of professionals and experts.

This New Left was not simply a continuation of the socialist tradition, it was also a rebuke to that tradition, and this is a major reason that so many of the (Old) Left could see nothing of any redeeming social value in the New. It really did break with their Old Left tradition. It really did represent something new. In addition to challenging the hierarchies of expertise, the student Left rejected a vision of socialism as essentially a redistribution of what there is to have within capitalism. They did not want "more," they wanted something qualitatively different. They wanted to break with what Jack Kerouac had called the chain of "production–consumption–production" of objects that could never satisfy our deepest needs for meaning. This was profoundly upsetting to older, more conventional leftists, who could only see in young radicals' political vision some inexplicable outbreak of self-indulgent countercultural utopianism. If there was a rupture on the left in the 1960s, it was because the New Left at its best had less in common with the socialist tradition of the Second, Third, and Fourth Internationals than with the utopian socialism of the nineteenth century, with anarchism, and with situationism.

I would like to conclude with some thoughts on the present decade of the 1990s. It is a key fact that the Old Left is dead for reasons that many radicals understood twenty-five years ago. The vision of socialism as an (at best) paternalistic, centrally-planned economy, a vision that led, perversely, both to Stalinism and to American neoconservatism, is no longer anyone's vision of human liberation.

It is our job, as scholars and activists, to resurrect the alternative vision of human liberation that had just begun to be developed by the New Left and the civil rights movement in the 1960s. This is a vision that includes not only economic justice, but also radical democracy and participation. It is this alternative left politics that inspired feminism and the environmental and European green movements, that now represents, I believe, the best (and perhaps the last best) hope for humankind.

Notes

Introduction   Barbara L. Tischler

1. See D. Michael Shafer, ed., *The Legacy: The Vietnam War in the American Imagination* (Boston: Beacon Press, 1990). Two recent review articles consider some of the newer books on the 1960s. See Maurice Isserman, "The Not So Dark and Bloody Ground, New Works on the 1960s," *The American Historical Review* 94, no. 4 (October 1989): 990–1010 and Winifred Breines, "Whose New Left?" *The Journal of American History* 75, no. 2 (September 1988): 528–545. Maurice Isserman and Michael Kazin offer an appreciation of the complex history of the New Left in "The Failure and Success of the New Radicalism," in Steve Fraser and Gary Gerstle, eds., *The Rise and Fall of the New Deal Order, 1930–1980* (Princeton: Princeton University Press, 1989), 212–242. Former Trotskyist movement leader, Tim Wohlforth, contributed a review essay, "America in the Sixties" to *New Left Review* no. 178 (July–August, 1989)

2. I appreciate input from the students from Columbia and Barnard Colleges, the School of General Studies, the Graduate School of Arts and Sciences, and the Master of Arts in Liberal Studies Program at Columbia University who took my seminar on "America in the 1960s" in the Spring of 1991. Sources on the 1960s can be found in Judith Clavir Albert and Stewart Edward Albert, *The Sixties Papers* (New York: Praeger, 1984) and the oral histories that form the basis of Milton Viorst's *Fire in the Streets*, (New York: Simon & Schuster, 1979). A new journal, *Vietnam Generation*, edited and published by Kalí Tal, brings new sources and new scholarship together, with a focus on the Vietnam War and its aftermath in the United States and abroad. Ken Wachsberger recently edited two volumes that provide valuable insights into the operation of the underground press in the 1960s and early 1970s as well as bibliographic information on new scholarship on the underground press. See *Voices from the Underground: Insider Histories of the Vietnam Era Underground Press* and *Voices from the Underground: A Directory of Resources and Sources* (Ann Arbor: Pierian Press, 1991).

3. See especially James Miller, *"Democracy Is in the Streets": From Port Huron to the Seige of Chicago* (New York: Simon & Schuster, 1987); Todd Gitlin, *Years of Hope, Days of Rage* (New York: Bantam, 1987); and David Caute, *The Year of the Barricades: A Journey Through 1968* (New York: Harper & Row, 1988). These are useful volumes, but they tend to focus on what their authors consider to be the most important aspects of the period, specifically within the New Left. Recent efforts to document all or a major part of the 1960s generally also focus on the familiar and the important. The PBS series, "Making Sense of the Sixties," that first aired in January of 1991, suffered from its own effort to cover almost everything and, as a result, it didn't analyze or make much sense of anything. The California Newsreel documentary, "Berkeley in the Sixties," was a more focused effort that still gave the impression that there was a "good" sixties that gave us the Free

235

Speech Movement and a "bad" time of violence, hippie excesses, and protests that all came to an end with the re-taking of the People's Park. The continued commitment to social change of the activists interviewed for this film gives a very different impression of the idea of a precise end to the 1960s, as most are still active in community organizing and working for social change.

Lyndon Johnson and the Democratization   Mark Stern
of the Party Process

1. Doris Kearns, *Lyndon Johnson and the American Dream* (New York: New American Library, 1976), 177.

2. *Public Papers of the Presidents: Lyndon B. Johnson, 1963-1964* (Washington, D.C.: U.S. Government Printing Office, 1965), I, 705. Hereafter references to this source are cited as: *PPP: LBJ, 1963–1964.*

3. Mark Stern, "Lyndon Johnson and the Democrats' Civil Rights Strategy," *Humboldt Journal of Social Relations* 16(1990): 1–29. Forthcoming.

4. Leslie McLemore, "The Mississippi Freedom Democratic Party: A Case Study of Grass Roots Politics" (Ph.D. diss., University of Massachusetts, 1971), 112–17. On the MFDP and the 1964 Democratic National Convention see also: David C. Colby, "Protest and Party: A Revisionist Study of the Mississippi Freedom Democratic Party" (Paper presented at the Annual Meeting of the Southern Political Science Association, November 1985).

5. Theodore H. White, *The Making of the President: 1964* (New York: Atheneum, 1965), 93.

6. F. Clifton White, *Suite 3505* (New Rochelle, N.Y.: Arlington House, 1967), 20–98; William A. Rusher, *The Rise of the Right* (New York: William Morrow, 1984), 87–127.

7. Barry Goldwater, *The Conscience of a Conservative* (New York: Hillman, 1960), 35.

8. *New York Times*, April 2, 1964.

9. Quoted in Stewart Alsop, "Can Goldwater Win?," *Saturday Evening Post*, 24 (August 24, 1963): 14.

10. Neil MacNeil, *Dirksen: Portrait of a Public Man* (New York: World Publishing, 1970), 238; *New York Times*, June 18, 1964; June 18, 1964, *Congressional Record*, 88th Cong., 2nd sess., 110: 14319.

11. *New York Times*, July 17, 1964, emphasis in original.

12. White, *Making of the President: 1964*, 217.

13. John H. Kessel, *The Goldwater Coalition: Republican Strategies in 1964* (Indianapolis, In.: Bobbs-Merrill, 1968).

14. *New York Times*, July 20, 1964.

15. *New York Times*, July 19, 1964.

16. Martin Luther King, Jr., News Release, July 16, 1964, Martin Luther King Papers, box 20–15, Martin Luther King Center for Social Change, Atlanta, Georgia. Hereafter materials from the King Center are cited as MLKC.

17. White, *Making of the President: 1964*, 221–231.

18. *PPP: LBJ, 1963–1964*, 890–891.

19. Hobart Taylor, Jr., to Lyndon Johnson, July 17, 1964, White House Central Files, Ex/Hu2, Box 2, Lyndon Baines Johnson Library, Austin, Texas. Hereafter, all materials

from this library are noted as LBJL. Materials from the White House Central Files are here-after noted as WHCF.

20. Roy Wilkins to Martin Luther King, Jr., James Farmer, Whitney M. Young, Jr., A. Philip Randolph, and John Lewis, July 22, 1964, Papers of the NAACP, Transfiles, "Government–National Elections, Miscellany, 1964," Library of Congress, Washington, D.C.. Hereafter, materials from the Library of Congress are noted as LC.

21. Lee White, Memorandum for the White House Files, July 6, 1964, WHCF, Ex/Hu2, Box 2, LBJL.

22. Roy Wilkins with Tom Mathews, *Standing Fast: The Autobiography of Roy Wilkins* (New York: Viking Penguin, 1984), 303. Johnson always publicly called for the public to understand that the riots were linked to legitimate, underlying grievances. See, for example, *New York Times*, July 12, 18, 1964; Lee White to Lyndon Johnson, Notes for Meeting with Negro Leaders, August 18, 1964, WHCF, Ex/Hu 2, Box 3, LBJL.

23. Lyndon Johnson, Telephone calls to Roy Wilkins July 27, 28, Daily Diary, July, 1964, LBJL. For a view of these events which sees the president as more directly manipulating this meeting see: Bruce Miroff, "Presidential Leverage over Social Movements: The Johnson White House and Civil Rights," *Journal of Politics* 43 (February 1981): 12–13.

24. James Farmer, *Lay Bare the Heart: An Autobiography of the Civil Rights Movement*, (New York: Arbor House, 1985), 298–299; Farmer, interviewed by Thomas H. Baker, April 30, 1969, 2, LBJL.

25. Statement of Civil Rights Organization Leaders, July 29, 1964, Papers of the NAACP, Transfiles, "Civil Rights, General, 1963–1964," LC; *New York Times*, July 30, 1964.

26. *New York Times*, August 2, 1964.

27. George H. Gallup, *The Gallup Poll: Public Opinion, 1936–1970* (New York: Random House, 1972), III, 1881, 1894, 1896, 1902. In July Goldwater was favored over Johnson in the South by 51% to 40%. By August the Goldwater–Johnson figures were 47% to 46%. See also: *New York Times*, August 24, 1964. Poll results confirm that the Johnson lead never was substantially diminished by Goldwater. See: *New York Times*, October 6, and November 3, 1964.

28. John Stewart, interviewed by Carl Solberg, June 21, 1970, 6, Minnesota Historical Society, Minneapolis, Minnesota. Hereafter cited as MHS.

29. Marion Barry, interviewed by Katherine Shannon, October 30, 1967, 42, Moorland-Spingarn Research Center, Howard University. Hereafter cited as MSRC.

30. McLemore, "The Mississippi Freedom" 128–129.

31. Joseph L. Rauh, Jr., interviewed by Anne Cooke Romaine, June 16, 1967, 310, MSRC. This oral history may be found in Anne Cook Romaine, "The Mississippi Freedom Democratic Party Through August, 1964," (Ph.D. diss., University of Virginia, 1969).

32. Ibid. Unless otherwise noted, the chronology of various pressures brought on Rauh and the Rauh quotations in this section are from this interview of Rauh by Romaine.

33. David J. Garrow, *Bearing the Cross: Martin Luther King, Jr., and the Southern Christian Leadership Conference* (New York: William Morrow, 1986), 347; U.S. Congress, Select Committee to Study Governmental Operations with Respect to Intelligence Activities, *Intelligence Activities and the Rights of American*, Book II, Final Report, 94th Cong., 2nd sess., April 26, 1976, 117–118. Approximately thirty FBI agents were involved in this electronic surveillance which included hidden room microphones and telephone taps on Martin Luther King, Jr.

34. Jack T. Conway, interviewed by author, July 21, 1990, 1–2. Transcript in possession of the author.

35. Joseph L. Rauh, Jr., "Remarks in Rebuttal of Joseph L. Rauh, Jr., Mississippi Freedom Democratic Party before the Credentials Committee of the Democratic National Convention, August 22, 1964, Appendix," Papers of Joseph L. Rauh, Jr., Box 86, LC.

36. Clayborne Carson, *In Struggle: SNCC and the Black Awakening of the 1960s* (Cambridge, Mass.: Harvard University Press, 1981), 124.

37. Conway interview, July 21, 1990, 12.

38. *New York Times*, August 19, 1964.

39. Rowland Evans and Robert Novak, *Lyndon B. Johnson: The Exercise of Power* (New York: New American Library, 1966), 435–448. On Humphrey as the most popular choice for the vice-presidential nomination among the Democratic delegates see: *New York Times*, July 31, 1964.

40. Harry McPherson, interviewed by T. H. Baker, March 24, 1969, Tape 2, 10, LBJL.

41. On Johnson's lecture: Bayard Rustin, telephone conversation with Ralph Helstein, August 19, 1964, FBI King File, MLKC. On the black leadership position see Arnold Aronson, "Memo to Cooperating Organizations," August 13, 1964, Papers of the National Urban League, Pt II, 1, A, Box 2, LC; Roy Wilkins to NAACP Branch and Youth Group Presidents, "Re: Support for Mississippi Freedom Party Delegation at Democratic National Convention in Atlantic City, New Jersey," August 12, 1964, Papers of the NAACP, III, B 375, LC; News Release, "Seat Freedom Delegates, NAACP Urges Democrats," August 21, 1964, Transfiles, NAACP, II, Government–National, Elections–Democratic Party, 1964, LC.

42. Evans and Novak, *Johnson and the Exercise of Power*, 452; George Reedy, News conference transcript, August 19, 1964, National Security Files, Volume 1, LBJL. Evans and Novak report the Johnson-Humphrey meeting as occurring on August 20, right after the president's meeting with the black leaders. The Reedy news conference places the president's meeting with the black leaders on August 19.

43. Stewart interviewed June 21, 1970, 6, MHS.

44. Hubert H. Humphrey, *The Education of a Public Man: My Life in Politics* (New York: Doubleday, 1976), 299.

45. Joseph L. Rauh Jr., "Remarks in Rebuttal," Rauh Papers, Box 86, LC.

46. Len Holt, *The Summer That Didn't End*, (London: William Heinemann, 1965) 168–169; White, *Making of the President: 1964*, 291–292. See also the oral history transcript in: "The Winona Incident," Appendix 1 in Pat Watters and Reece Cleghorn, *Climbing Jacob's Ladder: The Arrival of Negroes in Southern Politics* (New York: Harcourt, Brace & World, 1967), 362–375.

47. Rauh, interviewed by author, June 29, 1990, 2. Transcript in possession of author.

48. Conway interview, July 21, 1990, 2–3.

49. Rauh-Stern interview, June 28, 1990, 2.

50. Conway interview, July 21, 1990, 5–6. Material on the Johnson-Reuther relationship is drawn from this interview.

51. Conway interview, July 21, 1990, 5.

52. Rauh-Romaine interview, June 16, 1967, 338, MSRC.

53. Walter F. Mondale, interviewed by author, July 23, 1990, 1. Transcript in possession of author.

54. Mondale interview, July 23, 1990 1–2.

55. Conway interview, July 21, 1990, 4–5.

56. Rauh-Stern interview, June 29, 1990, 2.

57. Rauh-Romaine interview, June 16, 1967, 341–345, MSRC.

58. *New York Times*, July 26, 1964.

59. Aaron Henry, telephone interview with author, July 23, 1990, 1. Transcript in possession of author.

60. Milton Viorst, *Fire in the Streets: America in the 1960s* (New York: Simon & Schuster, 1979), 265; Rauh-Stern interview, June 29, 1990, 3.

61. Rauh-Stern interview, June 29, 1990, 2.

62. Wilkins, *Standing Fast*, 305–306.

63. Rauh-Romaine interview, June 16, 1967, 353, MSRC; James Forman, *The Making of Black Revolutionaries* (New York: Macmillan, 1972), 302.

64. McLemore, "The Mississippi Freedom," 153.

65. Forman, *Making of Black Revolutionaries*, 393; John Lewis interviewed by Steven F. Lawson, 1970, 8, Columbia University Oral History Collection, New York, New York.

66. Aaron Henry and Ed King to John W. McCormack, Chairman, Democratic National Convention, August 26, 1964, Rauh Papers, Box 86, LC.

67. Aaron E. Henry, Position Paper, August 29, 1964, Rauh Papers, Box 86, LC.

68. Aaron Henry quoted in: Garrow, *Bearing the Cross*, 349.

69. Allen J. Matusow, *The Unravelling of America: A History of Liberalism in the 1960* (New York: Harper & Row, 1984), 142.

70. Rauh interviewed by Paige Mulhollan, July 30, 1969, III, 7–8, LBJL.

71. Charles Diggs to Elizabeth Hirshfield, August 27, 1964, Mississippi Freedom Democratic Party Files, Box 4, MLKC.

72. Richard N. Goodwin, *Remembering America* (New York: Harper & Row, 1988), 302.

73. Evans and Novak, *Johnson and the Exercise of Power*, 481.

74. *New York Times*, November 4, and 5, 1964; Richard Rovere, "Letter from Washington," *New Yorker* (January 16, 1965): 126.

75. See list of reform committees provided in William Crotty, *Party Reform* (New York: Longman, 1983), 38.

76. Austin Ranney, *Curing the Mischiefs of Faction: Party Reform in America* (Berkeley: University of California Press, 1975), 182–183.

77. Democratic National Committee, *Preliminary Call for the 1968 Democratic National Convention* (Washington, D.C.: Democratic National Committee, 1967), Section II, "Qualifications of State delegations."

78. Ranney, *Curing the Mischiefs*, 184.

79. Crotty, *Party Reform*, 136.

Agent Orange on Campus   Jonathan Goldstein

1. "Scientists Speak Out on CB Weapons," *Bulletin of the Atomic Scientists* 22, no. 9 (November 1966): 39–40. According to the *New York Times*, after the 1966 protest by twenty-two American scientists, White House sources "left no doubt" that the Administration would continue using chemicals in South Vietnam (*New York Times*, September 21, 1966). Other media coverage of anti-CBW protest in 1966 included: *Le Monde*, January

18, 1966; *Science* 151, no. 3708 (January 28, 1966): 309; Philip Siekevitz and Richard Nagin, Letter-to-the-editor, *Science* 152, no. 3718 (April 1, 1966): 15; Jean Mayer, Letter-to-the-editor, *Science* 152, no. 3720 (April 15, 1966): 291; "Chemical, Biological Weapons," *Science* 153, no. 3743 (September 23, 1966): 1508; *Scientific Research* 1, no. 10 (October, 1966): 11.; Jean Mayer and Victor Sidel, "Crop Destruction in South Vietnam," *Christian Century* 83, no. 26 (June 29, 1966): 829–832.

For the purposes of this study, Michael Klare's definitions of chemical and biological warfare will be used. Chemical warfare involves "the military employment of chemicals toxic to men, animals, or plants." This would include battlefield weapons like the mustard gases of World War I, as well as agents which poison the food supplies or industrial crops of enemy countries. Chemical weapons include irritating and incapacitating agents which restrict the military effectiveness of enemy soldiers (or of an enemy civilian group, as the case may be) without necessarily producing permanent physiological injury. Examples are tear-and-nausea gases like DM (dipheny aminochlorarsine), CN (chloroacetophenone), and CS (O-chlorobenzalmalononitrile) and the "psycho-chemicals," or hallucinogens, which produce temporary mental derangement. Biological warfare consists of "intentional employment of living organisms or their toxic products to cause death, disability of disease in man, animals, plants or food supplies." Theoretically, a multitude of bacteria, viruses, rickettsiae, fungae, or toxins could be employed as BW agents. In order to be effective in warfare, however, the following characteristics must be present:

1. The agent must be lethal or incapacitating and should be capable of being produced economically in adequate quantities from available material.

2. The agent must retain its virulence during production, storage, and transportation.

3. The agent must be easily and effectively disseminated without exposing the user to injury.

4. The targets of such agents must have no widespread or natural or acquired immunity.

See Michael Klare, "CBW Research Director," *Viet-Report* 3, nos. 4 and 5 (January, 1968): 25.

2. Gabriel Kolko, "Universities and the Pentagon," *The Nation* 205, no. 11 (October 9, 1967): 328–332.

Information on each of the constituencies involved in the Summit–Spicerack controversy has been derived from various sources. The most helpful sources on the student movement were telephone interviews with Jules Benjamin (August 8 and 9, 1982) and student publications in Mr. Benjamin's personal archives, especially: Joel Aber, Jules Benjamin, and Robin Martin (a.k.a. Robin Maisel), *Germ Warfare Research for Vietnam* (Philadelphia: Philadelphia Area Committee to End the War in Vietnam, 1966), which included Fred Stanton's "ICR Song"; Robin Maisel, "Philadelphia Committee Fights Germ War Research," *Bring the Troops Home Now Newsletter* 1, no. 3 (June 9, 1965): 17–20; Joel Aber and Jules Benjamin, "Germ Warfare Research for Vietnam," *Bring the Troops Home Now Newsletter* 1, no. 15 (October 17, 1966): 7–8; and Jules Benjamin, "Weed Killer," in a 1966 University of Pennsylvania magazine, title uncertain. Also useful were a series of articles in the *Philadelphia Bulletin*, March 6, 7, 9, 14, 1966, entitled: "The Left— A View From Within," published after reporter Eugene Meyer infiltrated major left-wing student groups in Philadelphia, including CEWV and SDS. The student newspaper, *Daily Philadelphian*, from August 1965 through May 1967, indicated student opinion in its polls, editorials, letters to the editor, and reports of activities of the student government. The most useful sources of information on the viewpoint of the trustees and administration were: "Minutes of the Board of Trustees," vol. 30 (March 11, 1966–May 1, 1967); vol. 31 (May 4, 1967–May 28, 1968); and interviews with: ex-provost, David Goddard, February 1974, in person, and March, 1982, via telephone; trustee, Thomas Sovereign Gates, Jr., June 15, 1982; Donald S. Murray, assistant for federal relations to Penn president, Gaylord Harnwell, June 14, 1982, who also shared portions of his personal archive with me; and Fran Rozinski, administrative assistant to the board of trustees, March 11, 1982. The most useful documents reflecting faculty viewpoints were: University of Pennsylvania, "Faculty Senate Minutes and Agenda," 1965 and 1966; University and Pennsylvania, "Meeting of the Senate of the University of Pennsylvania," April 13, 1967 and May 3, 1967. The following publications also indicated faculty attitude: William Gomberg, "Freedom as a Disguise for Majority Tyranny," *BioScience* 17, no. 8 (August, 1967): 530–531; Edward Herman and Robert Rutman, "University of Pennsylvania's CB Warfare Controversy," *BioScience* 17, no. 8 (August, 1967): 526–529; Kolko, "Universities;" Albert Mildvan, letter circulated to faculty colleagues, February 22, 1967, in the papers of ex-faculty senate chairman, Julius Wishner; Julius Wishner, introduction to "University of Pennsylvania Integrated Statement of University Policy on Conduct of Research Program," *AAUP Bulletin* 54, no. 4, (December, 1968): 453–457; Julius Wishner, "University of Pennsylvania's Research Policy," *BioScience* 17, no. 8, (August, 1967): 529–530; and Julius Wishner, Letter-to-the-Editor, *Philadelphia Bulletin*, November 14, 1966. The following Penn faculty and staff were interviewed regarding the Summit–Spicerack controversy: Gabriel Kolko, history, now of York University, written interrogations, spring 1982; Sidney A. Bludman, physics, March 22, June 16, August 19, and September 3, 1982; Robert Davies, veterinary medicine, June 16, 1982; Edward Herman, finance, June 16, 1982; and Julius Wishner, psychology and ex-faculty senate chairman, March 24, 1982; and Karolyn Burdon, administrative assistant to the faculty senate, March 22, 1982. Professors Davies, Herman, Wishner, Kolko, and Rutman also shared all or portions of their Summit–Spicerack personal archives with me.

The most useful general sources on chemical and biological warfare research included: William Buckingham, *Operation Ranch Hand: The Air Force and Herbicides in Southeast Asia* (Washington: Office of Air Force History, 1982); Carol Brightman, "The Weed Killer," *Viet-Report* 2, nos. 4/5 (June/July 1966): 914, 33–45; Brightman, "'The Weed Killers'—A Final Word," *Viet-Report* 2, no. 7 (October 1966): 3–5; Klare, "CBW Research Directory," 24–36; Michael Klare, "The University and CBW Research—An Announcement," *Viet-Report* 3, no. 1 (January-February 1967): 36–88; Elinor Langer, "Chemical and Biological Warfare (I): The Research Program," *Science* 155 (January 13, 1967): 174–179; Elinor Langer, "Chemical and Biological Warfare (II): The Weapons and the Policies," *Science* 155, (January 20, 1967): 299–303; and Sol Stern, "War Catalog of the University of Pennsylvania," *Ramparts* 5, no. 3 (August 1966): 31–40. Efforts to procure the entire texts of the Summit and Spicerack contracts from the Defense Department under the Freedom of Information Act with the assistance of the office of Congressman Newt Gingrich, or from the University of Pennsylvania, were unavailing. Letters are on file from Robert Lorndale the associate secretary of the University of Pennsylvania, dated May 25, 1982; Donald L. Howarth, chief of the Freedom of Information Management Department of the

Air Force, dated August 4, 1982; and Robert W. Poor, acting chief of the Legal Office of the Department of the Army's Armament Research and Development Command, dated July 22, 1982.

 3. Langer, "Chemical (I)," 174–175; Langer, "Chemical (II)," 302; Buckingham, *Ranch Hand*, iii, 3, 9–11.

 4. "Chemical Agents for Guerrilla Warfare," *Chemical and Engineering News*, (August 16, 1965) 7; *Armed Forces Chemical Journal* 8, no. 4 (July–August, 1959): 18; "The Case for Gas Warfare," *Armed Forces Chemical Journal* 17, no. 2 (June 1963): 12–13; "Moral Aspects of CBR Warfare," *Armed Forces Chemical Journal* 17, no. 2 (June 1963): 6.

 5. Quoted in Stern, "Catalog," 38.

 6. Langer, "Chemical (I)," 174. According to Langer, CBW procurement figures after 1967 were classified.

 7. Buckingham, *Ranch Hand*, iii–iv; *The Effects of Herbicides in South Vietnam* (Washington: National Academy of Science, 1974), Part A Summary and Conclusions. For additional details of the defoliation program, see John Lewallen, *Ecology of Devastation: Indochina* (Baltimore: Penguin Books, 1971) and Ngo Vinh Long, "Leaf Abscission in Cambodia," *The Widening War in Indochina*, ed. Jonathan Grant, Laurence Moss, and Jonathan Unger (New York: Washington Square Press, 1971), 201–213. Long observed the defoliation program first hand while serving as a military map maker for the South Vietnamese government between 1959 and 1963. In the course of his official duties he "had occasion to be at one time or another in virtually every hamlet and village in the country." Long wrote the original version of his survey of defoliation for the English language edition of *Thoi Bao Ga* while he was a graduate student in Vietnamese and Chinese history at Harvard University. While the studies by Long, Lewallen, Buckingham, and the National Academy of Science essentially corroborate each other on the extent of ecological devastation, Long and Lewallen go further to corroborate NLF and DRV claims of damage to Vietnamese health, as well as the physical environment.

 8. *Le Monde*, March 23, 1966, quoting Agence France Presse Hanoi dispatch.

 9. *Le Monde*, August 17, 1965, quoting MacNamara statement made in Saigon. "No Place to Hide," *Armed Forces Chemical Journal* 18, no. 1 (March 1964): 5–6.

 10. Cyrus Vance statement to a foreign policy conference in Washington, in *DP*, November 1, 1965.

 11. Langer, "Chemical (II)," 303.

 12. Kolko, "Universities," 328–329; Donald Murray, interviewed by author, June 14, 1982.

 13. Stern, "Catalog," p. 32.

 14. Stern, "Catalog," 38; Brightman, "Weed Killers—A Final Word," 4. Donald Murray interview.

 15. Thomas Gates, Jr., interviewed by author June 15, 1982; *Who's Who in America*, 1976–1977, 1120.

 16. Minutes of the Board of Trustees, May 1, 1967; Donald Murray interview.

 17. Minutes of the Board of Trustees, May 1, 1967; Donald Murray interview.

 18. Minutes of the Board of Trustees, May 1, 1967.

 19. "Annual Report of the ICR," 1956, 4, in Benjamin, "Weed Killers," 14.

 20. Minutes of the Board of Trustees, May 1, 1967.

 21. Summit was the code-name for U.S. Army Chemical Corps contract DA-18-064-CML-2757 (A). *Technical Abstracts Bulletin*, Defense Department, 67–69, May 1,

1967, in Klare, "CBW," 33; "Annual Report of the ICR," 1959, 1960, in Brightman, "Weed Killers," 33; Stern, "Catalog," 37. *Armed Forces Chemical Journal* 19, no. 3 (September 1964): 13, cites a $134,000 Chemical Corps grant to Penn for a "data systems program."

22. Chemical Corps contracts DA-18-108-405-CML-630 and DA-18-108-CML-6556. "Annual Report of the ICR," 1957, 2 and 7, in Benjamin, "Weed Killers," 15; "Annual Report of the ICR," 1962, in Stern, "Catalogue," 35; "Annual Report of the ICR," 1959, in Brightman, "Weed Killers," 33; Jules Benjamin, letter to author, October 12, 1982.

23. Spicerack was the code-name for U.S. Army Air Force contract AF 08 (635)-3597. *Technical Abstracts Bulletin*, Defense Department, 67–11, June 1, 1967, in Klare, "CBW," 33.

24. David Goddard, letter to author, February 17, 1983.

25. Material in this and the preceding paragraph from the following sources: Jules Benjamin, interviewed by author, August 8 and 9, 1982; Kolko letter to author, April 26, 1982; Stern, "Catalog," 34–35; Herman and Rutman, "University," 526; Klare, "CBW," 33; Meyer, "The Left,"; *DP*, November 22, 1965, February 4, 15, June 14, August 15, September 28, November 18, 1966, and February 9, 1967.

In the ensuing controversy over Summit and Spicerack, rarely, if ever, did critics accuse Penn of actually brewing germs and toxic chemicals. Rather, the controversy was over the propriety of designing classified delivery systems for counterinsurgency weapons; neither was the propriety of developing systems to defend one's own country against CBW ever seriously challenged. It was the classified nature of the projects and their counterinsurgency applications that was found to be objectionable.

The nature of Spicerack, its predecessor Big Ben, and their Chemical Corps counterparts such as Summit, was specifically mentioned in the minutes of Penn trustees, where the work of these projects was described as determining "the posture of the United States, both defense and offense, in connection with BW and CW." ("Minutes of the Board of Trustees," May 1, 1967.) The actual Spicerack contract, as cited by Stern and Langer, called for "analyses and studies of the behavior, technical properties, and performance of particular agents, munitions, weapons, components or subsystems of CB weapons systems; estimation of the human effects of particular C and B agents; characterization of the aerosol behavior of the specific agents in field clouds; appraisal of the performance of candidate munition-agent combinations under environmental conditions; examination of various protection procedures in specific military situations; and the estimation of human factors and response to the C and B environment." Cornell Aeronautical Labs was subcontracted, under Spicerack, to "conduct a detailed target analysis to determine anticipated target neutralization requirements, protective measures against which weapon capability should be required, minimum acceptable casually infliction to achieve neutralization, and munition evaluation criteria, including evaluation of field and operational tests." *DP*, November 11, 1965, April 20, 1967; Kolko, "Universities," 330; Stern, "Catalog," 36–38; Langer, "Chemical (I)," 177; Herman and Rutman, "University," 527; Brightman, "Weed Killers," 9, 43; Brightman, "'The Weed Killers'—A Final Report," 5; *STOP* news release, April 25, 1967, in Benjamin archives.

26. *DP*, September 17, October 20, and 25, 1965. See occasional issues of Penn YAF's publication *Veritas* for red-baiting of Kolko, Herman, and especially Rutman.

27. Edward Herman, letter to author, November 9, 1982. Kolko's argument on the illegality of CB warfare drew heavily on the reasoning that, since the 1925 Geneva Protocol, which the United States did not sign, there emerged "from the practice of states a rule of

customary international law prohibiting at least the first use of chemical warfare. The vast majority of text-writers assert that CB warfare as defined in the Geneva Protocol is contrary to international law." (William O'Brien, "Biological Chemical Warfare and the International Law of War," *Georgetown Law Journal* 51 (1962): 36, 41.) Ironically, this legal study was sponsored by the ICR in an effort to legitimize its research, long before the 1965 controversy. *DP*, February 16, 1966.

28. Thomas Gates, Jr. interviewed by author, June 15, 1982. "If I told someone what research to do or not to do or what to publish," President Harnwell was quoted as saying, "another portion of the faculty would be down here knocking at the doors." (Langer, "Chemical (I)," 177.) Business Professor William Gomberg lamented after the CBW controversy that "measures were taken by one section of the faculty to impose restrictions on the individual autonomy of other members." (Gomberg, "Freedom," 530.)

29. "Who is to judge what is moral and immoral research?" Wishner asked his antiwar critics. "Are we to establish censorship of research?" Julius Wishner, interviewed by author, March 4, 1982. An editorial chairman of the *DP* summarized the Wishner view with the question: "If chemical warfare is deemed immoral today, might not mathematics, the basis of missile science, be considered immoral tomorrow?" (*DP*, March 31, 1967.) See also: Wishner letter to *The Bulletin* (Philadelphia), November 21, 1966; Wishner, "Introduction," 453; Wishner, "University," 529–520; "Faculty Senate Minutes," April 13, 1967, 16; *BioScience* 17, no. 8 (August 1967): 524–525.

30. *DP*, November 18, 1966.

31. In January, 1967, an unsuccessful attempt to launch a radical political party within the Penn student government was made by College for Women sophomore, Anita Dimondstein, a radical affiliated with SDS and unaffiliated with the Trotskyist YSA. She helped form a party that ran in the student government elections on a platform of "termination of all university DOD contracts." The party pledged "non-violent direct action tactics" if the university administration refused to cooperate. Although her political party won minimal support, Dimondstein continued her involvement as an editor of the *DP*, and as a participant in the April 16–27, 1967, sit-in and other demonstrations. (*DP*, January 17, 18, and 30, 1967.)

32. Gabriel Kolko, letter to the author, April 26, 1982. Examples of Kolko-generated publicity include: *Scientific American* 214, no. 2 (February, 1966): 53; "Chemical, Biological Weapons," *Science* 153, no. 3743 (September 23, 1966): 1508; Langer, "Chemical (I)"; Langer, "Chemical (II)"; *Scientific Research* 1, no. 10 (October, 1966): 11–12; and Kolko, "Universities." Gabriel Kolko letters to faculty, October 1, 13, and 15, 1965, Kolko archive; Herman and Rutman, "University," 526; *DP* October 21, 1965; Sidney Bludman, interviewed by author, March 22, June 16, August 19, and September 3, 1982; Sidney Bludman, letter to Marvin Kalkstein, Federation of American Scientists, December 16, 1966, Wishner archive.

33. Reproduced in *BioScience* 17, no. 8 (August 1967): 524.

34. "Faculty Senate Minutes," November 3, 1965; November 10, 1966, resolution reproduced in *BioScience* 17, no. 8 (August 1967): 524–525; Wishner interview March 24, 1982; Langer, "Chemical (I)," 177. Karolyn Burdon, administrative assistant to the faculty senate, made clear the advisory nature of senate resolutions in a March 22, 1982, interview with the author.

35. *The Militant*, newspaper of the Socialist Workers Party, the parent organization of Penn's YSA, covered Penn's CBW controversy as early as its November 15, 1965, issue. In

all probability *The Militant* was alerted to the Penn situation and continued to publicize it because of the involvement of YSAer's in CEWV.

36. *DP*, October 11, 1965.

37. *DP*, October 18, November 9, 1965.

38. *DP*, December 10, 13, 1975, July 31, 1967.

39. Other songs included "Exploitation Blues" and "Hitler Ain't Dead." Some were published in *Broadside* magazine. Aber, Benjamin, and Martin (Maisel), *Germ Warfare*, back cover; *DP*, April 6, 26, September 28, November 9, 1966.

40. *DP*, January 19, February 14, March 28, April 15, 18, November 4, December 6, 1965; February 9, March 10, 13; Meyer, "The Left," March 7, 1966.

41. *DP*, October 12 and 18, 1965.

42. *DP*, November 1, 1965.

43. *DP*, December 8, 1965.

44. *DP*, April 28, September 12, November 16, 1966.

45. *Scientific American* 214, no. 2, (February, 1966): 53; "Secret Research at Penn," *Time* 88, no. 12 (September 16, 1966): 62; "Controversies: Chemical Reaction." *Newsweek* 68, no. 12 (September 19, 1966): 34.

46. Interviews of Murray and Wishner, March 24, 1982; *DP*, February 22, 1967; "Trustees' Minutes," April 14, 1967, 317.

47. Julius Wishner interview; "Faculty Senate Minutes," April 13, 1967, Wishner Papers; *DP*, March 29, 1967; *The Bulletin*, March 19, 1967.

48. *DP*, April 5, 1967. On threatened gas mask protest by faculty, see: "Faculty Senate Minutes," May 3, 1967; *DP*, February 22, March 13 and 15, 1967.

49. *DP*, April 5, 10, 11, 21, 26, and 27, 1967.

50. "Markel has been here for three years, but this is his first step toward real commitment to the campus New Left," the *DP* reported on April 26. See also *DP*, April 20 and 27, 1967; Herman and Rutman, "University," 528; *Philadelphia Inquirer*, May 5, 1967.

51. *DP*, March 20, 28, April 5, 10, 11, and 21, 1967.

52. "Faculty Senate Minutes," April 13, 1967.

53. Wishner, letter to author, January 4, 1983.

54. "Faculty Senate Minutes," May 3, 1967; *Philadelphia Inquirer*, April 27, May 4 and 5, 1967.

55. David Goddard, letter to author, February 17, 1983. Wishner interview March 24, 1982; David Goddard, interviewed by author, February, 1974, and (via telephone) March 17, 1982; *Philadelphia Inquirer*, May 4 and 5, 1967.

56. Herman and Rutman, "University," 528; *Philadelphia Inquirer*, May 5, 1967.

57. Gates interview, "Trustees' Minutes," May 3 and 4, 1967.

58. Robert Davies, letter to author, November 5, 1982.

59. Wishner, "University," 454.

60. Herman, letter to author, November 9, 1982.

61. *Wall Street Journal*, October 25, 1967.

62. Kolko, "Universities," 332.

Antiwar Dissent in the College Press   Clifford Wilcox

1. Todd Gitlin, *The Whole World Is Watching: Mass Media in the Making and Unmaking of the New Left* (Berkeley: University of California Press, 1980), 1–18; Michael

Parenti, *Inventing Reality: The Politics of the Mass Media* (New York: St. Martin's Press, 1986), 19–23; Kathleen Turner, *Lyndon Johnson's Dual War: Vietnam and the Press* (Chicago: University of Chicago Press, 1985), 149–157.

2. Spyridon Granitsas, "Newspapers on Campus Are Popular," *Editor and Publisher* (December 5, 1970): 12.

3. The oldest daily is the *Yale Daily News*, which began publishing in 1873. This paper was followed by the *Harvard Crimson* in 1883 and shortly thereafter by the *Cornell Daily Sun*, the *Michigan Daily*, and the *Daily Illini*. Julius Duscha and Thomas Fischer, *The Campus Press: Freedom and Responsibility* (Washington, D.C.: American Association of State Colleges and Universities, 1973), 9; Howard H. Peckham, *The Making of the University of Michigan, 1817–1967* (Ann Arbor: University of Michigan Press, 1967), 107; George E. Stevens and John B. Webster, *Law and the Student Press* (Ames: Iowa State University Press, 1973), 88.

4. William Porter, "What Should Be the Role of the Student Newspaper?" in *The Student Newspaper: Report of the Special Commission on the Student Press to the President of the University of California* (Washington, D.C.: American Council on Education, 1970), 37.

5. Melvin Mencher, "The Curse of Gutenberg? The College Press," *The Quill* (May 1971): 12.

6. Philip G. Altbach, *Student Politics in America: A Historical Analysis* (New York: McGraw-Hill, 1974), 62, 93, 146, 159; Helen Lefkowitz Horowitz, *Campus Life: Undergraduate Cultures from the End of the Eighteenth Century to the Present* (Chicago: University of Chicago Press, 1988; reprint of 1987 Alfred A. Knopf edition), 163–164.

7. "Campus Newspapers," *National Review* 23 (January 26, 1971): 71; "The New Candor," *Newsweek* 70 (December 25, 1967): 66–67; "Opposition Press on Campus," *Time* 94 (December 12, 1969): 48; John Tebbel, "The Old New Journalism" *Saturday Review* 54 (March 13, 1971): 96–97. See Abe Peck, *Uncovering the Sixties: The Life and Times of the Underground Press* (New York: Pantheon Books, 1985) on the underground newspapers of the 1960s.

8. Douglas E. Kneeland, "The Campus Press, 1972—It's Changing Again," *The Quill* (March 1972): 10.

9. "The So-called System of Justice," *Michigan Daily*, July 31, 1927; "Education in the Union," ibid., July 18, 1937; "Roosevelt's Labor Policy," ibid., July 20, 1937; "Anniversary of the Spanish Civil War," ibid., July 21, 1937.

10. Altbach, *Student Politics*, 146–197.

11. James Miller, *Democracy Is in the Streets: From Port Huron to the Siege of Chicago* (New York: Simon & Schuster, 1987), 21–91; Kirkpatrick Sale, *SDS* (New York: Vintage Books, 1974), 35–59.

12. Edward Herstein (editorial director, *Michigan Daily*, 1964–65) and Ken Winter (managing editor, *Michigan Daily*, 1964–65), interview by author, tape recording, Ann Arbor, Michigan, March 2, 1990; William Porter (chairman, Department of Journalism, University of Michigan, 1966–1973), interview by author, tape recording, Ann Arbor, Michigan, March 2, 1990. The *Daily* advertised itself to prospective staff members by printing a short article headlined "We're Great." The article was simply a clipping from the *New York Times* that praised the training one received at the *Daily*: "A . . . minority of college newspapers, among them *The Michigan Daily*, *The Cornell Sun*, *The Harvard Crimson*, and *The Columbia Spectator* are truly professional training grounds for future

newspapermen, often more effective than journalism departments." (*Michigan Daily*, August 25, 1964).

13. Wayne Overbeck and Thomas M. Pasqua, Jr., *Excellence in College Journalism* (Belmont, Calif.: Wadsworth, 1983), 94–96; Michael Parenti, *Inventing Reality*, 42–59.

14. Informal reading in two other college newspapers provided the basis for a brief comparison of coverage on major national events reported in the *Michigan Daily* in the early 1960s compared to other members of the college press. The remainder of the body of the paper provides a detailed comparison of the Vietnam coverage between the *Michigan Daily* and the *Daily Illini*. On December 4, 1964, the FBI arrested suspects involved in the murder of three civil rights workers in Mississippi. The following morning the headline of the *Michigan Daily* read "FBI Arrests Twenty Men for Civil Rights Murders." No mention of the event ever appeared in the UCLA *Daily Bruin* or the *Arizona Daily Wildcat* (University of Arizona). The Berkeley Free Speech Movement (FSM) received similar coverage. News of the FSM was provided to University of Michigan students through front-page stories. On several days the headline of the *Daily* was devoted to the FSM: "Political Restrictions Spark Berkeley Riots" (October 2, 1964); "1100 Sit-in at Berkeley Administration Building" (December 3, 1964). The UCLA *Daily Bruin* mentioned the disruption at her sister University of California campus in a small Associated Press clipping in a "World Wire" page; the *Arizona Daily Wildcat* carried no mention of it. Furthermore, the *Michigan Daily* carried stories of American involvement in Vietnam far earlier than most student newspapers. Events which received the lead front-page headline in the *Michigan Daily* were sometimes covered in the UCLA *Daily Bruin* "World Wire" paste-up page, but not covered at all in the *Arizona Daily Wildcat*: "Troops Enter Saigon in Bloodless Coup," *Michigan Daily*, September 1, 1964; "Rusk Advises Viet Nam Leaders to End Quarrels," ibid., September 9, 1964.

15. "The President Acts," *New York Times*, August 5, 1964, 32; "Stern Crisis," *Washington Post*, August 6, 1964, A20; "Vietnam Sequel," ibid., August 12, 1964, A20; James Reston, "Some Basic Questions about Vietnam," *New York Times*, August 7, 1964, 28.

16. "U.S. Bombs Vietnamese Bases," *Michigan Daily*, August 5, 1964; Lawrence Kirshbaum, "Vietnamese Crisis Distorts Chances for Settlement," ibid. Kirshbaum went on to become managing editor of the *Daily* in 1966; Ken Winter, "A Choice Not an Echo," ibid., August 5, 1964; Edward Herstein, "What Really Happened in the Gulf of Tonkin?", ibid., August 11, 1964.

17. Melvin Small, *Johnson, Nixon, and the Doves* (New Brunswick N.J.: Rutgers University Press, 1988), 28; "Troops Enter Saigon in Bloodless Coup," *Michigan Daily*, September 13, 1964; "Khanh Arrests Leaders of Vietnamese Rebellion," ibid., September 17, 1964; Kenneth Winter, "Americans in Viet Nam: Policy of Contradictions," ibid., January 8, 1965.

18. Louis Manashe and Ronald Radosh, eds., *Teach-ins: U.S.A.* (New York: Frederick A. Praeger, 1967), 3–16.

19. W. Rexford Benoit, "Complexity Byword in Viet Protest," *Michigan Daily*, March 18, 1965; Robert Moore, "Faculty Teach-in Begins Tonight," ibid., March 24, 1965; Robert Moore, "Faculty Teach-in Gets Wide Spread Recognition," ibid., March 26, 1965; Roger Rapoport, "Protest, Learning, Heckling Spark Viet Rally," ibid.; Jeffrey Goodman, Robert Hippler, and Gail Blumberg, "Teach-in: An Opportunity," ibid.; "An Appeal to Our Students," (advertisement), ibid.

20. Michael Myers, "Wisconsin Conducts Vietnam Teach-in," *Michigan Daily*, April 2, 1965; Lynn A. Metzger, "MSU Will Hold Own 'Teach-in'", ibid., April 4, 1965; "Reviving the Practice of Democracy," ibid., April 10, 1965.

21. Marshall Lasser, "Hayden, Counter-Demonstrators Highlight Peaceful Days of Protest," *Michigan Daily*, March 27, 1966; Daniel Okrent and Gail Smiley, "Military Repulses Protesters at Pentagon after 100,00 Converge on Washington," ibid., October 22, 1967; Urban Lehner, "Tomatoes and Hatchets Hurt the March on Washington," ibid., October 22, 1967; Ron Landsman, "The Future of Dissent: More Blood, Less People," ibid., October 24, 1967.

22. John Meredith, " 'U' " Should Continue Ranking: Yes," *Michigan Daily*, November 16, 1966; Steve Wildstrom, " 'U' Should Continue Ranking: No," ibid; Neil Shister, "Pledge Not to Give Grades to Males," ibid., November 19, 1966; Susan Schnepp, "2:1 Margin Asks 'U' End Compilation," ibid., November 17, 1966.

23. See Elliot Carlson, "Classified Research Stirs Debate at Universities," *Wall Street Journal*, October 25, 1967, 1; reprinted in *Michigan Daily* October 26, 1967; Gabriel Kolko, "Universities and the Pentagon," *The Nation* 205 (October 9, 1967), 328–332.

24. Roger Rapoport, "On Classified Military Research," *Michigan Daily*, October 25, 1967.

25. Henry Grix, "Classified Research One Year Later," *Michigan Daily*, September 21, 1968.

26. Daniel Zwerdling, "Administration Allows Faculty to Observe Vietnam Moratorium," *Michigan Daily*, October 2, 1969; Henry Grix, "The Vietnam Moratorium: Faculty Action Now," ibid., October 4, 1969; Jim Beattie, "New Mobe Predicts 90% Moratorium Participation," ibid., October 14, 1969; "Million Protest Vietnam War; 20,000 Join 'U' Stadium Rally," ibid., October 16, 1969; Steve Koppman, Jim Neubacher, and Tammy Jacobs, "Classes Struck in War protest," ibid.

27. Joseph DeMartini, "Student Protest during Two Periods in the History of the University of Illinois, 1867–1894 and 1929–1942" (Ph.D. diss., University of Illinois, 1974), 80–83; Helen Lefkowitz Horowitz, *Campus Life*, 163–164.

28. Richard Hildwein (chairman, Illini Publishing Co., *Daily Illini*, 1969–1981), interview by author, tape recording, Champaign, Illinois, March 24, 1990; John Hundley (editor-in-chief, *Daily Illini*, 1969–1970), telephone interview by author, November 5, 1989; Carl Schwartz (editor-in-chief, *Daily Illini*, 1970–1971) telephone interview by author, November 4, 1989; Dick Sublette (publisher, *Daily Illini*, 1970–1981), telephone interview by author, October 1, 1989. Several former *Michigan Daily* and *Daily Illini* reporters and editors graciously shared much time in telephone and personal interviews with the author. The author expresses a debt of thanks to all of these people.

29. "Senate Defeats IM Building," *Daily Illini*, December 3, 1964; "Illini Stun UCLA, 110–83," ibid., December 5, 1964.

30. "U.S. Jets Rain Bombs, Rockets on Suspected Viet Cong Outposts," ibid., March 26, 1965; "U.S. Attack on Hanoi Possible," ibid., March 31, 1965; "Gruening Speaks at UI—Criticizes US Viet Policy," ibid., April 12, 1965; "We Don't Belong," ibid., April 14, 1965. "UM 'Teach-in,' " ibid., March 25, 1965.

31. "An Appeal to Our Students," *Michigan Daily*, March 26, 1965; Margaret Converse and Vicki Packard, "U.S. Intervention Denounced," *Daily Illini*, May 18, 1965; Jeffrey Goodman, Robert Hippel, Gail Blumberg, "Teach-in: An Opportunity," *Michigan Daily*, March 24, 1965; "An Editorial," ibid., March 26, 1965; "A Cold, Cold War," *Daily Illini*, May 18, 1965.

32. Bob Goldstein, "SDS Attack U.S. Policies," *Daily Illini*, November 8, 1966.

33. "Protesters End Dow Visit," ibid., October 26, 1967; Dan Balz, Don Ruhter, and Roger Simon, "Lincoln Memorial to Pentagon—Last Week's Gigantic March," *Daily Illini Spectrum*, October 28, 1967; Larry Finley, "Guilty," *Daily Illini*, November 30, 1967.

34. "DI Halts Business as Usual in Support of Moratorium," *Daily Illini*, October 15, 1969.

35. Howard Falk, "Reaching for a Gigaflop: The Fate of the Famed Illiac Was Shaped by Both Research Brilliance and Real-World Disaster," *IEEE Spectrum* (October 1976), 65.

36. Carl Schwartz, "Department of Defense to Employ UI Computer for Nuclear Weapons," *Daily Illini*, January 6, 1970; "Deceit Changes Concept of Illiac," ibid., February 6, 1970; "On Slotnick's Statement about Illiac," ibid.

37. John Hundley, telephone interview by author, May 5, 1991.

38. See Michael Schudson, *Discovering the News: A Social History of American Newspapers* (New York: Basic Books, 1978) for an illuminating discussion of objectivity and subjectivity in twentieth-century American journalism.

39. See Todd Gitlin, *The Sixties: Years of Hope, Days of Rage* (New York: Bantam Books, 1987) and James Miller, *Democracy Is in the Streets* on the differences between the early members of the New Left versus those of the late sixties.

40. In an advertisement describing a new format for itself the *Michigan Daily* stated: "Since the surge of campus-oriented news in the late Sixties and early Seventies, we've tended to overlook the trends that make the campus hum, that influence and change peoples' lives here at Michigan. We've gotten used to covering just the big national and international stories, and slighting the types of things we can cover best—what's happening right here in Ann Arbor." "Its A Bright New *Daily*," *Michigan Daily*, September 8, 1977.

41. David Margolick, "Michigan U. Daily, Muckraker of the 1960s, Strives for Relevance," *New York Times*, March 20, 1985.

Gentle Thursday   Glenn W. Jones

1. José E. Limón, "Western Marxism and Folklore," *Journal of American Folklore* 96, no. 379 (1983): 39.

2. Bob Brown, interviewed by author, 1986.

3. Rodney Needham, "Percussion and Transition," in *Reader in Comparative Religion: An Anthropological Approach*, ed. William A. Lessa and Evon Z. Vogt (New York: Harper & Row, 1979), 311–317.

4. Kathleen Stewart, "Nostalgia—A Polemic," *Cultural Anthropology* 33, no. 3 (1988): 232.

5. Fredric Jameson, *The Political Unconscious* (Ithaca, N.Y.: Cornell University Press, 1981), 79.

6. A complete ethnographic annotation of the specific "logic of practice," in Bourdieu's terms, of the sixties counterculture at Gentle Thursday would require an analysis of the impact of the sixties expansion of university enrollment to large portions of the white lower-middle and working classes as well as to increasing numbers of black and Mexican-American students. I am in the process of doing research for that larger project.

7. Dick Hebdige, *Subculture: The Meaning of Style* (New York: Methuen & Co. 1979), 13.

8. Jeff Nightbyrd, interviewed by author, 1988.

9. See Peter Stallybrass and Allon White's *The Politics and Poetics of Transgression* (Ithaca, N.Y.: Cornell University Press, 1986) for a discussion of the implications of Bakhtinian inversions like those at Gentle Thursday. Part of the motivation for and much of the impact of the first Gentle Thursday came from its location beneath the same main University of Texas tower used as a sniper's post by a deranged former marine only a few months before.

10. Thorne Dryer, "Flipped Out Week," *The Rag*, 1, no. 21 (April 10, 1967).

11. Dryer, "Flipped Out Week".

12. Michel de Certeau, *The Practice of Everyday Life* (Berkeley: University of California Press 1984), 37.

13. John Bryant, quoting the dean of student life in "Gentleness to Prevail as Controversy Ends," *The Daily Texan*, March 13, 1967.

14. Bryant, "Gentleness."

15. Unpublished UT administration memos "liberated" by the Austin underground and seen by the author.

16. Bryant, "Gentleness".

17. SDS flyer from Spring, 1967 in possession of the author.

18. Andrea Johnson, "Kissing, Kazoos, 'Flip' West Mall," *The Daily Texan*, April 14, 1967.

19. *The Austin-American Statesman*, "Happening," April 14, 1967.

20. Gary Thiher, "Gentle Thursday as Revolution," *The Rag*, April 17, 1967.

21. L. A. Kauffman, "The Anti-Politics of Identity," *Socialist Review*, 20, no. 1, 77.

22. John Clarke et al., "Subcultures, Cultures and Class," in *Resistance through Rituals: Youth Subcultures in Post-War Britain*, ed. Stuart Hall and Tony Jefferson (London: Hutchinson Education 1976), 67.

Being and Doing   Ellen Herman

1. For example, see Barbara Ehrenreich, *The Hearts of Men: American Dreams and the Flight from Commitment* (New York: Anchor Press/Doubleday, 1983); Todd Gitlin, *The Sixties: Years of Hope, Days of Rage* (New York: Bantam, 1987); Maurice Isserman, *If I Had A Hammer . . . The Death of the Old Left and the Birth of the New Left* (New York: Basic Books, 1987); Marty Jezer, *The Dark Ages: Life in the United States, 1945–1960* (Boston: South End Press, 1982).

2. Although this article treats one particular tendency among psychological experts, humanistic psychology, I use the term "psychological" broadly, not to designate the formal boundaries of an academic discipline or a professional job category, but to indicate an approach that emphasizes the analysis of mental processes, interpersonal relationships, introspection, and behavior in explaining both individual and social realities. In the period under review, the professions most closely associated with psychological approaches are those that originated in or grew into "helping" trades: psychiatry, clinical psychology, and social work. Clinical applications, in particular, multiplied and spread dramatically after World War II, and the spread of psychological thinking treated in this article can be traced in large measure to the popularization of psychotherapy and various forms of counseling.

But the mounting authority of the psychological worldview also had important, non-therapeutic origins in war and war mobilization, especially in the work psychological experts did for military institutions during World War II and throughout the early years of the cold war. Although this theme in the history of psychology is beyond the scope of this article, it is useful to keep in mind that psychology in the postwar era has been classified as a "behavioral science" (shorthand for a subset of the more general category, "social science") while still maintaining its identity as a natural science and building its reputation as a clinical specialty. Their status as "behavioral scientists" has allowed psychological experts to enter the realm of public policymaking where their roles have extended well beyond "helping" and where the psychological worldview has been applied directly to the political issues at the heart of American public life, from winning the international war against Communism to managing racial conflict at home.

3. "A Larger Jurisdiction for Psychology" is the title of Part 1 of Abraham H. Maslow's *Toward a Psychology of Being*, 2nd ed. (New York: D. Van Nostrand, 1969). See also Abraham H. Maslow, *The Psychology of Science* (Chicago: Henry Regnery, 1969), xvi.

4. Norman Vincent Peale, *The Power of Positive Thinking* (New York: Fawcett Crest, 1952), 29.

5. For his most comprehensive statement of this approach, see Carl L. Rogers, *Client-centered Therapy: Its Current Practice, Implications, and Theory* (Boston: Houghton Mifflin, 1951).

6. For a typical statement of these aspects of Maslow's psychology, see Abraham H. Maslow, *Motivation and Personality*, (New York: Harper & Row, 1954, 2nd ed., 1970).

7. For a general discussion of this trend, see Richard H. Pells, *The Liberal Mind in a Conservative Age: American Intellectuals in the 1940s and 1950s*, 2nd ed. (Middletown, Conn.: Wesleyan University Press, 1989), especially chapter 3.

8. Gordon W. Allport, *Becoming: Basic Considerations for a Psychology of Personality* (New Haven: Yale University Press, 1955), 100–101.

9. Carl Rogers, "The Emerging Person: A New Revolution" in Richard I. Evans, *Carl Rogers: The Man and His Ideas* (New York: E.P. Dutton & Co., 1975), 175.

10. Abraham H. Maslow, *The Journals of A. H. Maslow*, ed. Richard J. Lowry, 2 vols. (Monterey, Calif.: Brooks/Cole Publishing, 1979), 2:877, 1:646, 2:731.

11. Ibid., 2:1108.

12. Maslow, *Toward A Psychology of Being*, 8, emphasis in original. For an acknowledgement by Maslow that his ideas were similar to those of 1960s activists, especially in the counterculture, see *Journals*, 2:883.

13. Eldridge Cleaver, "On Becoming" in *Soul on Ice* (New York: Delta, 1968), 3–17.

14. Martin Luther King, Jr., "The Sword That Heals" in *Why We Can't Wait* (New York: New American Library, 1963), 30, emphasis in original.

15. Alvin F. Poussaint, "A Negro Psychiatrist Explains the Negro Psyche" in *Being Black: Psychological-Sociological Dilemmas*, ed. Robert V. Gutherie (San Francisco: Canfield Press, 1970), 23.

16. Emma Jones Lapsansky, " 'Black Power Is My Mental Health': Accomplishments of the Civil Rights Movement" in *Black America*, ed. John F. Szwed (New York: Basic Books, 1970), 3–15. For another example of the accomplishments of the civil rights movement defined psychologically, see Jean Smith, "I Learned to Feel Black" in *The Black Power Revolt: A Collection of Essays*, ed. Floyd B. Barbour (Boston: Porter Sargent, 1968), 207–218.

17. Hearings before the Subcommittee on Government Research of the Senate Com-

mittee on Government Operations, *Deprivation and Personality—A New Challenge to Human Resources Development*, pts. 1–2, 90th Cong., 2nd sess. April 1968, 265, emphasis in original. For a general consideration, by professional psychologists, of some of the issues raised by the civil rights movement, see Frances F. Korten, Stuart W. Cook, and John I. Lacey, *Psychology and the Problems of Society* (Washington, D.C.: American Psychological Association, 1970), especially the part titled "Psychology and Minority Groups," 257–303.

18. Doug McAdam, *Freedom Summer* (New York: Oxford University Press, 1988).

19. "The Port Huron Statement" in James Miller, *"Democracy Is in the Streets": From Port Huron to the Siege of Chicago* (New York: Simon & Schuster, 1987), 332–333, emphasis in original.

20. Maslow, *Journals*, 2:1090.

21. Abbie Hoffman, *Soon to Be a Major Motion Picture* (New York: Perigree, 1980), 26.

22. Ibid., 297, emphasis in original.

23. Abbie Hoffman, *Revolution for the Hell of It* (New York: The Dial Press, 1968), 61–62.

24. Betty Friedan, *The Feminine Mystique* (New York: Dell, 1963), chapter 13.

25. Pamela Allen, "Free Space" in *Radical Feminism*, ed. Anne Koedt, Ellen Levine, and Anita Rapone (New York: Quadrangle, 1973), 273.

26. Barbara Susan, "About My Consciousness Raising" in *Voices from Women's Liberation*, ed. Leslie B. Tanner (New York: New American Library, 1970), 240–241.

27. Kathy McAfee and Myrna Wood, "Bread and Roses" in Ibid., 419.

28. Naomi Weisstein, "Psychology Constructs the Female or The Fantasy Life of the Male Psychologist (with some attention to the fantasies of his friends, the male biologist and the male anthropologist)" in Koedt, Levine, and Rapone, *Radical Feminism*, 178–197.

29. Ibid., 181.

30. For an example of this perspective in a retrospective essay, see Ellen Willis, "Coming Down Again: After the Age of Excess," *Salmagundi*, no. 81 (Winter 1989): 124–140.

31. Examples of this position include: Robert Castel, Francoise Castel, and Anne Lovell, *The Psychiatric Society*, trans. Arthur Goldhammer (New York: Columbia University Press, 1982); Russell Jacoby, *Social Amnesia: A Critique of Conformist Psychology from Adler to Laing* (Boston: Beacon Press, 1975); Joel Kovel, "Politics of Therapy; Therapy of Politics," *Zeta*, March 1989, 106–110; Christopher Lasch, *The Minimal Self: Psychic Survival in Troubled Times* (New York: W.W. Norton, 1984); Philip Rieff, "The Emergence of Psychological Man" in *Freud: The Mind of the Moralist* (New York: Anchor Books, 1961) 361–392; Philip Rieff, *The Triumph of the Therapeutic: Uses of Faith after Freud* (New York: Harper Torchbooks, 1966); Richard Sennett, *The Fall of Public Man: On the Social Psychology of Capitalism* (New York: Vintage Books, 1978).

32. For more on this topic, see Ellen Herman, "Getting to Serenity: Do Addiction Programs Sap Our Political Vitality?," *Out/Look* 1, no. 2 (Summer 1988): 10–21 (reprinted in the *Utne Reader*, November/December 1988); "Against Therapy," *Z Magazine*, May 1990, 87–90; "Politics and Recovery," *Bridges* 1, no. 1 (Spring 1991): 138–142; "It's All in the Family: Lesbian Motherhood Meets Popular Psychology" in *Sisters, Sexperts, Queers: Beyond the Lesbian Nation*, ed. Arlene Stein (New American Library/E. P. Dutton, forthcoming); "Cures," *Z Magazine*, June, 1991, pp. 81–82; and "Toward a Politics of Self-Esteem?" *Z Magazine*, July/August, 1991, pp. 42–46.

The Stunt Man   Stephen J. Whitfield

1. Theodore Roszak, *The Making of a Counter Culture: Reflections on the Technocratic Society and Its Youthful Opposition* (Garden City, N.Y.: Doubleday Anchor, 1969), 292; E. L. Doctorow, *The Book of Daniel* (New York: Signet, 1972), 148, 152.

2. Roger L. Simon, *The Big Fix* (New York: Pocket Books, 1974), 37; Leo Rosten, *The Joys of Yiddish* (New York: Pocket Books, 1970), 108–109.

3. John Murray Cuddihy, *The Ordeal of Civility: Freud, Marx, Lévi-Strauss, and the Jewish Struggle with Modernity* (New York: Basic Books, 1974), 192; Mark Hertsgaard, "Steal This Decade," *Mother Jones* 15 (June 1990): 34.

4. Howard G. Chua-Eoan, "People," *Time* 132 (September 12, 1988): 69; Douglas Martin, "Abbie Hoffman Does Stand-Up for His Beliefs," *New York Times*, August 31, 1988, II, 1.

5. Abbie Hoffman, *Soon To Be a Major Motion Picture* (New York: G. P. Putnam's Sons, 1980), 99.

6. Hoffman quoted in Richard Lacayo, "A Flower in a Clenched Fist," *Time* 133 (April 24, 1989): 30; John P. Diggins, *The American Left in the Twentieth Century* (New York: Harcourt Brace Jovanovich, 1973), 165.

7. Tom Hayden, *Reunion: A Memoir* (New York: Random House, 1988), 377; "A Yippie Comes in from the Damp," *Time* 116 (September 15, 1980): 22.

8. Hoffman, *Major Motion Picture*, 100–102; Irwin Unger, *The Movement: A History of the American New Left, 1959–1972* (New York: Dodd, Mead, 1974), 135; James Madison, "The Federalist No. 10" (1787), in Alexander Hamilton et al., *The Federalist Papers* (New York: Bantam, 1982), 46, 48–49.

9. Abbie Hoffman, *Woodstock Nation: A Talk-Rock Album* (New York: Random House, 1969), 50–51, reprinted in *The Best of Abbie Hoffman*, ed. Daniel Simon (New York: Four Walls Eight Windows, 1989), 130–131; Hoffman, *Major Motion Picture*, 168–170.

10. Hoffman, *Major Motion Picture*, 145; James Miller, "*Democracy Is in the Streets*": *From Port Huron to the Siege of Chicago* (New York: Simon & Schuster, 1987), 285–286; Daniel Walker, *Rights in Conflict: The Violent Confrontation of Demonstrators and Police in the Parks and Streets of Chicago* (New York: Bantam, 1968), 41–53; Peter Burke, *Popular Culture in Early Modern Europe* (New York: Harper & Row, 1978), 191.

11. Walker, *Rights in Conflict*, 5, 9, 11; Mike Royko, *Boss: Richard J. Daley of Chicago* (New York: Signet, 1971), 187–198.

12. Cuddihy, *Ordeal of Civility*, 189–197; Jason Epstein, *The Great Conspiracy Trial: An Essay on Law, Liberty, and the Constitution* (New York: Random House, 1970), 332–433; Hayden, *Reunion*, 397.

13. Hoffman quoted in Hayden, *Reunion*, 397, and in J. Anthony Lukas, *The Barnyard Epithet and Other Obscenities: Notes on the Chicago Conspiracy Trail* (New York: Harper & Row, 1970), 50; Hoffman, *Major Motion Picture*, 208.

14. Hayden, *Reunion*, 389; Agnew quoted in Cuddihy, *Ordeal of Civility*, 197.

15. *Current Biography Yearbook 1981* (New York: H. W. Wilson, 1982), 207.

16. Abbie Hoffman, *Square Dancing in the Ice Age* (Boston: South End Press, 1982), 125–127.

17. Hoffman, *Square Dancing*, 30–40, and *Major Motion Picture*, 214.

18. "A Yippie Comes in from the Damp," *Time*, 22; Hertsgaard, "Steal This Decade," *Mother Jones*, 36.

19. Hoffman quoted in Danny Schechter, "Remember Abbie Hoffman?", *Real Paper* 8 (December 1, 1979): 18.

20. Roszak, *Making of a Counter Culture*, 292; Todd Gitlin, *The Sixties: Years of Hope, Days of Rage* (New York: Bantam, 1987), 236–237; Peter Clecak, *Radical Paradoxes: Dilemmas of the American Left, 1945–1970* (New York: Harper & Row, 1973), 264–265.

21. *New York Times*, April 14, 1989, IV, 17.

22. Normal Mailer, introduction to Hoffman, *Major Motion Picture*, xiii; Gitlin, *The Sixties*, 236n.

23. Benny Avni, "An Interview with Abbie Hoffman," *Tikkun* 4 (July–August, 1989): 17.

24. Nicholas von Hoffman, "Seize the Day," review of *Major Motion Picture* by Hoffman, *New York Review of Books* 27 (November 6, 1980): 3.

25. Hoffman quoted in Judith Gaines, "Friends Recall Abbie Hoffman's Radical Wit," *Boston Globe*, April 20, 1989, 34.

26. Hoffman, *Major Motion Picture*, 243.

27. James S. Kunen, "A Troubled Rebel Chooses a Silent Death," *People* 31 (May 1, 1989): 102; Marty Jezer, "Abbie in His Time," *Z Magazine* 2 (June 1989): 12; Walton quoted in *New York Times*, April 20, 1989, I, 16.

28. Hoffman, *Major Motion Picture*, 83–84.

29. Abbie Hoffman, *Steal This Book* (New York: Pirate Editions, 1971), 55, reprinted in *Best of Abbie Hoffman*, 231–232.

30. Fiedler quoted in Diggins, *American Left in the Twentieth Century*, 165; Abbie Hoffman, "Media Freaking," in *The Movement toward a New America: The Beginnings of a Long Revolution*, ed. Mitchell Goodman (New York: Alfred A. Knopf, 1970), 364.

31. Mark L. Levine, George C. McNamee, and Daniel Greenberg eds., *The Tales of Hoffman* (New York: Bantam, 1970), 141; Hoffman quoted in Hayden, *Reunion*, 385.

32. Hoffman, *Major Motion Picture*, 24–27, 84.

33. Hoffman, *Major Motion Picture*, 13; Paul Cowan, "Jewish Radicals of the 60's: Where Are They Now?", in *The Jewish Almanac*, ed. Richard Siegel and Carl Rheins (New York: Bantam, 1980), 218.

34. Hertsgaard, "Steal This Decade," *Mother Jones*, 36; Howard Goodman, "The Last Yippie," *Inside* magazine in Philadelphia *Jewish Exponent* 2 (Summer 1989): 66.

35. Hoffman quoted in Schechter, "Remember Abbie Hoffman?", *Real Paper*, 18.

36. Hoffman, *Major Motion Picture*, 166, 281.

37. Hilary Mills, *Mailer: A Biography* (New York: Empire Books, 1982), 55; *New York Times*, April 20, 1989, I, 16; *Boston Globe*, April 20, 1989, 34.

38. Avni, "Interview," *Tikkun*, 15.

39. Fred A. Bernstein, *The Jewish Mothers' Hall of Fame* (Garden City, N.Y.: Doubleday, 1986), 55, 62; Hoffman, *Major Motion Picture*, 9.

40. Hoffman, *Major Motion Picture*, 3–4; Florence Hoffman quoted in Bernstein, *Jewish Mothers'*, 61.

41. Hoffman quoted in *New York Times*, February 1, 1987, 18; Avni, "Interview," *Tikkun*, 16, 18; Levine et al., eds., *Tales of Hoffman*, 140–141.

42. Kunen, "Troubled Rebel," *People*, 108, 110.

43. E. L. Doctorow, "Commencement Address (May 21, 1989)," *Brandeis Review* 9 (Winter 1989/90): 30, and "The Brandeis Papers: 'A Gangsterism of the Spirit,'" *Nation* 249 (October 2, 1989): 353; Hoffman, *Square Dancing*, 24.

44. Hoffman quoted in Joel Makower, *Woodstock: The Oral History* (New York: Doubleday, 1989), 111–112; Hoffman, *Major Motion Picture*, 223.

45. Kunen, "Troubled Rebel," *People*, 107; Hoffman, *Major Motion Picture*, 232; *Current Biography 1981*, 206, 207.

46. J. Anthony Lukas, *Don't Shoot—We Are Your Children!* (New York: Random House, 1971), 388–391; Alinsky quoted in Sanford D. Horwitt, *Let Them Call Me Rebel: Saul Alinsky—His Life and Legacy* (New York: Alfred A. Knopf, 1989), 528.

47. Hertsgaard, "Steal This Decade," *Mother Jones*, 37, 48; Hoffman quoted in Lacayo, "Flower in a Clenched Fist," *Time*, 30, and in Bruce McCabe, "Times Changed; He Didn't," *Boston Globe*, April 14, 1989, 39.

48. *Boston Globe*, April 15, 1989, 22.

49. Free (pseud. Abbie Hoffman), *Revolution for the Hell of It* (New York: Dial, 1968), 167–168; Hoffman, *Major Motion Picture*, 165.

50. von Hoffman, "Seize the Day," *New York Review of Books*, 3.

51. "California: American Dream, American Nightmare," *Newsweek* 114 (July 31, 1989): 24.

52. Mailer, introduction to Hoffman, *Major Motion Picture*, xiii.

53. Kunen, "Troubled Rebel," *People*, 101, 108; Hoffman, *Square Dancing in the Ice Age*, 225–242.

54. Milton Viorst, *Fire in the Streets: American in the 1960's* (New York: Simon & Schuster, 1979), 429–430; Morris Dickstein, "Wild Child of the Media," review of *Major Motion Picture* by Hoffman, *New York Times Book Review*, September 21, 1980, 7, 26; Jezer, "Abbie in His Time," *Z Magazine*, 17.

55. Marvin Meyers, *The Jacksonian Persuasion: Politics and Belief* (Stanford, Calif.: Stanford University Press, 1968), ix.

56. Martin Peretz, "Cambridge Diarist: Who Cares?", *New Republic* 183 (September 27, 1980): 43; Doctorow, "Commencement Address," *Brandeis Review*, 30, and "Gangsterism of the Spirit," *Nation*, 353.

57. *New York Times*, February 1, 1987, 18; Hoffman, *Major Motion Picture*, vii.

58. Stanley Crouch, "Huey Newton, R.I.P.," *New Republic* 201 (September 11 and 25, 1989): 10–11; Jezer, "Abbie in His Time," *Z Magazine*, 15.

59. Hoffman, *Major Motion Picture*, 77–78; Clayborne Carson, *In Struggle: SNCC and the Black Awakening of the 1960s* (Cambridge, Mass.: Harvard University Press, 1981), 298; Stanley Rothman and S. Robert Lichter, *Roots of Radicalism: Jews, Christians, and the New Left* (New York: Oxford University Press, 1982), 136–139.

60. Hoffman, *Square Dancing*, ix–x, 27; Avni, "Interview," *Tikkun*, 17; Goodman, "Last Yippie," *Inside*, 65; mimeographed letter from Murray Kempton, in behalf of Abbie Hoffman and Friends Defense Committee, n.d., in possession of author.

61. *New York Times*, May 7, 1989, I, 28; Alex Haley, epilogue to *The Autobiography of Malcolm X* (New York: Grove Press, 1966), 445–446.

62. Hoffman quoted in *New York Times*, February 1, 1987, 18.

63. Avni, "Interview," *Tikkun*, 17.

Slogan Chanters to Mantra Chanters   Stephen A. Kent

1. Francine du Plessix Gray, "Blissing Out in Houston," *New York Review of Books*, December 13, 1973, 39.

2. Robert N. Bellah, "The New Consciousness and the Berkeley New Left," in *The*

New Religious Consciousness, ed., Charles Y. Glock and Robert Bellah, (Berkeley: University of California Press, 1976). 87. As Bellah suggests, the list of former activists who converted to sectarian religions in the early 1970s is striking. In addition to Rennie Davis, the Chicago 7 defendant who became involved in religion and psychotherapeutic groups (i.e., tantric yoga, psychic therapy, Arica, and est) was Jerry Rubin. The former Black Panther party leader, Eldridge Cleaver, became a born-again Christian, as did Bob Dylan. Bill Garaway, a former draft-resistance leader whom federal authorities twice prosecuted, also became a devout Christian, as did Dennis Peacocke, who began his political protests in the Berkeley Free Speech Movement and later joined the Socialist Workers party. The abbot of the prominent Zen monastery, Tassajara, was David Chadwick, who had been involved with the Student Nonviolent Coordinating Committee and SDS. Another former SDS leader, Greg Calvert, became involved in Sufism and Gestalt therapy. The feminist writer and organizer, Sally Kempton, joined Arica in 1972, but not long afterward became a disciple of Swami Muktananda. These are but a few examples of this phenomenon.

3. See Mayer N. Zald, "Theological Crucibles: Social Movements in and of Religion," *Review of Religious Research* 23, no. 4 (June 1982): 317–336 and David G. Bromley and Anson D. Shupe Jr., *"Moonies" in America: Cult, Church, and Crusade* (Beverley Hills: Sage Publications, 1979).

4. Steven M. Tipton, "The Moral Logic of Alternative Religion," *Daedalus 111*, no. 1 (Winter 1982), 185, 187. In Bellah's catalytic essay, "Civil Religion in America," (1967) he claimed that America was in the third great time of trial in its history. He argued that "successful negotiation of this third time of trial—the attainment of some kind of viable and coherent world order—would precipitate a major new set of symbolic forms." The new form of civil religion that would successfully reconcile the nation during this crisis "obviously would draw on religious traditions beyond the sphere of Biblical religion alone." Tipton, in essence, believed that the new religions and psychotherapies which he studied helped people resolve the crisis of living during this period of trial. (Robert N. Bellah, "Civil Religion in America," in *Religion in America*, ed. William G. McLoughlin and Robert N. Bellah [Boston: Houghton Mifflin, 1968], 20.)

5. See Meredith B. McGuire, *Religion: The Social Context* (Belmont, Calif.: Wadsworth, 1981) and Reginald W. Bibby, "Religion and Modernity: The Canadian Case," *Journal for the Scientific Study of Religion*, 18, no. 1 (1979): 1–17.

6. John D. McCarthy and Mayer N. Zald, "Resource Mobilization and Social Movements: A Partial Theory," *American Journal of Sociology* 82, no. 6 (1977): 1217–1218.

7. See Cyril Levitt, *Children of Privilege: Student Revolt in the Sixties* (Toronto: University of Toronto Press, 1984), 102; Anthony Oberschall, "The Decline of the 1960s Social Movements," in *Research in Social Movements, Conflicts, and Change*, ed. Louis Kriesberg, vol. 1 (Greenwich, Conn.: Jai Press, 1978), 281–283; and Judith Clavir Albert and Stewart Edward Albert, eds., *The Sixties Papers: Documents of a Rebellious Decade* (New York: Praeger, 1984), 28–29, 38–39.

8. McCarthy and Zald, "Resource Mobilization and Social Movements," 1218–1221, passim.

9. Levitt, *Children of Privilege*, 101 and Oberschall, "The Decline of the 1960s Social Movements," 281–283.

10. Oberschall, ibid., 281.

11. David Dellinger, quoted in Nancy Zaroulis and Gerald Sullivan, *Who Spoke Up? American Protest Agains the War in Vietnam* (Garden City, N.J.: Doubleday, 1984), 343.

12. Levitt, *Children of Privilege*, 105.

13. Jonathan H. Turner, *The Structure of Sociological Theory* (Chicago: the Dorsey Press, 4th ed., 1986), 263.

14. Mayer N. Zald and Roberta Ash, "Social Movement Organizations: Growth, Decay, and Change," *Social Forces* 44 (March 1966): 333, 334.

15. Stanley Karnow, *Vietnam: A History* (New York: Viking, 1983), 684.

16. Zald and Ash, "Social Movement Organizations," 335.

17. See Richard A. Cloward, "Illegitimate Means, Anomie, and Deviant Behavior," *American Sociological Review* 24, no. 2 (April 1959): 167–169 and Robert K. Merton, "Social Conformity, Deviation, and Opportunity-Structures: A Comment on the Contributions of Dubin and Cloward," *American Sociological Review* 24, no. 2 (April 1959): 187–189.

18. Paraphrased from Robert K. Merton, "Social Structure and Anomie," in *Social Theory and Social Structure* (New York: The Free Press, 1968), 186.

19. Robert Dubin, "Deviant Behavior and Social Structure: Continuities in Social Theory," *American Sociological Review* 24, no. 2 (April 1959): 149.

20. Daniel A. Foss and Ralph W. Larkin, "The Roar of the Lemming: Youth, Postmovement Groups, and the Life Construction Crisis," in *Religious Change and Continuity*, ed. Harry M. Johnson (Washington, D.C.: Jossey-Bass, 1979), 271, 274.

21. Rennie Davis, quoted in Gordon R. Lewis and Cal Thomas, "The Millennium: A Bad Beginning," *Christianity Today* (December 7, 1973), 51.

22. Albert and Albert, eds., *The Sixties Papers*, 247–279.

23. Ibid., 404, 418, 421–422, 428–430, and passim.

24. Jeanne Messer, "Guru Maharaj Ji and the Divine Light Mission," in Glock and Bellah, *The New Religious Consciousness*, 64–65.

25. Richard Levine, "When the Lord of All the Universe Played Houston: Many Are Called but Few Show Up," *Rolling Stone* (March 14, 1974), 50.

26. Peter M. Blau, *Exchange and Power in Social Life* (New York: John Wiley & Sons, 1964), 118–119.

27. See Stephen A. Kent, "Relative Deprivation and Resource Mobilization: A Study of Early Quakerism," *British Journal of Sociology*, 33, no. 4 (December 1982) and "Mysticism, Quakerism, and Relative Deprivation: A Sociological Reply to R. A. Naulty," *Religion* 10 (1989): 160–172.

28. Michael Rossman, *New Age Blues: On the Politics of Consciousness* (New York: E. P. Dutton, 1979), 22.

29. Rodney Stark and William Sims Bainbridge, "Towards a Theory of Religious Commitment," *Journal for the Scientific Study of Religion*, 19 (1980): 121.

30. McCarthy and Zald, "Resource Mobilization and Social Movements," 1235.

31. Robert Wuthnow, "The New Religions in Social Context," in Glock and Bellah, *The New Religious Consciousness*, 278.

32. Steven M. Tipton, *Getting Saved from the Sixties: Moral Meaning in Conversion and Cultural Change* (Berkeley: University of California Press, 1982), 244.

33. Thomas Robbins and Dick Anthony, "Getting Straight with Meher Baba," *Journal for the Scientific Study of Religion*, 11, no. 2 (June 1972): 192.

34. Ibid., 205.

35. See Foss and Larkin, "The Roar of the Lemming," 271; Levine, "When the Lord of All the Universe Played Houston," 44; and Gray, "Blissing Out in Houston," 39.

Apocalypse Then   David Sanjek

1. For more discussion of this film and its relationship to sixties cinema, see Ethan Morden, *Medium Cool: The Movies of The Sixties* (New York: Alfred A. Knopf, 1990), 87.

2. For a cogent discussion of the ideological dimension of the commercial film industry, see David James, *Allegories of Cinema: American Film in the Sixties* (Princeton: Princeton University Press, 1989), 5–12.

3. Axel Madsen, "Fission–Fusion–Fission," *Sight and Sound* 37, no. 3 (1968): 125.

4. Lawrence Alloway, *Violent America: The Movies 1946–1964* (New York: Museum of Modern Art–New York Graphic Society, 1971), 30.

5. Lawrence Alloway, "The Long Front of Culture," in ed. *Pop Art Redefined*, ed. John Russell and Suzi Gablik (New York: Praeger, 1969), 42.

6. For a cogent discussion of recontextualization in the reading of commercial film, see James, *Allegories*, 189–195, where he examines the blaxploitation genre and the manner in which it allowed black audiences to identify with African-American performers as heroes and heroines, albeit in films that allowed a vicarious release of anger even if they never challenged the power of the state or the system of Hollywood distribution and its representation of the black community.

7. The extended statement of this definition is contained in Tom Doherty, *Teenagers and Teenpics: The Juvenilization of American Movies in the 1950s* (Boston: Unwin Hyman, 1988), 3–10.

8. See Steve Puchalski, "Attack of the Cycle Psychos: Bikers on Film," *Shock Express* 2, no. 5 (1988/89): 16–21 and "Taste Purple! Hear Green! A History of Hallucinogens in Cinema," *Shock Express* 3, no. 1 (1989): 26–32 for the fullest documentation of films in these genres.

9. Richard Rush's description of bikers as "distasteful" is quoted in Chris Auty's review of *Hell's Angels On Wheels* included in Tom Milne, ed., *The Time Out Film Guide* (London: Penguin, 1989), 257–258. The improvisatory nature of much of the footage in this film is discussed by cinematographer Laszlo Kovacs in Michael Goodwin, "Camera: Laszlo Kovacs," *Take One* 2, no. 12 (1971): 12–16.

10. For discussions of *The Trip* and *The Wild Angels* see Thomas McGee, *Fast and Furious: The Story of American International Pictures* (Jefferson, N.C.: McFarland, 1984): 167–180; Thomas McGee, *Roger Corman: The Best of the Cheap Acts* (Jefferson, N.C.: McFarland, 1988): 55–61, 62–66 and Gary Morris, *Roger Corman* (Boston: Twayne, 1985): 70–77. All three detail Corman's memorable experience with dropping acid. They also discuss the potential presence of stylistic autobiography in *The Trip* as the film's imagery recycles elements from Corman's own films, particularly the cycle of Edgar Allan Poe adaptations.

11. As Doherty details (*Teenagers*, 158–160), American International Pictures defused any potential cultural criticism in their films. In reference to criticism of their 1950s horror films, for example, studio executive James H. Nicholson states, "Our stories are pure fantasy with no attempt at realism . . . we strive for unbelievability." (ibid., 160) Furthermore, the box office failure of Corman's *The Intruder* (1962), one of his few such failures and the only film of his that explicitly criticizes social institutions, in this case the racism latent in American society, may have made the director gun shy of once again being seen as an explicit social critic.

12. For the most complete filmography of the mondo genre to date, see Charles Kilgore and Michael Weldon, "Mondo Movies," *Psychotronic Video* 3 and 4 (1989) 3:28–39, 4:34–43.

13. Alloway, *Violent America*, 65.

14. Stephen Farber, "End of the Road?," *Film Quarterly* (Winter 1969–1970): 9.

15. Another potential reason for the contradictary depiction of Natalie is Coppola's stormy relationship with actress Shirley Knight, a fact apparently recorded in the documentary made by George Lucas during the shooting of *The Rain People*. Could the film not, perhaps, allegorize the battle between the director and the actress? Certainly in Coppola's works, Natalie is the notable exception—a strong female character. For a discussion of the production of *The Rain People*, see Michael Goodwin and Naomi Wise, *On The Edge: The Life and Times of Francis Coppola* (New York: William Morrow, 1989), 83–94.

16. The campus-revolt cycle was at its height in 1970 with the release, in addition to *Zabriskie Point* and *The Strawberry Statement* in June, of *Getting Straight* and *The Magic Garden of Stanley Sweetheart* in May, *The Revolutionary* in July, and *RPM* in September. The year before a notable non-American film that can be classed in this genre, and one of its best representations, was released: Lindsay Anderson's *If*. For a detailed discussion of the campus revolt genre, see Seth Cagin and Philip Dray, *Hollywood Films of the Seventies: Sex, Drugs, Violence, Rock 'n' Roll and Politics* (New York: Harper & Row, 1984), 114–133.

17. Ibid., 61.

18. For a discussion of rack focus, see Goodwin, "Camera," 13–16 and John Belton and Lyle Tector, "The Bionic Zoom: The Aesthetics of the Zoom," *Film Comment* 16, no. 5 (1980): 11–17.

19. There is, I am suggesting, a connection between the aesthetic of rack focus and the ethics Rush's characters unsuccessfully attempt to embody. As Belton and Tector state, "If, as Jean-Luc Goddard proposes, every tracking shot is a moral statement, probing the physicality of the world around him, then every zoom makes an epistemological statement, contemplating man's relationships not with the world itself but with his idea or consciousness of it." (ibid., 12.)

20. Ibid., 131.

21. Ian Cameron and Mark Shivas, "An Interview with Richard Lester," *Movie*, 16 (1968–1969), 24.

22. Joseph Gelmis, *The Film Direct as Superstar* (New York: Doubleday, 1970), 243.

23. Ibid., 244.

24. For a detailed discussion of the "product placement" phenomenon, see Mark Crispin Miller, "End of Story," in *Seeing Through Movies*, ed. Miller (New York: Pantheon, 1990), 186–246.

25. Ibid., 245.

26. There are any number of notable examples of the use of the prerelease audience survey, one of the most memorable of which is *Fatal Attraction* (1989). In the original cut of the film, Glen Close's character committed suicide, but audiences indicated on their response cards a desire to see her punished, and the final release print had her killed by the family she had terrorized. In effect, the film depicted, and then narratively fulfilled, the audience's fear of any and all attacks upon the nuclear family and its attendant ideology.

27. Andrew Britton, "Blissing Out: The Politics of Reaganite Entertainment," *Movie* 31, no. 2 (1986), 4.

The Arts and the Vietnam Antiwar Movement   Alexis Greene

1. Ian Hamilton, *Robert Lowell* (New York: Random House, 1982), 321–322.

2. Allen Ginsberg, *Planet News* (San Francisco: City Lights Books, 1968), 118.

3. Robert Bly, *The Teeth-Mother Naked At Last* (San Francisco: City Lights Books, 1970), 14.

4. Ibid., 15.

5. Denise Levertov, *Relearning the Alphabet* (New York: New Directions, 1970), 13.

6. Lucy R. Lippard, *A Different War* (Seattle, Wash.: Real Comet Press, 1990), 27–28.

7. Hamilton, *Robert Lowell*, 360.

8. C. W. E. Bigsby, *Twentieth-Century American Drama*, vol. 3 of *Beyond Broadway* (Cambridge, Eng.: Cambridge University Press, 1985), 321.

9. Joseph Chaikin, *The Presence of the Actor* (New York: Atheneum, 1977), 1.

10. R. G. Davis, *The San Francisco Mime Troupe: The First Ten Years* (Palo Alto, Calif.: Ramparts Press, 1975), 149–150.

11. Megan Terry, *Viet Rock and Other Plays* (New York: Simon & Schuster, 1967), 104–105.

12. Robert, Pasolli, *A Book on the Open Theatre* (New York: Avon Books, 1972), 77.

13. Carlo Goldoni, *L'Amant Militaire*, trans. Joan Holden in R. G. Davis, *The San Francisco Mime Troupe: The First Ten Years* (Palo Alto, Calif.: Ramparts Press, 1975), 193.

14. Theodore Shank, "Political Theatre as Popular Entertainment: The San Francisco Mime Troupe," *The Drama Review*, 18, no. 1 (March 1974): 113.

15. Stefan Brecht, *The Bread and Puppet Theatre*, vol. 1 (London: Methuen, 1988), 507.

16. Ibid., 550.

17. Elizabeth Anne Barron, "A Structural Analysis of Representative Plays of Megan Terry" (Ph.D. diss., University of Louisville, 1983), 80.

18. Ibid., 81.

19. Brecht, *The Bread and Puppet*, 527.

20. Ibid., 547.

21. Stefan Brecht, "Family of the f.p.," *The Drama Review* 13 (Fall 1968): 139.

22. Alan Geyer, "A Need for Nationhood," *Worldview* 13 (July–Aug. 1970): 3, quoted in Charles DeBenedetti, *An American Ordeal* (Syracuse, N.Y.: Syracuse University Press, 1990), 289.

23. Jean-Claude van Itallie, introduction to *Behind the Scenes: Theatre and Film*, ed. Joseph F. McCrindle (New York: Holt, Rinehart and Winston, 1971), viii–x.

"Not My Son, Not Your Son, Not Their Sons"   Amy Swerdlow

1. For the political background of the wsp women see: Elise Boulding, *Who Are These Women?* (Ann Arbor, Mich.: Institute for Conflict Resolution, 1962).

2. See: Barrie Thorne, "Resisting the Draft: An Ethnography of the Draft Resistance Movement" (Ph.D. diss., Brandeis University, 1971); Leslie Cagan, "Women and the Anti-Draft Movement," *Radical America* 14 (September–October 1980): 9.

3. See: Amy Swerdlow, "The Politics of Motherhood: Women Strike for Peace and the Test Ban Treaty of 1963" (Ph.D. diss., Rutgers University, 1984).

4. Jean Bethke Elshtain and Sheila Tobias described the wsp encounter with HUAC

this way: "The Women Strike for Peace didn't proclaim that the emperor had no clothes; rather it put him in a position where, to his own astonishment, he found he had disrobed himself with his own tactics and strategies." Jean Bethke Elshtain and Sheila Tobias, *Women, Militarism, and War: Essays in History, Politics, and Social Theory* (Savage, Md.: Rowman & Littlefield, 1990), 4.

5. *Memo,* August 1969, 10, Swarthmore College Peace Collection, Swarthmore, Penn. Hereafter noted as SCPC.

6. *Sacramento Women for Peace Newsletter* July–August 1969, 2, WSP Document Collection, SCPC.

7. Ibid.

8. Leo Frumkin, L. A. chairman, GI Civil Liberties Defense Committee to WSP, *La Wisp,* September 1969, 6.

9. Philadelphia WSP, *Newsletter,* January 1968, 9.

10. A WSP anti-draft resolution, which augmented its original policy statement of 1962, was agreed upon as a guide to action. It declared: "We are opposed to the U.S. policy of military intervention all over the world, and the reliance on military means for solving problems which are essentially social and political. We oppose the draft of young men for destruction and killing in Vietnam and anywhere in the world to further this policy of intervention. We oppose all conscription because we want a free society dedicated to the pursuit of human rights." Statement before the House Armed Services Committee in opposition to continuation of a Selective Service System, Mimedgraphed copy, May 3, 1967, WSP Document Collection, SCPC.

11. Veronica Sissons, "Who Buys that Dream?" *La Wisp,* September 1969, 3.

12. Berkeley-Oakland Women for Peace, pamphlet, "Your Draft-Age Son: A Message for Peaceful Parents" April 1968, 8, WSP Document Collection, SCPC.

13. The suit named Long Beach Draft Board No. 25, Woodrow Wilson High School of Long Beach, Long Beach Unified School District, Los Angeles County Board of Education, and the State Board of Education. *Los Angeles Times,* December 16, 1969; Long Beach, Calif. *Press-Telegram,* December 15, 1969.

14. *La Wisp,* December 1969, 1.

15. Irma Zigas, interview with author June 26, 1979.

16. Ibid. Because of fears that records might be stolen from the office, or subpoenaed by the government, WSP kept no draft counseling records in Nassau county so there is no way of accurately knowing how many young men were actually kept out of the army.

17. Ibid.

18. Ibid.

19. Nashville, Tennessee, Women for Peace and Social Justice, *Newsletter,* n.d.

20. *La Wisp,* June 1967.

21. Charlotte E. Keyes, "Suppose They Gave a War and No One Came," *McCalls* (October 1966): 26, 187–191.

22. "Young World," *This Week,* April 13, 1969. *Plain Rapper,* January 10, 1969, 2.

23. Ibid., 1–2.

24. Statement to the Press by Evelyn Whitehorn, August 25, 1967, Xerox, WSP Document Collection, SCPC.

25. Women's Statement of Conscience to be presented to General Hershey, nation-wide director of Selective Service, at a nation-wide demonstration of women, Wednesday, September 20, 1967, WSP Document Collection, SCPC.

26. This WSP demonstration in support of draft resistance actually took place one

month before a delegation of writers, college professors, and other professionals visited the attorney general's office to declare, with more specificity than WSP had, that they would "counsel, aid, and abet draft resisters." See: Demise Levertov, "The Intellectuals and the War Machine," *North American Review* (January 1968):11.

27. *The New York Times* September 15, 1967.

28. *The New York Times*, September 21, 1967.

29. *The Sun* (Baltimore), September 21, 1967.

30. As a result of the WSP confrontation with Capitol police, Secretary of the Interior Steward Udall, decided, according to *The Washington Post*, to take another look at the regulation limiting the number of demonstrators at the White House; WSP pressed suit, and won a revocation of the limitation of White House picketers.

31. *The Washington Post*, (September 22, 1967): A-24, Radio station WWDC accused the "impatient women of breaking the rules. All the kicking and pushing was an outgrowth of this decision to defy the police and push through their barricade. Under the circumstances, WWDC rejects the tiresome cries of police brutality. To try to make the police the scapegoats for the misbehavior of these demonstrators does no credit to their cause." Vice-president Perry S. Samuels, Transcript of WWDC Editorial #1, September 22, 1968, WSP, Doc. Coll. SCPC.

32. "For Immediate Release," WSP, Washington, D.C., September 22, 1967, WSP Document Collection, SCPC.

From Maternal Pacifism to Revolutionary Solidarity   Gerald Gill

1. *New York Times*, November 28, 1965.

2. Joyce Ladner, *Tomorrow's Tomorrow: The Black Woman* (Garden City, N.Y.: Doubleday, 1971), 105.

3. G. Louis Heath, ed., *Off the Pigs!: The History and Literature of the Black Panther Party* (Metuchen, N.J.: The Scarecrow Press, 1976), 342.

4. For polling data, see John E. Mueller, *War Presidents and Public Opinion* (New York: John Wiley & Sons, 1973) 146–147.

5. With the exception of Bell Hooks, few feminist theoreticians have written about African-American women and militarism. See Bell Hooks, *Feminist Theory: From Margin to Center* (Boston: South End Press, 1984), 124–131 and *Talking Back: Thinking Feminist, Thinking Black* (Boston: South End Press, 1989), 91–95. Anthologies such as Ruth Roach Pierson, ed., *Women and Peace: Theoretical, Historical and Practical Perspectives* (London: Croon Helm, 1987), Sharon MacDonald, Pat Holden, and Shirley Ardener eds., *Images of Women in Peace and War: Cross-Cultural and Historical Perspectives* (Madison: The University of Wisconsin Press, 1988), and Jean Bethke Elshtain and Sheila Tobias, eds., *Women, Militarism, and War: Essays in History, Politics and Social Theory* (Savage, Md.: Rowan & Littlefield Publishers, Inc., 1990) provide no essays linking African-American women and war and peace perspectives.

6. Lawrence S. Wittner, *Rebels Against War: The American Peace Movement, 1933–1983*, rev. ed. (Philadelphia: Temple University Press, 1984), 156–157; Juanita Nelson, "A Matter of Freedom," *Liberation* (September 1960): 12–16; Pam McAllister, *You Can't Kill the Spirit* (Philadelphia: New Society Publishers, 1988), 87–89.

7. Catherine Foster, *Women for All Seasons: The Story of the Women's International League for Peace and Freedom* (Athens: The University of Georgia Press, 1989), 38–39. See *Four Lights* (June 1967): 4; *Four Lights*, May 1968 Supplement; *Four Lights* (July

1968): 1; *Four Lights*, May 1969. Rochelle Gatlin, *American Women Since 1945* (Jackson: University Press of Mississippi, 1987), 255–256.

8. Amy Swerdlow, "Ladies' Day at the Capitol: Women Strike for Peace Versus HUAC," *Feminist Studies*, 8 (Fall 1982): 493–520. See "Frances Mary Albrier, Determined Advocate for Racial Equality: An Interview Conducted by Malca Chall, 1977," Regional Oral History Office, Bancroft Library, University of California at Berkeley, 224–225. Although the text of the interview indicates that Albrier was a member of WILPF, the historical context of her protests more closely resemble WSP than WILPF.

9. *National Guardian*, June 20, 1963.

10. Coretta Scott King, *My Life With Martin Luther King, Jr.* (New York: Holt, Rinehart and Winston, 1969), 208–209, 292–293; Jim Bishop, *The Days of Martin Luther King, Jr.* (New York: G. P. Putnam's Sons, 1971), 402, 404; William D. Watley, *Roots of Resistance: The Nonviolent Ethic of Martin Luther King, Jr.* (Valley Forge, Penn.: Judson Press, 1985), 102; *National Guardian*, May 16, November 7, 1963; *New York Amsterdam News*, June 5, 1965; *New York Times*, June 9, November 28, 1965.

11. *New York Times*, November 28, 1965; *San Francisco Examiner*, April 16, 1967; *Washington Post*, January 16, 1968; Coretta King, "Statement at WILPF Conference," in *My Country Is the Whole World: An Anthology of Women's Work on Peace and War*, ed. Cambridge Women's Peace Collective (London: Pandora Press, 1984), 183–184.

12. Octavia Vivian, *Coretta: The Story of Mrs. Martin Luther King, Jr.* (Philadelphia: Fortress Press, 1970), 105–106; *Muhammad Speaks*, July 5 and 12, 1968; Phyl Garland, "Coretta King: In Her Husband's Footsteps," *Ebony*, September 1968, 156.

13. *Atlanta Constitution*, October 16, 1969; *Chicago Defender*, October 18, 1969; *Time*, October 24, 1969; *Washington Post*, April 25, 1971; Thomas R. Peake, *Keeping the Dream Alive: A History of the Southern Christian Leadership Conference from King to the Nineteen Eighties* (New York: Peter Lang, 1987), 278–279.

14. Gatlin, *American Women Since 1945*, 116.

15. Barbara Ransby, "Eslanda Goode Robeson, Pan-Africanist," *Sage* 3 (Fall 1986): 22–26; John Oliver Killens, "Lorraine Hansberry: On Time!" *Freedomways* 19 (Fourth Quarter 1974): 274; Lorraine Hansberry, *To Be Young, Gifted and Black* (New York: Signet Books, 1970), 247; Steven R. Carter, "Commitment Amid Complexity: Lorraine Hansberry's Life in Action," *MELUS* 7 (Fall 1980): 45, 49.

16. Fred Halstead, *Out Now!: A Participant's Account of the American Movement against the Vietnam War* (New York: Monad Press, 1978), 257; Susan Kling, *Fannie Lou Hamer: A Biography* (Chicago: Women for Racial and Economic Equality, 1979), 35, 39, 42; Fannie Lou Hamer, "Sick and Tired of Being Sick and Tired" in *The Failure and the Hope: Essays of Southern Churchmen*, Will D. Campbell and James Y. Holloway (Grand Rapids, Mich.: William B. Eerdmans, 1972), 162; "Hunger—American Style," Fannie Lou Hamer Papers, Reel 2, Widener Library, Harvard University, Cambridge, Mass. Hereafter noted as WL.

17. Diane Nash is also known by the name Diane Nash Bevel. Diane Nash, "Inside the Sit-Ins and Freedom Rides: Testimony of a Southern Student," in *The New Negro* ed. Mathew H. Ahmann (Notre Dame, Ind.: Fides Publishing, 1961), 43–44; Martha Norman, interviewed by author, March 1, 1991, Cambridge, Mass.; Clayborne Carson, *In Struggle: SNCC and the Black Awakening of the 1960s* (Cambridge: Harvard University Press, 1981), 134; Diane Nash Bevel, interviewed by author, June 29, 1991, Amite County, Miss.

18. Joanne Grant, ed., *Black Protest: History, Documents and Analyses 1619 to the*

Present (Greenwich, Conn.: Fawcett, 1968), 415–416; Michael Ferber and Staughton Lynd, *The Resistance* (Boston: Beacon Press, 1971), 32; Bernice Johnson Reagon, "Coalition Politics: Turning the Century" in *Home Girls: A Black Feminist Anthology*, ed. Barbara Smith (New York: Kitchen Table/Women of Color Press, 1983), 364; Ronald Fraser et al., eds., *1968: A Student Generation in Revolt* (New York: Pantheon Books, 1988), 54, 103; letter, Gloria House to Gerald Gill, January 1, 1991.

19. Diane Nash Bevel, "Journey to North Vietnam," *Freedomways* 7 (Spring 1967): 119; *Muhammad Speaks*, February 10, and 24 1967; *Afro-American*, February 4, 1967; Nash interview.

20. *Muhammad Speaks*, February 10 and 24, 1967.

21. Inez Smith Reid, *"Together" Black Women* (New York: The Third Press, 1975), 16; Sara Evans, *Personal Politics: The Roots of Women's Liberation in the Civil Rights Movement and the New Left* (New York: Alfred A. Knopf, 1979), 196n; Frances Beal, "Double Jeopardy: To Be Black and Female" in *The Black Woman: An Anthology* ed. Toni Cade (New York: Mentor Books, 1970), 99; Frances M. Beal, "Slave of a Slave No More: Black Women in Struggle," *Black Scholar* 6 (March 1975): 4–5.

22. Philip S. Foner, ed., *The Black Panthers Speak* (Philadelphia: J. B. Lippincott, 1970), 2, 46; Jan Zahler Lebow, "From 'Pussy Power' to Political Power: The History of Women in the Black Panther Party" (unpublished seminar paper, UCLA, Fall 1986); *Black Panther*, September 14, 1968; "*Black Scholar* Interviews Kathleen Cleaver," *Black Scholar* 3 (December 1971): 54–55.

23. *Black Panther*, May 4 and August 2, 1969.

24. *Black Panther*, October 25, 1969; Lebow, "From 'Pussy Power'"; Heath, *Off the Pigs!*, 339, 342; Assata Shakur, *Assata: An Autobiography* (Westport, Conn.: Lawrence Hill, 1987), 150–151, 190–191.

25. *Muhammad Speaks*, November 1, 1968; Bettina Aptheker, *The Morning Breaks: The Trial of Angela Davis* (New York: International Publishers, 1975), 58–59; Angela Davis, *Angela Davis: An Autobiography* (New York: Random House, 1974), 130–131, 140; Angela Y. Davis, *If They Come in the Morning* (New York: New American Library, 1971), 190–191.

26. Davis, *Angela Davis*, 151, 190; Angela Davis, "I Am a Black Revolutionary Woman," in *The Voice of Black America: Major Speeches by Negroes in the United States*, ed. Philip S. Foner (New York: Simon & Schuster, 1972), 1179–1180; *Black Panther*, November 1, 1969; *Muhammad Speaks*, May 29, 1970; Davis, *If They Come in the Morning*, 190–191.

27. See Rosalyn Terborg-Penn, "African Feminism: A Theoretical Approach to the History of Women in the African Diaspora" in *Women in Africa and the African Diaspora*, ed. Rosalyn Terborg-Penn, Sharon Harley, and Andrea Benton Rushing (Washington, D.C.: Howard University Press, 1987), 45–50. See Patricia Hill Collins, *Black Feminist Thought: Knowledge, Consciousness, and the Politics of Empowerment* (Boston: Unwin Hyman, 1990), 142, 155–156.

28. Judith Hole and Ellen Levine, *Rebirth of Feminism* (New York: Quadrangle Books, 1971), 108–109, 116–119; Myra Marx Ferree and Beth B. Hess, *Controversy and Coalition: The New Feminist Movement* (Boston: Twayne Publishers, 1985), 42–43; Gatlin, *American Women Since 1945*, 115, 116; Flo Kennedy, *Color Me Flo: My Hard Life and Good Times* (Englewood Cliffs, N.J.: Prentice-Hall, 1976), 62; Maren Lockwood Carden, *The New Feminist Movement* (New York: Russell Sage Foundation, 1974), 29–30, 61, 116–117, 134.

29. *Muhammad Speaks*, November 8, 1968; *New York Amsterdam News*, April 5, 1969; Shirley Chisholm, *Unbought and Unbossed* (Boston: Houghton Mifflin, 1970), 94–99; Shirley Chisholm, " 'All We Are Saying' Is—" *Freedomways* 12 (Second Quarter 1972): 118.

30. Chisholm, " 'All We Are Saying,' " 119.

31. Ibid., 119.

32. Gatlin, *American Women Since 1945*, 116, 123; Foster, *Women for All Seasons*, 44, 45; Alice Echols, *Daring to Be Bad: Radical Feminism in American 1967–1975* (Minneapolis: University of Minnesota Press, 1989), 55–56; The Damned, *Lessons from the Damned: Class Struggle in the Black Community* (Washington, N.J.: Time Change Press, 1973), 96–101; Mary Ann Weathers, "An Argument for Black Women's Liberation as a Revolutionary Force" in *Voice from Women's Liberation*, ed. Leslie B. Tanner (New York: New American Library, 1971), 304–307; Patricia Haden, Donna Middleton, and Patricia Robinson, "A Historical and Critical Essay for Black Women" in *Voices from Women's Liberation*, 323.

33. Mueller, *War, Presidents and Public Opinion* 146–147; see Pan-African Research Associates polls in *Muhammad Speaks*, May 21, June 4, October 22, November 5, and December 17, 1965.

34. *Movement*, March 1966, Underground Newspapers, Reel 271, WL.

35. *Jet*, (April 21, 1966): 50; *Chicago Defender*, April 1 and 22, 1967; *Muhammad Speaks*, April 29, June 10, 1966, April 5 and 12, 1968, and June 13 and 27, 1969. See also Heather Brandon, *Casualties: Death in Viet Nam: Anguish and Survival in America* (New York: St. Martin's Press, 1984), 93–94, 211 212.

36. Josephine Carson, *Silent Voices: The Southern Negro Woman Today* (New York: Delta Books, 1969), 145; Ladner, *Tomorrow's Tomorrow*, 99–100, 105–106; Bob Blauner, *Black Lives, White Lives: Three Decades of Race Relations in America* (Berkeley: University of California Press, 1989), 66; *Newsweek*, July 10, 1967, 34, 36.

37. *New York Times*, January 19, 1968; Eartha Kitt, *Alone With Me: A New Autobiography* (Chicago: Henry Regnery, 1976), 237, 245–246.

38. Kitt, *Alone With Me*, 250–254, 257; *Muhammad Speaks*, February 2, 1968; *New York Amsterdam News*, January 27, February 3, 10, 24 and March 9, 1968.

39. *Chicago Defender*, October 18, 1969; *Daily Cal*, October 16, 1969; Schomburg and Collection for Research in Black Culture, Small Periodical File on Hamer, 1925–1974, New York Public Library, New York, N.Y.; *Guardian*, April 27 and May 4, 1968; *National Guardian*, May 7, 1966 and September 30, 1967; *Muhammad Speaks*, April 18, 1966 and May 5, 1967; Jocelyn H. Cohen, Ellen Dwyer, and Jean C. Robinson, *Women in Social Protest: The US Since 1915*, a photographic postcard series (Bloomington, Ind.: Helaine Victoria Press, 1989), picture of demonstration, 1967; *Four Lights*, June 1967; Halstead, *Out Now!*, 282; Smith Reid, *"Together" Black Women*, 297.

40. Halstead, *Out Now!*, 282.

41. *New York Times*, October 23, 1967.

42. *New York Amsterdam News*, October 18, 1969; *Bison 1970* (Howard University Yearbook), 176, 177; Nick Kotz and Mary Lynn Kotz, *A Passion for Equality: George Wiley and the Movement* (New York: W. W. Norton, 1977), 287.

43. Kotz and Kotz, *A Passion for Equality*, 287; *Muhammad Speaks*, May 1 and June 5, 1970; Frances Fox Piven and Richard A. Cloward, *Poor People's Movements: Why They Succeed, How They Fail* (New York: Pantheon Books, 1977), 325.

44. Grant, *Black Protest*, 415–416; Ferber and Lynd, *The Resistance*, 32; Evans, *Per-*

sonal Politics, 196n; The Damned, *Lessons from the Damned*, 93–94; *Muhammad Speaks*, August 5, 1966; Mimeograph sheet, Black Women Enraged, n.d., Conrad Lynn Papers, Box 36, Boston University Library, Boston, Mass.

45. Flier, "Black Women!!," SNCC Papers, Reel 52, WL.

46. The Damned, *Lessons from the Damned*, 93–94; *Muhammad Speaks*, April 22, 1966, February 3, and October 13, 1967; *National Guardian*, April 8, 1967.

47. Evans, *Personal Politics*, 179–192; Gatlin, *American Women Since 1945*, 93; Janet Jemmott, "Memo to all SNCC Staff Regarding Vietnam and the Draft," n.d., SNCC Papers, Reel 52 WL; Phil Hutchings, interviewed by author July 18, 1975; Gwen Patton, "Position Paper: Why Black People Must Develop Own Anti-War and Anti-Draft Union . . . Heed the Call!" n.d. SNCC Papers, Reel 52, WL.

48. Letter, Gwendolyn M. Patton to Gerald Gill, December 7, 1979; NBAWADU, "For Us Women," SNCC Papers, n.d., Reel 9, WL; *Muhammad Speaks*, February 9, 1968; *Bay State Banner*, February 22, 1968.

49. Lawrence M. Baskir and William M. Strauss, *Chance and Circumstance: The Draft, the War and the Vietnam Generation* (New York: Alfred A. Knopf, 1978), 84–85; *Muhammad Speaks*, September 8, 1967; *Peace and Freedom*, January and November 1971.

Voices of Protest   Barbara L. Tischler

1. For a comprehensive analysis of the GI antiwar movement with reference to influential and supportive civilian organizations, see David Cortright, *Soldiers in Revolt: The American Military Today* (Garden City, N.J.: Anchor Press/Doubleday, 1975). See also "GI Resistance: Soldiers and Veterans against the War, *Vietnam Generation*, 2, no. 1 (1990).

2. Stokely Carmichael, "We Are Going to Use the Term, 'Black Power' and We Are Going to Define It Because Black Power Speaks to Us," from a speech on July 28, 1966 in *Notes and Comment* (Chicago: Student Nonviolent Coordinating Committee, 1966) in John H. Bracey, Jr., August Meier, and Elliott Rudwick, eds., *Black Nationalism in America* (Indianapolis: Bobbs Merrill, 1970), 470–476.

3. Dan Freeman and Jacqueline Rhoads, *Nurses in Vietnam: the Forgotten Veterans* (Austin: Texas Monthly Press, 1987), 67.

4. *Fun, Travel, and Adventure* (Fort Knox, Ky.) no. 1 (June 23, 1968): 1.

5. "Anniston Women's Project Report," *GI News and Discussion Bulletin*, no. 9 (September–October 1971): 20.

6. Renny Christopher, "'I Never Really Became a Woman Veteran Until . . . I Saw the Wall': Review of Oral Histories and Personal Narratives by Women Veterans of the Vietnam War," *Vietnam Generation* 1, nos. 3–4 (Summer–Fall 1989): 33–34.

7. See Sara Evans, *Personal Politics* (New York: Vintage, 1979) and Betty Friedan, *The Feminine Mystique* (New York: W. W. Norton, 1963). For an analysis of radical feminists and the Women's Liberation movement, see Alice Echols, *Daring to Be Bad: Radical Feminism in America* (Minneapolis: University of Minnesota Press, 1989).

8. Mark Gerzon, "The Soldier," in *Unwinding the Vietnam War*, ed. Reese Williams (Seattle: The Real Comet Press, 1987), 150.

9. "41 WACs Are First to Serve in Vietnam: 3,000 GIs in Area Suddenly Spruce Up," *Philadelphia Bulletin*, January 25, 1967.

10. Sheila Moran, "Our 'Soldiers in Skirts' Are Going Off to War," *Philadelphia Bulletin*, April 30, 1967.

11. "Anniston Women's Project Report," 20.

12. Major General Jeanne Holm (ret.), *Women in the Military: An Unfinished Revolution* (Novato, Calif.: Presidio Press, 1982), 234.

13. For a comprehensive bibliography of works relating to women's experiences in the Vietnam War, see *Vietnam Generation* 1, nos. 3–4 (Summer–Fall 1989): 274–277.

14. "Bragg Briefs," reprinted in *GI News and Discussion Bulletin*, no. 8 (August 1971): 15.

15. "Women in the Green Machine," *Fragging Action*, 2, no. 1 (June 1972): 5.

16. "Anniston Women's Project Report," 22.

17. "CID Attacks WACs," *Bragg Briefs*, 4, no. 5 (June 1971): 2, 10.

18. "Sex Lectures for WAF," *Helping Hand*, 1, no. 2 (1971): 4.

19. Lily Adams, quoted in Kathryn Marshall, *In the Combat Zone: Vivid Personal Recollections of the Vietnam War from the Women Who Served There* (New York: Penguin, 1987), 207.

20. "Men and Women Must Unite against the Brass," *AFB*, 2, no. 10 (December 1970–January 1971): 7.

21. C. S. W., "WAF Harrassment [sic.] 3" *Offul Times* no. 4 (August 20, 1972): 3.

22. "Sister Says, 'Hell No, I Won't Go,'" *Up Against the Bulkhead*, 2, no. 9 (September 1971): 5.

23. See, for example, *All Hands Abandon Ship* (Newport Navy Base), January and October 1971.

In the Belly of the Beast   Gerald R. Gioglio

1. Leon Friedman, "Conscription and the Constitution: The Original Understanding," in ed. M. Anderson *The Military Draft: Selected Readings on Conscription* (Stanford, Calif.: The Hoover Institution Press, 1982), 231–296.

2. Gerald R. Gioglio, *Days of Decision: An Oral History of Conscientious Objectors in the Military During the Vietnam War* (Trenton, N.J.: Broken Rifle Press, 1989).

3. See David Cortright, *Soldiers in Revolt, The American Military Today* (Garden City, N.Y.: Anchor/Doubleday, 1975) and Lawrence M. Baskir and William A. Strauss, *Chance and Circumstance: The Draft, the War and the Vietnam Generation* (New York: Alfred A. Knopf, 1978).

4. Andy Stapp, *Up Against the Brass* (New York: Simon & Schuster, 1970).

5. Committee on Veterans' Affairs, United States Senate, *Myths and Realities, A Study of Attitudes toward Vietnam Era Veterans* (Washington, D.C.: U.S. Government Printing Office, 1980), xxviii, 346.

6. See Baskir and Strauss, *Chance and Circumstance*.

7. Arlo Tatum and Joseph Tuchinsky, *Guide to the Draft* (Boston: Beacon Press, 1969).

8. Cortright, *Soldiers in Revolt*, 16.

9. Ibid., 17.

Legacies of the 1960s   Barbara Ehrenreich

1. These thoughts were presented as the keynote address to the annual meeting of the New England American Studies Association in April of 1990. I thank Barbara Tischler for her efforts in transforming what was originally a talk into a written essay.

2. See Peter Steinfels, *The Neoconservatives* (New York: Simon & Schuster, 1979).

3. Bruno Bettelheim, "Disturbing Student Parallels," *New York Times*, March 23, 1969 (excerpted from his statement before the House Special Subcommittee on Education).

4. John Silber, quoted in "Campus Protest Takes New Shape," *New York Times*, November 20, 1967.

5. Nathan Glazer, quoted in Wini Breines, *Community and Organization in the New Left, 1962–1968: The Great Refusal* (New York: Praeger, 1982), 3.

6. Daniel Bell, quoted in Breines, *The Great Refusal*, 2.

7. Irving Kristol, "A Different Way to Restructure the University," in *Confrontation: The Student Rebellion and the Universities*, ed. Daniel Bell and Irving Kristol (New York: Basic Books, 1969), 150.

8. Eugene D. Genovese, quoted in Breines, *The Great Refusal*, 2.

9. Irving Howe, quoted in Breines, *The Great Refusal*, 3.

10. *New York Times*, March 23, 1969.

11. William Appleman Williams, quoted in "Campus Protest Takes Shape," *New York Times*, November 20, 1967.

12. David Truman, quoted in "Columbia Starts to Discipline 500 for Campus Sit-In," *New York Times*, May 20, 1968.

13. Edward Shils, "Dreams of Plenitude, Nightmares of Scarcity" in *Students in Revolt*, ed. Seymour Martin Lipset and Philip G. Altbach (Boston: Houghton Mifflin, 1969), 15.

14. Robert Nesbet, "Knowledge Dethroned," *New York Times Magazine* (September 28, 1975): 34.

15. Bruno Bettelheim, "Children Must Learn to Fear," *New York Times Magazine* (April 13, 1969): 125.

16. "Agnew Develops His Father Image," *New York Times*, October 13, 1968.

17. Norman Podhoretz, *Breaking Ranks* (New York: Harper & Row), 288–289.

18. Michael Novak, "Needing Niebuhr Again," *Commentary* (September, 1972): 60.

19. Podhoretz, *Breaking Ranks*, 288.

20. John Chamberlain, "We Did Not Begin as a Permissive Society," *Conservative Digest* (July, 1975): 32.

21. Samuel T. Francis, "The Message from MARS: The Social Politics of the New Right," in *The New Right Papers*, ed. Robert W. Whitaker (New York: St. Martin's Press, 1982), 66.

Contributors

Barbara L. Tischler is a member of the Department of History and Director of Admissions and Financial Aid in the School of General Studies at Columbia University.

Morris Dickstein is a member of the Department of English at Queens College, City University of New York. He is the author of *Gates of Eden: American Culture in the Sixties*.

Barbara Ehrenreich is a member of the Department of Sociology at Queens College, City University of New York. She is the author of *Fear of Falling*.

Gerald Gill is a member of the Department of History at Tufts University.

Gerald R. Gioglio is a member of the Department of Sociology at Ryder College, and the Publisher of Broken Rifle Press.

Jonathan Goldstein is a member of the Department of History at West Georgia College.

Alexis Greene is an independent scholar and arts critic in New York City.

Ellen Herman is in the Ph.D. program in American Studies at Brandeis University, and an Editor at South End Press.

Glenn W. Jones is in the Ph.D. program in Folklore at Indiana University.

Stephen A. Kent is a member of the Department of Sociology at the University of Alberta.

David Sanjek is Archives Director at BMI (Broadcast Music, Inc.).

Mark Stern is Associate Professor of Political Science and Director of the University Honors Program at the University of Central Florida. He is the author of *Calculating Visions: Kennedy, Johnson, and Civil Rights* (Rutgers University Press, 1992).

Amy Swerdlow is a member of the Department of Women's Studies at Sarah Lawrence College.

Stephen J. Whitfield is a member of the Department of American Studies at Brandeis University.

Clifford Wilcox is in the Ph.D. program in the History of Education at the University of Michigan.